HOLDEN ON HOLD'EM

HOLDEN ON HOLD'EM

How to Play and Win at the Biggest Deal in Town

Anthony Holden

Little, Brown

LITTLE, BROWN

First published in Great Britain as a paperback original in 2008 by Little, Brown

Copyright © Anthony Holden 2008

The moral right of the author has been asserted.

A CIP catalogue record for this book
is available from the British Library.

ISBN 978-1-4087-0055-6

Typeset in Baskerville by M Rules
Printed and bound in Great Britain by
Clays Ltd, St Ives plc

Papers used by Little, Brown are natural, renewable and recyclable
products made from wood grown in sustainable forests and certified
in accordance with the rules of the Forest Stewardship Council.

Mixed Sources
Product group from well-managed
forests and other controlled sources
www.fsc.org Cert no. SGS-COC-004081
© 1996 Forest Stewardship Council

Little, Brown
An imprint of
Little, Brown Book Group
100 Victoria Embankment
London EC4Y 0DY

An Hachette Livre UK Company
www.hachettelivre.co.uk

www.littlebrown.co.uk

Let drums be rolled, corks popped and flags unfurl'd;
George and Ione, welcome to the world!

With much love from Grantonio

Contents

APPENDICES

PART ONE

The Basics

In which we learn the colourful history of Texas Hold'em – and get a first, A-B-C lesson in how to play the game

1

Hold Me, Darling

'This is poker?' asked an incredulous *Life* magazine on 16 August 1968. Inside an issue leading on the Nixons and the Agnews, a partnership that would last all of five years, there lay buried an article introducing mainstream America to something rather more enduring: a 'wild' new variant of its national game of poker, called 'Hold Me'. Above a colour photograph of no fewer than twelve men crowded around a green-baize table, most of them wearing suits and ties amid a profusion of splashed chips, exposed cards and overflowing ashtrays, the magazine sniffed that 'the decorous mob scene below looks more like a group therapy séance down at the poker-chip factory'.

There were several other names for this radical new variation of America's favourite pastime: originally called Hold Me, Darling, it had already bred regional variations such as Tennessee Hold Me, and – in Texas only – Texas Hold'em. 'It started somewhere in the South or Southwest a few years ago,' according to *Life*, 'and is threatening to catch fire with the rest of America's 47 million poker addicts, who bet an estimated $43 billion yearly.'

The magazine went on to explain the rules of Hold Me. 'The game's fascination lies in the number of players involved – up to 22 can play. This leads to big action and huge pots, both dear to all gambling card-players, and to great precision in analysing hands, especially dear to brainy poker experts.' Alongside the article was an explanatory piece by the Alabama poker authority A. D. Livingston, which presciently declared: 'I believe the game is a major event in the history of poker and I predict it will replace stud for the rest of the century.'

If he could have foreseen the twenty-first-century advent of the internet and televised poker, Livingston might well have added, 'and beyond, way beyond' – despite Cassandra-like predictions in the early 1990s from the poker pundit Mason Malmuth that 'there will be a decrease in the number of major tournaments . . . No-limit hold'em will be a game that a few old-timers will remember'.

This late sixties issue of *Life* magazine is exhibit A for anyone investigating the origins of Hold'em, the game that has so comprehensively monopolised the poker community during the TV and internet boom of the early twenty-first century. Exhibit B is an essay by Texas oilman and high-stakes player Crandell Addington, in *Super/System 2*, the 'Bible' of poker manuals edited by Doyle 'Texas Dolly' Brunson – world champion of poker in 1976–77, doyen of living players, and the man who christened Texas Hold'em 'the Cadillac of poker games'.

Addington was among the Texan 'road players' who first played Hold'em in and around San Antonio in the early 1960s, when poker was still illegal in all American states but Nevada and California. He adds his own name, as well as those of his fellow 'roadies' Brunson, Bryan 'Sailor' Roberts, Johnny Moss, Amarillo 'Slim' Preston and Jack 'Treetops' Straus to that of Felton 'Corky' McCorquodale, the man traditionally credited with introducing no limit Texas Hold'em (NLHE) to Las Vegas in 1963. Addington insists that the game did not arrive at Benny

Binion's downtown Horseshoe casino, as poker legend would have it, but across the street at the Golden Nugget cardroom then run by Bill Boyd.

Boyd's room at the Nugget was an authentic 'sawdust joint' – red-flocked wallpaper on the walls, and oiled sawdust covering the floors. 'It didn't exactly attract the same number of high-roller casino patrons that the Strip casinos reeled in by their thousands,' recalls Addington. This meant there was 'very little opportunity to catch a drop-by player or "producer" ['fish', in modern parlance; see Glossary] at the poker room'. But Sid Wyman, the boss of the Dunes, was one entrepreneur who could see the game's potential, not least as a spectator sport. In 1969 he invited these Hold'em pioneers to play a high-stakes no limit game just outside the entrance to the Strip hotel-casino's main showroom – opened in 1955 by Hollywood musical star Vera-Ellen, by then hosting a Welsh-Irish-German opera singer born Jim Haun who had changed his name to the more exotic 'Rouvan'. Here, says Addington, 'we were able to catch lots of drop-ins' – occasional players to whom poker still meant five-card stud – not least the Dunes' majority owner, who went by the name of Major Auterburn Riddle.

Where once stood the Dunes now stands the Bellagio, opened in 1998 by the one-man force behind contemporary Las Vegas, Steve Wynn, who himself fired the cannon from his latest Strip resort, Treasure Island, that appeared to trigger the implosion of the Dunes – watched by millions on live television and since immortalised in the closing credits of Wayne Kramer's 2003 movie *The Cooler*. So the spot where no limit Hold'em was first played on the Strip is now the home of Vegas's leading card-room – rivalled only by the sleek poker room Wynn opened in 2005 in the 215-acre, $2.7-billion Wynn, the eponymous hotel-casino he built after selling his Mirage chain to Kirk Kerkorian's MGM Grand group in 2000 for $4.4 billion.

It was in the Bellagio cardroom, in the first few years of this century, that the biggest cash game in the history of poker was played. A Texas banker named Andy Beal challenged a group of professionals, who called themselves 'The Corporation', to play heads-up, fixed limit Hold'em for stakes so high as to lift even them beyond their comfort zones. More than merely a gifted player, Beal was also a high-calibre mathematician, especially interested in such arcane mysteries of number theory as Fermat's Last Theorem. At home in Dallas Beal wrote a custom-built poker program through which he ran literally millions of hands, to calculate (and memorise) the odds in any given situation. To avoid giveaway 'tells', he attempted to eliminate his personality by donning wraparound shades and headphones to shut out distracting noise and all backchat. Then battle commenced, with the betting limits gradually escalating to an astonishing $100,000–$200,000.

It lasted, on and off, for more than three years, with sessions where Beal would win as much as $12 million, others where the pros would win more. One of Beal's edges was to get them to play at 7 a.m., not a starting-time favoured by many of the world's top players. But most sessions would, of course, run to marathon lengths, giving the edge back to the pros, who could take over from each other while Beal played his long, lone game. In the end, if not by much, he finished a loser; but he is made to sound like a winner in Michael Craig's thrilling account of the episode in a 2005 book, *The Professor, the Banker and the Suicide King* (continued in Craig's account of a brief revival of hostilities the following year in *Bluff* magazine, April–May 2006).

The Corporation that responded to Beal's challenge was led by Doyle Brunson – yes, that same Texas Dolly, by then in his seventies, who had sat down with Crandell Addington and others in search of 'producers' outside the Dunes showroom back in the sixties. To make his point about those producers, Addington describes a memorable hand involving the aforementioned

Major Riddle, the Dunes boss who is the stuff of many a Vegas legend, not least as the first casino owner to stage a topless cabaret on the Strip in 1957 ('There was initial uproar in the State Legislature,' according to the hotel's official history, but 'the show set a record for attendance in a single week at 16,000'). As the first hand of the many to be played in this book, it contains several object-lessons for beginners.

> On one hand, all but Texan Johnny Moss and Major Riddle folded, leaving a huge heads-up pot. Johnny was in the lead and never checked his hand; Riddle never hesitated to call Johnny's bets from before the flop or after the river. When all the cards came out, the board was K-K-9-9-J. Moss moved in on Riddle, and Riddle called him. Moss rolled a pair of nines out of the hole for four of a kind. Major Riddle rolled a pair of deuces out of the hole. See what I mean about the five-card stud players and their learning curve? Riddle had a wired pair, and he was not about to lay them down, not realizing that he had the worst hand possible in this situation, and could not even beat the five cards on the board.

One of the other players, an Alabaman named Joe Rubino who specialised in Kansas City lowball, registered an objection as Moss scooped in the huge pot. Since Riddle could not beat the board with his pair of deuces, argued Rubino, he should be able to take back his last bet. 'It didn't take but a second,' recalls Addington, 'for Johnny to tell him that sometimes the board is the best possible hand in Texas Hold'em, and that his comment showed how little he knew about the game.' Oh, and Moss also told Rubino a couple of things about 'minding his own business when he was not involved in a pot'.

As the game caught on in Vegas, during the late 1960s and early 1970s, the amount required to sit down at a no limit Texas Hold'em table soared as high as $10,000 to $100,000 – the equivalent of $60,000 to $600,000 in 2005, when Addington was recalling those early days. By 1973, with the Dunes mired in perennial financial difficulties, Sid Wyman had moved across Las Vegas Boulevard (aka the Strip) to the Aladdin (now Planet Hollywood). Here Johnny Moss hosted a cardroom spreading NLHE not just for the handful of local professionals, but for plenty of the 'drop-ins' on whom they fed. 'It was so well attended,' says Addington, 'that games often ran for days at a time, and fortunes changed hands.' Among the drop-ins was, yes, Major Riddle, whose poor play cost him so much that he lost control of the Dunes to 'parties represented by Sid Wyman'.

Riddle then acquired control of a Strip casino called the Silverbird (formerly the Thunderbird, subsequently the El Rancho), where in the late 1970s Doyle Brunson and Eric Drache were hosting high-stakes games, including NLHE. In 1976 Johnny Moss had opened the first cardroom on the Strip at its oldest casino, the Flamingo, while the late Chip Reese opened a bona fide cardroom at the Dunes, as opposed to that showcase table outside the showroom. Between them, these and other Vegas entrepreneurs not merely disproved the 1940s theory that gambling could never move from downtown Las Vegas to the remote, dusty, blisteringly hot stretch of desert that eventually became known as the Strip. They also showed that neither the Golden Nugget nor Benny Binion's downtown Horseshoe Casino – the pride of Glitter Gulch, 'where the *real* gamblers go' – held a monopoly on poker in Las Vegas, least of all on Texas Hold'em, as the game that started life as Hold Me, Darling had by now, perhaps inevitably, become known.

Bill Boyd, Sid Wyman, Johnny Moss, Doyle Brunson, 'Sailor' Roberts, Amarillo Slim, Jack Straus, Crandell Addington – nearly all the legendary players we have already met, with the notable exception of Major Riddle, were sooner or later

accorded places in the Poker Hall of Fame established in 1979.
As indeed was the toughest entrepreneur of them all, if not
himself much of a player, Benny Binion – none too surprising,
since Binion founded the Hall of Fame on a suggestion from his
then poker manager Eric Drache, as a marketing ploy for an
annual tournament he started in 1970 called the World Series of
Poker (WSOP). In 2005 Binion's son and successor Jack was also
enrolled in the Hall of Fame, for his role in maintaining and
building the World Series through the latter decades of the
twentieth century.

Today, thanks to the TV and online poker boom of the early
twenty-first century, the WSOP has grown into a massive
annual jamboree involving some fifty thousand registered players from all over the world – almost nine thousand of whom
paid (or won) the $10,000 entry fee to play in the 2006 'main
event', a ten-day no limit Hold'em tournament whose winner is
crowned world champion, with a first prize that year of $12 mil-
lion, by far the largest in all sport. Of the fifty-four events at the
2008 World Series, more than forty involved some form of
Hold'em. Back in 1970, the first WSOP at Binion's ended in a
steak dinner in the Sombrero Room, where the handful of par-
ticipants were asked to vote on whom they considered the best
all-round player. Down to a man, of course, each player voted
for himself. 'I couldn't understand why the fuck anybody would
want to vote,' said Amarillo Slim. 'We played for a lot of money,
and that was the vote.' So they were all asked to vote again, this
time for the player they considered the best – apart from themselves. The answer came up Johnny Moss, who thus found
himself elected the first official world champion of poker.

The following year the title was decided, as it has been ever
since, by a knockout tournament (or 'freezeout'), whose entry fee
of $10,000 has remained unchanged since the third WSOP in
1972. In the 1980s Eric Drache transformed the event by coming
up with the idea of the 'satellite' – a single-table, ten-player,

$1000-entry freezeout whose winner would play in the main event for a mere thou; 1983 saw Tom McEvoy become the first world champion to have won his way into the event via this route. By 1991 the first prize (won that year by local pro Brad Daugherty) had become a guaranteed $1 million; as of 2000, and the arrival of internet poker, rising young professionals like Chris 'Jesus' Ferguson and Carlos 'The Matador' Mortensen started to win first prizes in excess of a million. In the first few years of this century, through sheer force of numbers, the centre of gravity in the WSOP main event has shifted from pros to amateurs, with each of the nine players to reach the final table becoming dollar-millionaires – and that awesome first prize, by 2006, of $12 million.

Poker mythology gives Benny Binion the credit for launching the event that has done more than any other, before the launch of television's World Poker Tour in 2003, to make Hold'em the world's favourite poker game. But the honours should be shared with the man who gave Binion the idea – handed it him, at no charge, on a silver platter – by inviting him in 1969 to a 'Texas Gamblers Reunion' in Reno, Nevada. Among those present was, guess who, Crandell Addington.

Tom Moore was the reason that Hold'em had, in Addington's well-chosen word, 'gypsied' its way from San Antonio to Reno, Nevada, en route to Las Vegas. In 1969 Moore staged the week-long reunion to boost the slow season at his Holiday Hotel. The twenty or so players to show up included all the usual suspects: Moss, Preston, Brunson, Roberts, McCorquodale, Addington, 'Puggy' Pearson, Benny and Jack Binion. Even the legendary pool player Minnesota Fats came along for the ride – as did the notorious hitman Charles Harrelson, a convicted contract killer, father of the actor Woody.

They had such a wild time at Moore's riverside casino, play-ing a series of poker games across the different disciplines, as to nickname the event 'The World Series of Poker'. The winner that first year was Crandell Addington – who never again managed to win the world title, once it was so called, but went on to finish in the top ten no fewer than eight times, a record unequalled as of 2007. The following year Moore sold his interest in the Holiday and passed the WSOP baton to his pal Benny Binion, who put his son Jack in charge. They invited the same dozen big-time poker players – plus a few more, including the amateurs 'Doc' Green and Curtis 'Iron Man' Skinner – to come to the Horseshoe in downtown Vegas for a few days in May and play the game in all its many forms. But the main event, from the very start, gave the world title to the winner of the Texas Hold'em freezeout.

Texas Hold'em was introduced to Europe in the 1980s by the Irish bookmaker and poker entrepreneur Terry Rogers. Nicknamed the 'Red Menace' because of his ginger hair and bursts of belligerence, Rogers was one of the first Europeans to travel to Vegas each May for poker's World Series. At the 1980 event he was the only bookmaker not to write off Stu 'The Kid' Ungar too soon, quoting him at 20-1 while all else were offering 100-1; Ungar went on to win the first of his three world crowns, beating Doyle Brunson in the heads-up.

Back in Ireland, Rogers founded the Eccentrics Club in Dublin, where the inaugural Irish Open tournament saw Colette ('Collect') Doherty sent to Vegas as the first European, man or woman, to play in the World Series' main event. Another Eccentrics Club member, carpet millionaire J. J. 'Noel' Furlong, went on to win the world title in 1999. Before his death that year, Rogers handed control of the Irish Open to his friend and partner 'Gentleman' Liam Flood, who really deserves to share the credit for introducing Hold'em to Europe. The advent of poker on television saw Flood, another bookmaker and professional poker player, become a popular tournament director;

as a player he was a finalist in the first two series of Channel 4's *Late Night Poker* and won the $125,000 first prize in the 2007 PartyPoker European Open.

Back in the US, the popularity of Hold'em was swiftly boosted by the advent of a tournament circuit, and the first few manuals offering tips on the game, by the likes of Brunson, David Sklansky, 'Mad' Mike Caro and Mason Malmuth (see Bibliography). In 1988 the game finally became legal in the casinos of southern California, spreading across the country to Atlantic City, New Jersey, in the early 1990s.

John Dahl's 1998 movie *Rounders* also, undoubtedly, played its role in the growth of Hold'em. Starring Matt Damon, Edward Norton and John Malkovich, it also used the players themselves to recreate the famous showdown between Johnny Chan and Erik Seidel at the 1988 final table. The movie was the inspiration for the 2003 world champion, Chris Moneymaker, whose name alone – plus his amateur status, as in 'If that guy can win it, anybody can' – also triggered a poker boom symbolised by the subtitle of his 2005 memoirs: *How an Amateur Poker Player Turned $40 into $2.5 Million at the World Series of Poker*.

By then television had joined the internet in promoting Hold'em into the stratosphere, starting in Britain with *Late Night Poker*, which debuted in 1999; its pioneering format proved influential throughout the world, thanks to the system devised by the late Rob Gardner of seeing the players' hole cards via a glass panel around the rim of the table. Across the Atlantic, the inventor of Transformer toys played a crucial role when he switched from chess to poker in his sixties because chess was giving him headaches; bored with ESPN's coverage of the World Series, which simply pointed its cameras at a group of unhealthy-looking men playing cards, Holocaust survivor Henry Orenstein devised and patented the under-the-table camera, later known (because of its shape) as the 'lipstick' camera, which could also share the players' hole cards with the viewer.

ESPN or CBS Sports had been airing short segments on the WSOP since 1979. But the capacity to see hole cards, allied with snappy graphics keeping tally of the pot, changing odds and so on led to an explosion of poker on cable television that turned the leading players into celebrities – even, in some cases, brands – whom the average Joe could find himself sitting down next to at a tournament. Joe's liability, what's more, was limited to the buy-in, which he could win in a low-entry-fee satellite, usually online. The new economics of poker were born, and the biggest beneficiary was that most telegenic of all card games, Hold'em, where the flop sits handily beside the sponsor's logo.

If the first version of poker arrived in the United States in the 1820s, imported by French sailors landing in Louisiana, it took another hundred and fifty years for 'community card' variants to catch on. Then, just as the poker revolution was catching fire in the early twenty-first century, a Texan dealt a lethal blow to the game invented in his home state.

On 13 October 2006 – Friday the thirteenth, or 'Black Friday' as it soon became known in the poker world – President George W. Bush signed into law an outrageous piece of legislation that at least temporarily crippled online poker in the US. The 'Unlawful Internet Gambling Enforcement Act', which rendered it illegal to transfer funds between online gaming sites and financial institutions from banks to credit card companies, had been cynically sneaked through Congress in the early hours of Saturday, 30 September 2006, on the last vote before both Houses rose for the mid-term elections. In a nakedly opportunist move, apparently designed to appease the religious right and other fundamentalist voters, Senate majority leader (and then presidential hopeful) Bill Frist attached the anti-gaming act to the completely unrelated 'Safe Ports Act', a 'war on terrorism'

measure that passed on a mere voice vote. It made little difference to US politics – the Republicans lost control of the House,
anyway – but it dealt a lethal blow to online poker, which the
legislation treated as a game entirely of luck, like craps or
roulette.

As far as Texas Hold'em was concerned, the wretched Bush
acquiesced in this fundamental assault upon a game of
supreme skill invented in (and indeed named after) the state of
which he had once been governor. The consequences are still
with us, perhaps to be resolved by the next occupant of the
White House. The first was to see the number of entrants in
the world championship event of the 2007 World Series of
Poker fall for the first time in the tournament's thirty-eight-year
history.

Nine months later, nonetheless, on 11 May 2007, the Texas
State Legislature formally passed Resolution 80(R) HCR 109,
declaring:

> WHEREAS, The popularity of the poker game Texas Hold'em
> has increased dramatically over the past several years, and each
> day untold numbers of people throughout the world play this
> exciting game of skill, intuition and good old-fashioned luck;
> and
>
> WHEREAS, A true phenomenon of our time, Texas
> Hold'em has taken the world by storm, captivating countless
> card enthusiasts with its deceptively simple format; whether
> betting and bluffing across casino tables and kitchen tables,
> raising and folding in the virtual world of online card rooms,
> or moving 'all-in' at charity poker tournaments, poker players
> everywhere have embraced this fascinating and challenging
> game; and
>
> WHEREAS, The game's invention dates back to the early
> 1900s when it is traditionally held that the first hand of the
> popular card game was dealt in the city of Robstown, and

from there it traveled northward in the hands of 'rounders' and up the sleeves of cardsharps who quickly recognized the game's potential for mass appeal; and

WHEREAS, Poker legends such as Crandell Addington and Doyle 'Texas Dolly' Brunson helped further popularize the game in and around Texas in the 1950s, and they and others eventually brought Texas Hold'em to Las Vegas, where it was first played at the Golden Nugget casino in 1967; three years later, the inaugural World Series of Poker was held at the Horseshoe Casino, featuring no-limit Texas Hold'em to determine the world champion, and that annual tournament has continued to grow in both size and stature with each passing year; and

WHEREAS, The popularity of Hold'em has no doubt been spurred by the advent of online gaming and by the broadcast of televised poker tournaments, most notably the World Series of Poker's 'Main Event', a $10,000 no-limit Texas Hold'em tournament that attracts top poker professionals, talented amateurs, celebrities, and poker wannabes from around the globe hoping to become the next world champion of poker; and

WHEREAS, It is said that Texas Hold'em takes a minute to learn and a lifetime to master, and this telling statement underscores the high level of skill necessary to win consistently; a successful Hold'em player relies on reason, intuition and bravado, and these same qualities have served many Texans notable well throughout the proud history of the Lone Star state; now, therefore, be it

RESOLVED, That the 80th Legislature of the States of Texas hereby formally recognize Robstown, Texas, as the birthplace of the poker game Texas Hold'em.

There is no evidence beyond this eyebrow-raising document that Texas Hold'em dates back to the early 1900s; and nothing but 'tradition' to suggest that the first hand was dealt in the small, south-east Texas town of Robstown, a suburb of Corpus Christi in Nueces County. Robstown was not even founded until 1906, when it was named for a prominent son of Corpus Christi, Robert Driscoll.

Johnny Moss, never the most reliable of witnesses, claimed to have played Hold'em in the 1930s. In his forthcoming book *The Story of Poker*, James McManus will suggest that Hold'em arrived in Dallas, the 'unofficial gambling capital' of Texas, around 1925. 'No one knows for sure where and when the first hand of hold'em was dealt,' he has already written in *Card Player* magazine. 'One plausible guess is that a dozen or so Texas ranch hands wanted to play a little stud, but found they had only one deck. The most creative cowboy must've got to thinking: If five cards were shared by all players, as many as twenty-three of them could be dealt two-card hands . . .'

McManus quotes Moss claiming to have played limit at the Elks Club and no limit at the Otters Club, both in Dallas, in the 1930s. But he also points out that, when the authoritative *Oswald Jacoby on Poker* appeared in 1940, it mentioned 'no game called or resembling Hold'em'. The same goes for *Foster's Complete Hoyle*, which appeared in 1963. Five years later, the A. D. Livingston who introduced the game to America in that 1968 issue of *Life* magazine, could not find a single reference to Hold'em, or even Hold Me, Darling, in his extensive collection of poker books.

But let the Texas legislators have their self-regarding moment in the sun; at least they called Hold'em a game of skill, thus belying the law enacted by their pal Bush – which was all but endorsed in the UK by an absurd court ruling (in the Crown's case against London's Gutshot Club) adjudging poker to be a game of luck because the deck is shuffled before the deal. If Texas Hold'em is a game of luck, how come you see the same players at final tables month in, month out? How come so many expert players make a handsome living from the game?

Luck (or chance) is but one element of poker; much of the skill lies in knowing how to minimise it. That, among many other things, is what this book will now attempt to teach you.

2

How the Game Works

This chapter is here for beginners. If you already
know how to play poker, including Texas Hold'em,
you can skip straight on to Chapter 3.

Hold'em is the simplest of poker games to follow, but one of
the most complex to play – so full of possibilities as to
require consummate skill, especially in 'reading' your opponents, at the highest level. It will take you a moment to learn, in
the time-worn truth, and a lifetime to master.

The game was devised, as we have seen, so that as many
people as possible can play at the same table – sometimes ten,
usually nine, then (in tournaments) fewer as players get knocked
out, until two players are left 'head to head', or 'heads-up'. This
one-on-one version can itself be a two-player variant of Hold'em;
there are even heads-up tournaments these days.

Each player is dealt two cards, face down. These are your
'hole' cards, or 'pocket' cards. Between betting intervals, five
'community' cards will then be dealt in the middle of the table –
at first three simultaneously (the 'flop'), then one (fourth street,
or 'the turn'), then the last (fifth street, or 'the river'). Between
them, these five communal cards are called 'the board'.

The purpose of the game is to combine either or both of
your hole cards with the communal cards in the middle so as to

create the best possible five-card poker hand. Occasionally it is possible that the board wins – i.e. no player still in the hand can improve on the five community cards, in which case the pot will be split between the surviving players.

With a professional or non-playing dealer, a button will pass clockwise round the table to indicate which player is nominally dealing the hand. The two players to the dealer's left are called 'the blinds'; before the deal, they are obliged to put in compulsory bets to start building a pot. Dealer's left is called the 'small blind', the next seat the 'big blind' (usually double the small blind). This works out the same for every player, who has to do both once a round. In the later stages of a tournament, as the level of the blinds increases, putting pressure on the players with fewer chips, every player will also have to put in an 'ante' each hand, which will also increase with the level of the blinds.

After the deal, before the flop, the betting starts in the seat after the big blind. This player has three options: to 'call' (i.e. match) the blind, raise it (by at least as much), or to fold (surrender his or her cards, taking no further part in the hand). And so it goes around the table, with each player either calling, raising, reraising or folding – and the small blind must match the big blind, and both blinds any raise that may have been made, to stay in the hand. The blinds also have the option to raise.

Once this betting round is complete, the dealer will 'burn' a card (a tradition originally designed to prevent cheating) and reveal the flop. There follows a second round of betting, where the first player to speak may now 'check' (or bet nothing, but stay in the hand), before another burn and the turn, then another betting round before the river. One final round of betting follows before the 'showdown', if more than one player remains in the pot.

Bluffing is a common tactic in Hold'em i.e. 'representing' a good hand by betting with lesser ones, or 'rags', in the hope of scaring your opponents into folding (see pages 57–8, 85–6 and 123).

The other key element to the game is 'position'. The first player to speak, i.e. the first to the dealer's left still in the hand, or 'under the gun', is in the worst position, or 'out of' position. The last player to speak is in the best position, as you get to know what all the other players are up to before making your own decision. Usually, of course, this is the button, or nominal dealer; next best is the 'cut-off' seat, immediately before the button. Again, this evens out with each round, as position changes for all players with each hand. But the best Hold'em players maximise their use of position, regardless of the quality of their hand. Players in late position often try to 'steal' the pot with a bluff if they sense weakness around the table before it is their turn to act.

Finally, the version mostly played in this book (as on television) is no limit Hold'em, at which any player can bet as much as he wants or has in front of him at any given time. There is also limit Hold'em, where the betting rounds have fixed limits, and pot limit Hold'em, where the maximum bet is the total of the pot (see Chapter 7). But no limit Hold'em has become, to Anglicise Doyle Brunson, the Rolls-Royce of poker games.

The basics

The ranking of hands

A poker hand is always made up of the best five cards available to you. So the first thing to do is read, mark, learn and inwardly digest the ranking of hands, from worst to best:

Ace-high (e.g. As-Th-6h-3c-2d)
> no cards of the same denomination, no five of any one suit, no five consecutive cards, the highest hand being defined by the highest card(s),

is beaten by

One pair (e.g. Ks-Jh-Jd-Th-6s)

    two cards of the same denomination – the higher the pair, the better,

is beaten by

Two pairs (e.g. Qs-Qh-6d-6c-2s)

    two × two cards of the same denomination, the highest upper pair deciding between two such hands,

is beaten by

Three of a kind (e.g. 6s-6h-6c-4s-2h)

    three cards of the same denomination, or 'trips' – the higher, the better,

is beaten by

Straight (e.g. 5h-6c-7s-8h-9h)

    five consecutive cards of different suits, can begin or end at the ace (A-2-3-4-5 or T-J-Q-K-A)   the higher the sequence, the better,

is beaten by

Flush (e.g. Ad-Jd-9d-6d-5d)

    five cards of the same suit, the highest card(s) deciding,

is beaten by

Full house (e.g. Ks-Kh-Kd-7h-7s)

    three of a kind and a pair, the trips deciding the winner,

is beaten by

Four of a kind (e.g. 8s-8h-8d-8c-Qd)

    four cards of the same denomination – the higher, the better,

is beaten by

Straight flush (e.g. 3h-4h-5h-6h-7h)

    five consecutive cards of the same suit, ranked according to the highest top card,

is beaten by

Royal flush (Ts-Js-Qs-Ks-As)

    top five consecutive cards of the same suit.

A straight flush is a rare event indeed, a royal flush a once-in-a-lifetime hand. If you ever come up against one in a Hold'em game, you'll lose as much money as the fortunate player holding it can sucker out of you. If you ever hold such a hand yourself at Hold'em, give thanks to the poker gods and pray that your opponent(s) call your well-judged bet on the river. This is the ultimate example of what they call a 'monster hand'.

Concentrate on the ranking of hands until your knowledge of it becomes second nature. These are the only lines you have to learn by heart to be able to perform poker. The rest consists of subtleties that you'll go on learning for ever. Poker, like life, is a game where every master of the game is still also its student. In poker, there is a hierarchy. But it can, as in life, be beaten.

Soon the ranking of hands will be subliminal second nature to you. Now let's play some hands, to begin to learn the infinite subtleties of Hold'em. For now, just ask yourself which player is winning the following hand of Hold'em. Each player has been dealt two hole cards, known only to himself. An initial bet – 'the blind' – has been called, a card from the deck has been burned by the dealer, and a flop has been dealt.

The flop

As we saw, the flop is the name for the three communal cards in the middle of the table. Players use their two concealed or hole cards together with the three cards available to all players to make a five-card hand – with two more still to come. For now, remember: no matter how many cards are available to you, your final hand will always be the best five cards on offer.

Right? So who's winning here?

Player A	Player B	Player C
As-2s	**7d-7c**	**Jd-Td**

Player D	Player E	You
9d-7s	**Ks-Ac**	**Kh-2h**

With A-K, or 'Big Slick' (see panel overleaf), Player E is bound to play the hand even if he's worried that another player might have a pair – as does Player B. But sevens are only a medium-sized pair. Either one of them may raise, but Players A and C both have suited hands – as do you, but theirs are also connectors, and yours is the weakest pre-flop. If there's any action at all, which seems highly likely, Player D should certainly fold. Now here comes the flop.

The flop: **7h-Ah-9h**

This a great flop for you. Here's why:

- Player A has a pair of aces, but he's behind.
- B, who now has a 'set', or three of a kind – 'trip' sevens – is ahead of him.
- C has four cards to an 'inside' straight (7-9-T-J). He needs an 8 to complete it.
- D (a 'loose' player who has wrongly stayed in the hand) has two pairs, sevens and nines.
- E has a pair of aces with a king 'kicker' or strong side card.
- But you are winning the hand, with a flush in hearts (Ah-Kh-9h-7h-2h). Since you have the king of hearts, and the ace is 'on the board', you also know your flush cannot be bettered. Any player with two hearts in the hole (say Qh-8h) would be likely to lose a bundle to your higher Ah-Kh flush.

There can be no higher flush out there. You should make a strong bet (or raise) at this point because (for now) you are holding 'the nuts', the best hand available. But it might swiftly get worse, as we shall see in a minute, after we've taken a look at:

Nicknames of pocket hands

A-A	American Airlines	**J-4**	Flat Tyre
A-K	Big Slick	**10-4**	Broderick Crawford
A-Q	Big Chick	**10-2**	Doyle Brunson
A-J	Ajax, or Jackass	**9-9**	German Virgins
A-10	Johnny Moss	**9-5**	Dolly Parton
A-8	Dead Man's Hand	**8-8**	Snowmen
K-K	Cowboys	**7-7**	Sunset Strip
K-Q	Royal Wedding	**7-2**	(The) Hammer
K-J	Kojak	**6-6**	Route 66
K-9	Canine	**5-10**	Woolworth
Q-Q	Siegfried and Roy	**4-5**	Jesse James
Q-J	Maverick	**4-4-4**	Grand Jury
Qs-Jd	Pinochle	**3-8**	Raquel Welch
Q-9	Quinine	**3-3**	Crabs
J-J	Fish Hooks	**2-9**	Twiggy
J-5	Motown	**2-2**	Ducks

The nuts

What each player seeks is the nuts, the holy grail of hands, the best cards available. Consider the following three-card flops and try to work out which hole cards would be strongest. What hand would give you the nuts?

Flop 1: **2s-Kh-Jh**

You'll notice that – as yet – no two pocket cards can connect a sequence of five consecutively to make a straight. Nor is a flush (yet) available, as there are no three cards of any one suit. So the best cards to be holding in your hand would be K-K, since this would give you top three of a kind or 'trips'. Other strong hands (in descending order) would be J-J, 2-2, K-J, K-2 or J-2. But having the second-best hand gets you nowhere in poker. You might as well be holding 'rags'. Your hand must beat all others at the table to win.

Flop 2: **Jh-Td-Qh**

On this flop, you'll see that 8-9 in your hand would give you a low straight (8-9-T-J-Q), which would of course be beaten by 9-K (for a higher straight, 9-T-J-Q-K) or, best of all, A-K (the top straight, T-J-Q-K-A). So A-K, or Big Slick, would be the nuts here, likely to win good money off a lower straight.

Flop 3: **Qs-As-Qc**

The first thing to notice is that, thanks to the flop, every player is already holding a pair of queens. A single ace in the hole would give you two pair, aces and queens. But a single queen (one of only two remaining in the deck) would be better, giving you three of a kind or trip queens.

A pair of aces in the hole (a.k.a. 'aces wired', or 'pocket rockets') would give you a powerful full-house, trip aces and paired queens (A-A-A-Q-Q). But even that would be beaten by a player holding pocket queens (a pair of queens in the hole). The odds against it are high (see table, p. 67), leaving the 'boat' in danger of losing a lot of money, but pocket queens would give their fortunate possessor an unbeatable (at this stage) four of a kind or 'quad' queens (Qh-Qd-Qs-Qc) – the nuts. The only thing that can go wrong for this hand, over the next two communal cards, is an unlikely royal flush in spades, or freak quad aces.

Always remember that the board can win. If no one still in the hand can improve on the five cards in the middle, the pot is split between those still playing at the end (or show-down).

Hold'em: a card-by-card breakdown

You've seen how hole cards combine with communal cards to make a poker hand. Now consider the infinite niceties of the game of Hold'em, where each player makes the best five-card hand out of their two hole cards and not just three, but five communal cards. After the flop, there follows the fourth, then the final card. So each player has seven cards available to them, out of which the best five represent their hand.

Let's pick up on our earlier example, as the fourth communal card (fourth street or the turn) is added to the flop in the centre of the table. You're winning for now. But will you win the hand? The turn brings the 8s.

The board: **7h-Ah-9h-8s**

Player A	Player B	Player C
As-2s	**7d-7c**	**Jd-Td**

Player D	Player E	You
9d-7s	**Ks – Ac**	**Kh-2h**

This 8s is a useful card for you. Player C has made his 'gutshot' straight, but is losing to your flush. So you're still ahead. But then 'fifth street' or 'the river' brings the 9c

The board: **7h-Ah-9h-8s-9c**

Player A	Player B	Player C
As-2s	**7d-7c**	**Jd-Td**

Player D	Player E	You
9d-7s	**Ks-Ac**	**Kh-2h**

This last card is disastrous for you – because two players now have full houses, which beat your flush. Player B has a low full house, sevens full of nines (7-7-7-9-9). But Player D (who should never have called the first bet) will win the hand with nines full of sevens (9-9-9-7-7). And what would the nuts be?

Paired nines in the hole, of course, giving you quads, which hasn't happened here, and rarely will. If a seventh player was holding Ad-Ac – 'aces wired' in the hole – they'd have the best full house available, aces full of nines (A-A-A-9-9), but that, as you don't know, is not possible here because Players A and E are both holding aces.

Note that whenever a pair has fallen on the board (i.e. when the board itself is paired), a full house (and a less likely four of a kind) becomes a possible hand.

Another sample hand

Now let's look at another example to see how the nuts can change as first three, then four, then five communal cards make up the board in a sample hand of Hold'em. After the initial deal, each player is holding:

Player A	Player B	Player C
Kh-Kd	**6d-7c**	**Qh-9h**

Player D	Player E	You
4s-4c	**As-2s**	**Jd-Qd**

The flop: **Ts-4h-Ks**

So, at this point, Player A has boss trips (K-K-K), while Player D has a potentially expensive set of fours. Player C has four cards to a straight (9-T-Q-K), in need of a jack to fill it. You also have four cards to a straight (T-J-Q-K). Player E has ace-high and four cards to a spade flush. Player B is holding rags (i.e. nothing worth having), though he could make an unlikely straight by the final river card (6-7-8-9-T).

Ostensibly you have a decent 'draw'. You are drawing to an 'open-ended' straight, i.e. a card on either side of the four you already have in sequence – either an ace or a 9 – would fill up your straight. Player C has a lesser 'inside straight' or gutshot draw. Only a jack would fill his straight. Regardless, Player A is in a powerful position and betting at you, as fourth street brings the Jc. Now the board reads:

Ts-4h-Ks-Jc

Who's winning now? This is a lively hand. Lucky old Player C has filled his straight (9-T-J-Q-K) and is ahead. You now have paired jacks to go with your inside straight draw. Player E is still four cards to a flush. A and D both have trips, and are looking for the board to pair – to make a full house or four of a kind. Player B has lost the hand; he is, as they say, 'drawing dead'. No card that could fall on the river would give him a winning hand. He's lost even by the time fifth street brings the 9s.

Ts-4h-Ks-Jc-9s

You've now made your straight, the same straight as Player C. Maybe you'll both end up splitting the pot with 9-T-J-Q-K? Then again, maybe not. Just for the record, here are each player's final hands:

Player A	Player B	Player C
Kh-Kd-Ks-Jc-Ts	**Ks-Jc-Ts-9s-7c**	**Ks-Qh-Jc-Ts-9h**
Trip kings	King high	Straight
Player D	Player E	You
4s-4c-4h-Ks-Jc	**As-Ks-Ts-9s-2s**	**Ks-Qd-Jc-Ts-9s**
Trip fours	Flush – WINNER!	Straight

Player E has won the hand with a 'nut flush' or ace-high flush in spades. He wins all the money – and you, if you care to call his bet, could wind up losing a fortune.

The nuts revisited, from flop to river

Hold'em, you will have noticed, is a game where any hand may be winning one minute, then losing the next. Study another sample, to see how the lead in any one hand can change dramatically:

Player A	Player B	Player C
2s-7h	**Ah-9d**	**As-Ac**
Player D	Player E	You
3h-4h	**Kd-8d**	**Jh-Jd**

Before the flop's been dealt, your hole cards should give you a clue as to whether you may be able to make a strong hand. Player A has 2-7 off-suit, theoretically the worst hole cards in Hold'em, as it's the lowest gap too wide to bookend a straight. Player C is currently winning with the best possible pre-flop hand, pocket aces. Player D has low 'suited connectors', two cards that could well make a flush or a straight. Player B has an ace, with a middling kicker. Player E has an unexciting king, while you have a strong hand with paired jacks. Notice how, if hole cards are suited (as with D's and E's), they have a far better chance of making a flush. The flop brings:

2h-Ad-Kh

Take a moment to consider this flop. Whose hand would you like to be holding if you saw these three cards on the board? Would you care to be Player D, with four cards to both flush and straight draws? Or Player C, with boss trips? At this stage of the hand, it's impossible to tell who ultimately will win it – but for now, since he has the nuts, Player C is definitely the favourite. In any hand of Hold'em, as you'll see when we come to the next chapter, it's usually the amount that players bet – even more than the cards they are holding – that will decide the winner. For now, though of course you don't know it, you're losing, since your jacks are bettered by Player C's trip aces, B's pair of aces and E's paired kings, as fourth street brings a 2d:

2h–Ad–Kh–2d

Suddenly, Player E is excited by the prospect of his diamond flush-draw. He has the king of diamonds and the ace is out there, so he knows no other flush will beat him if the river brings a diamond. Player D is still hanging in with four cards to a straight and four to a flush. Player A (who should have folded his 7-2 before the flop) now has low trips. B, E and you all have two pairs. But you're all going down to Player C, who has aces full of 'deuces' . . . until fifth street falls:

2h–Ad–Kh–2d–2c

Yes, suddenly everything has changed again. No flush is possible, since the board is showing no three cards of the same suit. No straight is possible. Everyone's got trip deuces and anyone with a pair has a full house. You have twos full of jacks, beaten by Player E's twos full of kings, beaten by Player B's twos full of aces – and all these have been busted by Player C's aces full of deuces. But this river card was a disaster for him, because it turned Player A's trip deuces into quad deuces. He's won the hand – but would he ever have been in it? Imagine the embarrassment of turning over 7-2 to claim all that dough . . .

Player A	Player B	Player C
2s-2h-2d-2c-Ad	**Ah-Ad-2h-2d-2c**	**As-Ac-Ad-2h-2d**
Four of a kind – WINNER!	Full house	Full house

Player D	Player E	You
2h-2d-2c-Ad-Kh	**2h-2d-2c-Kd-Kh**	**2h-2d-2c-Jh-Jd**
Three of a kind	Full house	Full house

You can probably see by now that this hand would never really happen – Player A would not even have called the opening blind, let alone Player C's pre-flop raise – so here are some sample hands to help you master the reading of the cards, and at the back of the book, in Appendix C, there are some tables giving statistical guides to the odds against being dealt certain hands, and their improving on the flop.

As with the ranking of hands, you should study these until they are engraved on your subconscious.

Sample Hold'em: best hands
Board

Example 1

	Board			
	Ah-8s-Ts-Ad-Js	(1)	**Qs-9s**	(Straight flush)
		(2)	**7s-9s**	(Straight flush)
		(3)	**As-Ac**	(Four of a kind)
		(4)	**A-J**	(Full house)
		(5)	**A-T**	(Full house)
		(6)	**A-8**	(Full house)
		(7)	**J-J**	(Full house)
		(8)	**T-T**	(Full house)
		(9)	**8-8**	(Full house)
		(10)	**As-Xs**	(Nut flush)
		(11)	**Ks-Xs**	(Flush) etc.

Example 2

2s-Tc-2h-Ks-Qc	(1)	**2d-2c**	(Four of a kind)
	(2)	**K-K**	(Full house)
	(3)	**Q-Q**	(Full house)
	(4)	**T-T**	(Full house)
	(5)	**K-2**	(Full house)
	(6)	**Q-2**	(Full house)
	(7)	**T-2**	(Full house)
	(8)	**A-J**	(Top straight) etc.

Example 3

7d-9c-6h-Qs-4h	(1)	**T-8**	(Top straight)
	(2)	**8-5**	(Straight)
	(3)	**5-3**	(Low straight)
	(4)	**Q-Q**	(Three of a kind)
	(5)	**9-9**	(Three of a kind) etc.

Example 4

Td-7d-Qc-5c-3c	(1)	**Ac-Xc**	(Nut flush)
	(2)	**Kc-Xc**	(Flush)
	(3)	**Jc-Xc**	(Flush)
	(4)	**Tc-Xc**	(Flush)
	(5)	**9c-Xc**	(Flush) etc.

A word to the poker wise

Beginner's luck

Ten tips for those still on a learning curve – in a home game or in a cardroom.

1 Concentrate. Even if you don't intend to play the hand, keep an eye on what's happening. Don't, for instance, fold out of turn; it annoys the other players, not least because it gives their opponents information (viz. that you're not going to play the hand).

2 Even more important, don't bet out of turn. Again, it
   bugs the other players – and it can cost you. Different
   games have different rules about these things, but you're
   bound to lose out – perhaps by forfeiting the right to
   raise if someone comes in ahead of you.

3 Keep concentrating. Just because you're not in the hand,
   that doesn't mean you can't learn something about the
   other players – and the game – from the way they play it.

4 Under the same heading, always post your blind – large
   or small – without having to be nagged to. That, too, is
   very tiresome to the other players, even to the dealer (if
   you have one).

5 Protect your cards. Put a chip, or a personal talisman, on
   your hole cards, even if you wind up folding them. If a
   dealer scoops them up by mistake, it's your fault, not his.
   Your hand is dead – as it is if it hits the 'muck', or
   discarded cards, for whatever reason.

6 If you want to show your cards, wait till the hand is
   over – or you might get shot. If you show them to one
   player, maybe the guy you were up against, you must
   show them to all.

7 If you've bluffed someone out of a pot, showing them
   your cards – and thus their own mistake   is a perfectly
   legitimate tactic. But do it sparingly. It gets up their
   noses, and they're going to come after you.

8 If you're going to raise, say so. A single chip of larger
   denomination than the bet is deemed a call, unless you
   say 'Raise'. Likewise, a player with a fistful of chips in the
   middle, or 'across the line', cannot raise unless he pre-
   announces it, or indeed go back to his stack for more. A
   player guilty of doing this, even by mistake, is making a
   'string' bet, which is illegal.

9 Don't take any notice of Kenny Rogers. Sure, you have
   to know when to hold 'em, know when to fold 'em. But

feel free to count your money while you're sitting at the table. Knowing the size of your own stack, and indeed everyone else's, is a crucial part of playing the game well.

10 Always remember the wise words of David Mamet, and everyone else who has ever played poker. It doesn't matter who wins the most hands. It's the person who wins the most money . . .

Once you've mastered these fundamental truths, commit to memory two immortal poker sayings.

(1) 'Never play with mugs' – i.e. players who don't know what they're doing – because they're likely to chuck their money in on anything, and may well prove lucky enough to beat your strong, well-played hand. It's more fun, believe it or not, playing with skilled players – just as long as they are less skilled than you. But, before you get too cocky, be sure to remember, (2) 'If you can't spot the sucker in your first half-hour at the table . . . it's you!'

Now it's time to move up a notch, and introduce you to two little letters, 'EV', which are the key to accurate play at Hold'em.

PART TWO

How to Play Better – and Win

In theory and in practice, intermediate and advanced, tournaments and cash games, no limit, pot limit and fixed limit, online and in bricks & mortar casinos or home games

3

In Theory

Expected Value (EV)

In his entertaining 2007 poker novel *Texas Poker Wisdom*, Johnny Hughes has his protagonist, Matthew 'Slick' O'Malley, run through various ritual procedures en route to his regular poker game.

First, Matt studies his worn, dog-eared notebook. 'His string of wins and losses showed so many smaller wins and losses you wouldn't know he was playing very high. "I'm too conservative," Matt thought, "tighter than Dick's hat band". He kept promising himself to open up his game.' Then he runs through his notes on 'some eighty poker players around West Texas', from the good ones he wants to avoid to losers like Tim and Williard. 'Those geese are like Williard,' Matt thinks. 'They keep coming closer to you until you stand up. Then they retreat.'

Matt does a few yoga moves, then scans his list of starting Hold'em hands, in early, middle and late position. He takes 'another gambler's oath to stick with his starting-hand discipline'; Matt has been making 'the same tired promises to himself to play only face-cards since he was in knee-britches'. Even more important were 'his self-promises about his real enemies: anger and boredom'.

When his nephew, Dylan, arrives, Matt warns him that it's 'a nest of rattlesnakes over there. Harder to beat than a broken drum.' So how does Matt know who's 'over there'? He's already used his binoculars to check out the cars outside the venue. 'I can see the cars of Farm Boy, Dee, Dagwood, Tim, Bidal, and two cars I don't know. It is best to wait until a game warms up before you show up. When folks get behind, they start playing bad and making mistakes. That's the gambler's fallacy, trying to play higher and get even when you are behind . . . The odds are you won't.'

This is all sound advice from a seasoned player, useful way beyond west Texas. A good player will get himself in the best physical and psychological shape for a game; top professional Howard ('The Professor') Lederer, for instance, is reluctant to stay in the hotel where a tournament is being played, arguing that 'you should have to make a positive effort to get there and play, to go there and win'. Note, too, how Edward G. Robinson's eventually victorious Lancey Howard, a.k.a 'The Man', is always immaculately dressed and groomed during the marathon poker game at the end of *The Cincinnati Kid*, while Steve McQueen's Kid grows ever more stubbly and dishevelled.

The internet has changed all that; one of its great advantages is that you don't have to get washed and shaved – you don't even have to get dressed – before facing its mightiest poker chal-lenges. Nor is it too easy to get out the binoculars and check out the cars, to see who might be playing. But there *are* online equivalents.

At any of the major poker websites, the screen-names of the players involved are all waiting there for you to see before you choose (or not) to sign on. Regular players will know those names, have personal databases on them, or check them out on the internet tools available (see Chapter 8). They may or may not be rested, but they know they would be foolish to play when drunk, depressed or otherwise distracted.

I could go on. My point is that all the usual rules for playing your best poker apply as much online as they do in home games or casinos, ring games or tournaments. So the guidelines that follow apply to both online and 'real' play (with some obvious extras for the latter at the end). Read, mark, learn and inwardly digest these precepts until they become second nature at the table, whether online or bricks and mortar.

You may (like me) be hopeless at mental arithmetic, but we must begin with a little maths lesson. Then we'll get straight to the tables, in the thick of the action. After absorbing these principles, you'll know how you *ought* to play. Whether or not you *do* then play as you know you should – and we all, like Johnny Hughes's Matt O'Malley, break our own rules from time to time – is entirely a matter for you. But stick to these essential guidelines, and you'll wind up a winner more often than not.

Expected Value

The theory of expected value (EV) is the natural domain of the new generation of player, borne of the online boom. In the 1950s and 1960s, players like Doyle Brunson had complex strategies and played sophisticated games, yet survived without reference to, or knowledge of, EV theory. Crucially, though, every considered decision a player makes at the poker table, whether he knows it or not, is an application of EV theory to Texas Hold'em. When Brunson realised that making aggressive moves with flush draws added to his long-term profit, he was learning that those plays have positive EV. When he smelt weakness in an opponent's bet and moved over the top with a raise, he did so because he figured he would win the pot often enough to make it a 'winning' play – that is to say, evidence pointed to the fact that the play had a positive EV. Today's players are not playing a different game from the old greats. The language we use to talk about poker may be different but the idea is still the same: to make as many plays as you can that add to your long-term profit. This is now, always has been and always will be what makes a winning player.

What is expected value (EV)?

Consider the following challenge: toss a coin, and you will win $2 if it turns up heads, but lose $1 if it turns up tails.

If your instinct is that this is a proposition worth taking, you would be right to follow it. This is because it has what is called a 'positive' EV. Expected value is a cash value that represents the 'worth' of a given bet or proposition. Even though a single toss of that coin *can* result in your losing $1, overall it is still a winning proposition, given the expectation of the law of averages that the coin will come up heads half the time, tails the other half. If you were to take this bet over and over *ad infinitum*, you would wind up very rich.

EV theory can be used to calculate an exact figure that represents the worth of each toss of the coin, i.e. half the time you will win $2, half the time you will lose $1.

EV = probability of winning × what you stand to win (your return) – probability of losing × what you stand to lose (your loss).

$$EV = (Pw \times R) - (Pl \times L).$$

So in this case, $EV = (0.5 \times \$2) - (0.5 \times \$1) = \$0.50$.

With each toss of the coin, you are making a theoretical $0.50. If you took this proposition enough times to smooth out the short-term luck factor, you would end up earning $0.50 × the number of times the coin was tossed.

EV in Texas Hold'em

So how does this relate to playing Texas Hold'em? Any decision at the poker table can be analysed in the same way. Any time you make a call, bet or raise, there is a probability of your going on to win the hand, and an amount you stand to win. There is also a probability of your going on to lose the hand, and an amount you stand to lose. You can use the same method as above to work out the EV of any play. If you consistently make positive EV plays in your poker career, you will be much like the man taking the coin-toss proposition over and over. You will wind up rich.

The calculation above can be simplified and made quicker, so as to be more useful at the table. In the example above, the coin-toss proposition was a winning one because $(Pw \times R) - (Pl \times L)$ was positive, i.e. $(Pw \times R)$ was greater than $(Pl \times L)$. A necessary result of the above condition is that a proposition has a positive EV if the ratio R:L is greater than Pw:Pl. To apply this to the coin-toss example, it has positive EV because you stand to win twice as much as you stand to lose, and you don't lose more than twice as often as you win. In Hold'em, the R:L ratio is called pot odds (or implied odds, or reverse implied odds in some circumstances – to be explained later) and Pw:Pl is your odds of winning the hand, or just your 'odds'.

Once you have the four figures (your return, your loss, the probability of winning and the probability of losing), you can compare the two ratios and confirm if the proposition has positive EV.

Example 1: You hold Ac-4c. The board on the turn is showing Kc-Th-7d . . . 2c. There is $1500 in the pot. Your opponent pushes all-in for $375, and foolishly flips up Ah-Ad before you have had a chance to act. Should you call?

As there is no money that can be extracted further down the road, your return is simply the $1875 in the middle of the table (the $1500 already in the pot plus his $375). Your loss is the bet you are facing: $375. The pot odds are therefore $1875 to $375. In this case they stand at 5-1.

The odds of your winning the hand are the ratio of the number of river cards that win you the hand to the number that lose you the hand. In this case the 35 non-clubs against the nine remaining clubs, which simplifies to just under 3.9-1.

The pot odds here exceed the odds against your winning the hand, so this has positive EV – a winning proposition. Make the call. To see the actual EV figure for this call, you can go back to the very first formula above:

$EV = (Pw \times R) - (Pl \times L)$.

Pw is 9/44 (there are 44 unseen cards, 9 of which win you the pot) and likewise Pl is 35/44.

$EV = (9/44 \times \$1875) - (35/44 \times \$375) = \$85.23$

Every time you make this play, you are earning $85.23 in EV regardless of the actual outcome. The more the pot odds exceed your odds of winning, the greater the EV of the play to you.

The above example was, however, one of the simplest decisions you will find yourself called upon to make. In reality, it is obviously not this easy to calculate your odds of winning the hand. It is also not always this easy to calculate exactly what you expect to win. This is where things become a lot more complicated; and mastering the techniques in the following sections is what separates solid players from the best.

Figuring what you stand to win

Pot odds are simply the ratio of the amount of money currently in the pot to the amount it is going to cost you to continue. If you are facing a bet when an opponent has more money in his stack (money behind), you can expect to extract at least some of it on later streets if you hit. If you hit your flush against your opponent's A-A in Example 1, you know that all you are going to win is the $1875 in the middle. You don't need to think about how much more you can extract since your opponent is all-in. In Example 2, the bet is made on the turn and the opponent has money behind for you to target once you've made your flush. This is where implied odds come in.

Example 2: You hold Ac-4c. The board on the turn is showing Kc-Th-7d . . . 2c. There is $1000 in the pot. Your opponent again holds Ah-Ad and bets $500. He has another $2000 in his stack and you have at least that much more yourself (you have him 'covered'). If you call and hit your flush, you figure that he will check the river, and call when you bet $750. If you call and miss your flush, you will fold when he bets on the river. Should you call?

Simply looking at pot odds would suggest no. The pot odds are 3-1 and the odds against your winning the hand are again 3.9-1. But you have not included the $750 you expect to make on the river. You are still facing a $500 bet, but what you stand to gain (your return) is now the $1500 in the middle *plus* the $750 you plan to extract on the river. The relevant ratio is $2250:$500 which comes out to 4.5-1. All of a sudden, calling is a winning play.

$$EV = (Pw \times R) - (Pl \times L)$$
$$EV = (9/44 \times \$2250) - (35/44 \times \$500) = \$62.50$$

Implied odds should *not*, however, be used as an excuse for making poor calls. You must *not* see the $2000 in his stack and decide to include all of this in the 'what you stand to gain' column. We are not talking about the maximum you could gain, but a reasonable estimation of what you can *expect* to gain. In the example above, in fact, it would have been even more accurate to say that he will call your $750 bet 90 per cent of the time, and so to add in $(0.90 \times \$750) = \$675$ to the return figure rather than the full $750. In practice, make sure you include only what you truly believe you can extract from your opponent, and even then discount this figure a little due to the possibility that he will fold.

In some cases you can hit the hand you are chasing, and still end up losing the pot. Here there is a danger of miscalculating the probability of winning the hand (see section below on true odds). You must factor into your calculation the disastrous scenario where you hit your hand and still lose. Imagine you are chasing the same club flush as in the examples above, but your opponent has a set of kings. In this case, if you make your flush as the board pairs, your opponent will make a full house, and you are not likely to be able to get away from the hand without going broke. Your opponent effectively has his own implied odds against you. If your opponent has a hand that can beat you occasionally, even when you do hit your hand, this calls for a consideration of reverse implied odds.

Example 3: The situation is the same as Example 2, but this time your opponent holds Kd-Kh for top set. If you hit your flush on the river, as he hits a full house, you will go broke. Should you call?

The odds against you making your flush are still 3.9-1. When calculating your return, however, only seven of the nine times you hit do you go on to win the pot. The 'what you stand to gain' column needs to reflect this, *plus* the big loss that occurs the two times he makes his full house – you lose the $500 bet plus the $2000 he is going to bet on the river. What you stand to gain is now:

Pot odds $(7/9 \times \$1500)$ + implied odds $(7/9 \times \$750)$ − reverse implied odds $(2/9 \times \$2500) = \$1194.44$.

So your true ratio is $\$1194.44:\$500 = 2.39\text{-}1$, which is lower than the 3.9-1 odds that you make your flush. Make the fold.

The EV if you had elected to call is: $EV = (9/44 \times \$1194.44) - (35/44 \times \$500) = -\$153.41$

This play is now a disastrous call.

As David Sklansky points out in his seminal book *The Theory of Poker*, reverse implied odds are also a concern when you cannot deduce your opponent's hand accurately, but you suspect that a good deal of the time you are ahead. You cannot simply compare your return (the money in the pot) with your loss (the bet you currently face) and try to figure if you have the best hand often enough to make a call here worthwhile. If your opponent *does* have you beat, he may very well bet again on the turn and the river, costing you *way* more money than just the bet you currently face. Your loss here is greater than the bet you are now facing. This will take your true odds way down and will often make calling a negative EV play.

Carrying out all these calculations in the heat of battle is, of course, less than feasible. In practice, you cannot possibly calculate these odds exactly in the time you have to make a decision. But reverse implied odds should always be on your mind, and can certainly turn a marginal call into a losing play. Always think of reverse implied odds when your draw is not to the nuts. Drawing to a king-high flush is a dangerous example. Most of the time you hit, you will wind up winning the pot; but those few times you hit your flush, and run into someone who has been betting the ace-high flush, you are going to be crippled. Any time you have a flush draw, one or two cards (depending on the exact distribution of cards) are going to make your flush as the board pairs. This could have made your opponent a full house. Tread carefully.

Figuring the odds of your winning the hand

What if you can still hit your hand and lose? How does this affect your calculation of the odds for or against your winning the hand? If you know your opponent's hand, you can discount cards that only *seem* like outs, and leave yourself with a lower number of *true* outs. As we have seen, when drawing to a flush against an opponent with a set, you most often have seven true outs instead of nine. The exception comes when one of the cards that would make a flush and pair the board is already in your hand.

Example 4: You hold Ac-7c. The board on the turn is showing Kc-Th-7d . . . 2c. Your opponent holds Kd-Kh. How many *true* outs do you have?

There are, as usual, nine clubs remaining. Tc would make your flush but make your opponent's full house, so it is not a true out. No other club pairs the board. So you have eight true outs. Whenever you are making a calculation of the odds of going on to win the hand, you *must* be careful to count only true outs.

In complicated situations, the calculations you use return a decimal probability between 0 and 1. It is therefore crucial to be able to convert a decimal probability into an odds ratio. Call the figure in your calculation returns X. Divide 1 by this figure, giving you a number greater than 1. Then subtract 1 from this second figure. The odds ratio is this number to 1.

$$[(1/X)-1]:1.$$

For example, if your calculation returns a figure of 0.2, the odds ratio is:

$$(1/0.2)-1:1$$
$$= (5-1):1$$
$$= 4:1.$$

You will need to be able to switch from a probability figure to the odds ratio with ease in the following sections.

What if the bet you are facing is on the flop and there are two cards to come. How do you calculate your odds now? This is where things get a little more complicated. Even though there are two streets on which you can hit your hand, you are not simply twice as likely to do so. If you hit on both the turn *and* the river, you haven't hit two flushes. You've hit one twice. Simply adding the probability of hitting on the turn to the probability of hitting on the river double-counts those times you hit on both.

Example 5: You hold Ac-4c. The board on the flop is showing Kc-Th-7c. What are the odds you make your flush?

You are going to hit your flush unless you miss on both streets. The probability of two events occurring is the probability of the first multiplied by the probability of the second. The probability of your missing on both streets is therefore the probability of your missing on the turn multiplied by the probability of your missing on the river. Once you have this, to calculate the probability of your *not* missing on both (that is, the probability of your hitting your flush), simply subtract this figure from 1. On the turn, there are 47 unseen cards (the 52 in the deck minus the two in your hand and the three on the board). Thirty-eight of them are not clubs. On the turn, you have seen another card. There are now 46 unseen cards, 37 of which are not clubs.

So the probability of making your flush is $1 - (38/47 \times 37/46) = 0.35$. Note that this does not match the 0.364 for the 'true' figure for nine outs in the table on page 51. This is because this calculation just looks at the odds of making a flush without factoring in your opponent's cards. In the table, we are assuming we know his two cards and that our nine outs are still live.

Using the conversion formula above, the odds of you making your flush are $(1/0.35)-1:1$, which works out as $1.86:1$.

As we have seen, sometimes your opponent can have a hand that can beat you even when you make the hand you are chasing. In the following example, we look at chasing a flush against an opponent with a set on the flop. This is not now simply a case of looking at true outs because you could hit one of your true outs on the turn (a flush card that doesn't pair the board) but then he could hit on the river and make his full house or quads. Equally problematic is when he makes his full house or quads on the turn and you hit a card you considered to be a true out on the river.

Example 6: You hold Ac-4c. The board is showing Kc-Th-7c. Your opponent holds Kd-Kh. What are the odds of you winning the hand?

This is about as complicated as a situation can get. There are no easy shortcuts for figuring the probability here. You need to take a 'brute force' approach and work through every way in which you can win the pot, then add the probabilities together before converting to an odds ratio.

There are only two ways for you to win this pot:

One: You hit a true out on the turn and your opponent doesn't hit a redraw on the river;

OR

Two: You both miss the turn and you hit a true out on the river.

Any other eventuality sees you lose the pot. Let's calculate the probabilities of One and Two.

One: There are 45 unknown cards on the turn. Eight of them are true outs (non-board-pairing clubs). Once you have hit a true out, there are then 44 unseen cards on the river, 34 of which do not pair the board, so are not redraws for your opponent. Therefore the probability of this outcome is (8/45 × 34/44) = 0.1374.

Two: There are 45 unknown cards on the turn. Eight of them are true outs for you and seven of them complete his hand. Therefore there are 30 out of 45 cards on the turn that miss both of you. There are now 44 unseen cards on the river, seven of which are true outs for you. The probability of this outcome is (30/45 × 7/44) = 0.106.

The combined probability of either event is 0.1374 + 0.106 = 0.243. Using the conversion formula, the odds are therefore 3.11:1.

Again, you can't make calculations as complicated as this in the thick of the action, in the time you have to make a decision. Thankfully, there are two ways of avoiding this burden.

Probability shortcuts
2% per out per street
When you calculate the odds of hitting an out on the next card, you are effectively dividing your number of outs into the number of unknown cards and then converting to an odds ratio. The number of unknown cards varies, depending on whether you are about to see the flop, turn or river, and whether you are factoring in what cards you think your opponent holds, but it is always close to 50. Each out you have therefore contributes a roughly 1/50 (or 2%) chance to your winning the hand.

When there are two cards to come, you have two shots at hitting your card, so each out contributes roughly 2 × 1/50 (or 4%) chance to your winning the hand. In truth, the odds of your hitting on the next two cards is 1 minus the odds of your missing both, which is slightly different to two times the odds of your hitting on the next card. Fortunately, the difference is so slight that the '2% per street per out' approximation is close enough to be usable at the table.

Let's revisit Example 5: You hold Ac-4c. The board on the flop is showing Kc-Th-7c. What are the odds you make your flush, assuming all your clubs are outs and your opponent doesn't have a hand with a redraw?

You have nine outs. You have two streets to come. So you have a $(9 \times 2 \times 2) = 36\%$ chance of hitting your flush. Divide this by 100 to give a 0.36 chance of making your flush. This is close enough to the true figure of 0.364 that you can confidently use it without making a significant EV error.

The 2% per street per out method is not always this close to the true figures, though. On the next page is a table comparing the figures returned by the 2% per street per out rule and the true figures. The method becomes less accurate at the higher number of outs, underestimating with one card to come and overestimating with two cards to come. Finally, this method does not deal with the subtleties of opponents' redraws, so you must know when and by how much to discount these figures.

Outs	2 cards to come		1 card to come	
	2% per street per out estimate	True figure	2% per street per out estimate	True figure
1	4%	4.5%	2%	2.3%
2	8%	8.8%	4%	4.5%
3	12%	13.0%	6%	6.8%
4	16%	17.2%	8%	9.1%
5	20%	21.2%	10%	11.4%
6	24%	25.2%	12%	13.6%
7	28%	29.0%	14%	15.9%
8	32%	32.7%	16%	18.2%
9	36%	36.4%	18%	20.5%
10	40%	39.9%	20%	22.7%
11	44%	43.3%	22%	25.0%
12	48%	46.7%	24%	27.3%
13	52%	49.9%	26%	29.5%
14	56%	53.0%	28%	31.8%
15	60%	56.1%	30%	34.1%
16	64%	59.0%	32%	36.4%
17	68%	61.8%	34%	38.6%
18	72%	64.0%	36%	40.8%
21	84%	70.0%	42%	47.7%

This shortcut and a good estimate of the number of true outs are all you need in order to calculate your odds of winning the hand fairly accurately. The table overleaf shows the most common Texas Hold'em hands that occur on the flop and turn, and the number of outs each hand has.

Matchup	Your cards	Opponent's cards	Board cards	Outs
Set vs set	4s-4c	Ks-Kd	4h-8h-Kc	1
Overpair vs set	Jh-Jc	6d-6c	7h-6s-2d	2
Two pair vs two pair	Ac-6c	As-Kc	Ah-Kh-6d	2
Gutshot vs pair + flush draw	6c-8s	Ad-Kd	7d-Td-Ac	3
Gutshot vs pair	5d-6d	Ac-Kc	8d-9c-Kh	4
Two overcards vs pair	Ad-Kd	Jc-Qh	4s-6c-Jh	6
Flush draw vs set on turn	Ah-Kh	Qs-Qh	Qc-7h-3h-2d	7
Flush draw vs set on flop	Ah-Kh	Qs-Qc	Qc-7h-3h	8
Flush draw vs pair	6h-Th	Ac-Ad	Kh-4h-Jd	9
Gutshot + two live cards	Js-Tc	Ad-Kc	2s-7d-8c	10
Flush draw + gutshot	5s-6s	Ad-Ah	2s-3c-Js	12
Flush draw + live card	Ah-5h	Kd-Kc	Qh-8h-2s	13
Flush draw + two live cards	Ad-Kd	Qs-Qc	7d-Td-3c	15
Flush draw + gutshot + one live card	Ts-Js	Td-Th	9s-7c-3s	15
Flush draw + open-ended straight draw	7h-8h	Ac-Ks	5h-6h-Kd	15
Flush draw + gutshot + two live cards	Jc-Qc	7d-7h	Tc-Ad-2c	18
Flush draw + open-ended straight draw + live card	Qd-Kd	Qs-Qc	Td-3h-Jd	18
Flush draw + open-ended straight draw + two live cards	Js-Ts	Ac-9d	9s-8s-4h	21

As noted, the 2% per street per out rule fails to take into account any redraws your opponent may have. The exact odds of winning a hand depend not only on the cards you hold, but on the type of hand you are up against. For complete statistics on Hold'em match-ups taking into account both hands, see Appendix C, p. 297.

This section has shown you how to calculate figures for what you expect to gain in a hand, and the odds of your going on to win the hand. With these figures you can calculate the EV of a play and determine whether it is a winning play. The following section will look at how to think about EV when considering different types of play: calling for value, betting for value, bluffing and semi-bluffing.

EV and different types of play

EV and calling for value

The examples in the last section all featured situations where you know you don't have the best hand, but you have a decent chance of improving to go on and win the hand. Calling in a situation like this is known as 'calling for value'. The methods already described determine if a specific call for value is correct. In real Texas Hold'em situations, there are some subtleties that must be considered to avoid falling into traps of making negative EV calls and turning down positive EV calls.

The first subtlety comes when you face a bet on the flop and your opponent has enough money and a strong enough hand to bet at you again on the turn. It is wrong to compare the odds of making your hand by the river with the odds you are getting on your money (implied odds included). This method would work only if you get to see both the turn *and* the river for the cost of the bet you are currently facing. As I have said, your opponent isn't going to be this generous. The correct way to think in these situations is to treat the decision on the flop in isolation.

Example 7: You hold Ac-4c. The board on the flop is showing Kc-Th-7c. There is $1000 in the pot. Your opponent has Ah-Ad and bets $1000. You both have $10,000 behind. If you call and hit, your opponent will call a $750 bet on the turn. On the river, you will bet $1500 and you estimate he will call half of the time. Should you call on the flop?

His play on the turn if you miss is uncertain – he may bet enough that you have to fold (a zero EV play for you). He may outplay you and trap you into making a negative EV call, or he may bet small enough to let you make a positive EV call. Unless you greatly outclass your opponent, it is natural to assume the play on the turn, should you miss, is EV neutral and won't factor in our calculation of your return. You should really be considering the odds of your hitting on the next card (your relevant odds) and the odds you are getting on your money now. Unfortunately, the relevant odds here are slim, but on the plus side; if you do hit, you will have two streets to extract money from him. The calculation for your return now looks like:

Pot odds ($2000) + implied odds ($750 + (0.5 × $1500) = $3500

So your ratio is $3500:$1000 = 3.5-1. Your relevant odds are a little under 3.9-1, so you can see that this is a negative EV play. If you had mistakenly considered the odds of hitting your hand on the turn *or* river (about 1.75-1), you would have jumped into a negative EV play.

An alternative but equally valid method in this situation is to compare the odds of your hitting on either of the next two cards with the effective odds the pot is offering you. Your effective odds compare what you stand to win not only with the bet you face now, but the bet(s) you are likely to face on later streets. It is simpler, particularly in no limit and pot limit Hold'em, to treat the decision on the flop in isolation. With the relevant odds method, you are not required accurately to predict your opponent's future actions when you miss your hand and can concentrate on making one positive EV play at a time. In limit Hold'em your opponent cannot choose the bet size on the turn, so merely predicting whether your opponent will check or bet will allow you to calculate your effective odds accurately.

Sometimes there are cards in the deck that don't really make your hand but that you can include as outs in your calculations.

Example 8: You hold 7c-8d and the board on the turn is showing 5h-2c-6h . . . Kd. Your opponent holds Ac-As and incorrectly believes with 100% certainty that you hold two hearts in your hand. He has no idea which hearts these may be. How many outs do you have on the river?

There are eight outs that make your straight (any 4 or 9). However, there are seven more cards (2h 3h 7h 8h Th Jh Qh Kh and Ah) that will convince your opponent you have made a flush. If one of these cards comes on the river, you can win the pot by betting, and representing the heart flush he fears you to have. So in total, you have 15 outs (eight true outs and seven 'phantom' outs) and should calculate your odds accordingly. It is easy to see that ignoring phantom outs can result in your passing up solidly positive EV plays.

NB: Make sure you do not double-count outs – 4h and 9h are included in your eight true outs and must therefore not be double-counted as phantom outs as well.

EV and betting for value

When you bet in a situation where you believe you have the best hand, you are betting for value. On the flop and turn, your opponent may still have a chance to improve and win the hand. You should notice that this situation is the exact reverse of those covered so far about calling for value. Now you are holding the hand your opponent held, and vice-versa.

You call for value if the bet size is small enough that the call carries positive EV. Every time you do so, you make theoretical money from your opponents. It follows that when you hold the stronger hand, and it is your opponent considering calling for value, you must prevent him from making positive EV calls against you. If you can somehow trap him into making negative EV calls, so much the better. The way you achieve this is to ensure that you bet enough that you offer your opponent two choices: fold (zero EV) or call (negative EV). In practice, this means figuring the bet size that would make calling a zero EV play, and betting more than this.

Example 9: You hold Ad-Ah. On the flop, the board is showing Kc-Th-7c and there is $1000 in the pot. Your opponent holds Ac-4c. You both have $10,000 on the table. To simplify the calculations, assume that you will not lose any further money if your opponent hits his flush on the turn. This means you do not have to consider his implied odds. How much do you need to bet to ensure he cannot make a positive EV call?

First off, consider the odds of your opponent hitting on the turn (35:9 = 3.9:1). If you were to bet an amount that offered him pot odds greater than this, he could make a positive EV call. If you were to bet an amount that offered him exactly the same pot odds, his call would have zero EV. To find this figure, subtract 1 from the left-hand side of his odds ratio, and divide the pot size by this figure.

Bet size = $1000/(3.9-1) = $346.15.

His pot odds are now: 1346.15:346.15, which is 3.9-1, exactly the same as the odds of his making the hand on the turn – his relevant odds.

Any amount greater than this will offer him a negative EV play since the pot odds will be lower than the odds of his hitting his hand. Let's pick a nice round number above this figure and see what options he has. You bet $400.

Option 1: Call. His EV as we have seen is $(Pw \times R) - (Pl \times L)$ = $(9/44 \times \$1400) - (35/44 \times \$400) = -\$31.82$.

Option 2: Fold. The EV of folding is always zero.

You have made a bet that leaves your opponent with the choice of either a zero or a negative EV play. He *should* fold, but if he calls, you are delighted to note that he is making a play that is 'worth' –$31.82 to him, or conversely +$31.82 to you. The skill when you find yourself in this situation is to pick a bet size above the amount required to offer him zero EV on calling, but still small enough to entice him into making the negative EV call. The more you bet, the more negative the EV of his call becomes; but the less likely a (good) player is to make the call. Judging the amount is a subtle art, and will be discussed later in the advanced sections on opponents' playing styles.

EV and bluffing

Bluffing (or pure bluffing, as it is considered here) is making a bet when you know that you do not have the best hand and have no chance of improving to a hand that will win the pot. The maths behind making a winning bluff are fairly simple, and very similar to those used to calculate if a call is a winning play. When you bluff, you win the pot if your opponent folds. If your opponent folds, there is no more betting so you do not have to worry about implied or reverse implied odds. Instead of *calculating* your odds of improving to win the hand, you *estimate* the odds of your opponent folding, and compare these odds to the odds you are being offered on your bet. A bluff is a winning play if the odds of your opponent folding exceed the pot odds of the bluff.

Example 10: You hold 6h-5d. On the river, the board is showing 3h-4s-Ts-Jd . . . 3s. Your opponent holds Kc-Kd. There is $1500 in the pot and you both have $10,000 at the table. He has a strong hand but you know he is scared that you have a flush; and you estimate that if you bet $750, he will fold 40% of the time. Should you make the bluff?

First, you need to convert the 40% chance of his folding into an odds ratio. You have seen above that this is done in the following way:

40% = (40/100) = 0.4
So the odds are [(1/0.4)–1]:1
= 1.5-1.

Now check the pot odds you are getting. You stand to win $1500 if your bluff is successful, and you stand to lose $750 if your bluff fails. Your pot odds are therefore: $1500:$750 = 2:1.

You can see that the pot odds exceed the odds of your winning the hand. This is a positive EV play because of the folding equity from the times your opponent folds. Make the bluff.

Calculating whether this was a positive or negative EV play required an accurate estimation of the odds of your opponent folding. Again, this is a skill that comes only with experience and will be further discussed throughout the rest of this book.

In practice, bluffs are often made when the chances of your going on to win the hand if you are called are not strictly zero. You might be betting primarily to drive your opponent out of the hand, and win it there and then; but if the bluff fails, and you go on to see the next card, there are a small number of miracle cards that could still win you the pot. The intention of the bet is half-bluff, half-hoping to hit if you do get called. It is a semi-bluff.

EV and semi-bluffing

Semi-bluffs have folding equity as well as the chance of winning you a pot (probably quite a big pot) if you do get called and hit your hand. In effect, you have implied odds as well as folding equity, and you can add these benefits together to calculate a semi-bluff's value. Of course you could get called and miss your hand, but there are now two benefits to the play, and the EV is calculated accordingly.

Example 11: You hold As-Qc. The board on the turn is showing Kc-Th-7d . . . 2c. There is $1000 in the pot and your opponent holds Ad-Ah. He is a timid player who often fears that when the pot gets big, his opponents have a set. So he checks to you. If you bet $1000, you estimate that he will fold 35% of the time. If he calls, and you hit one of your four outs (the four jacks) on the river, there will be $3000 in the pot, and you know that he will check and call a bet of $2500. If he calls and you miss on the river, he will check, you will check and he will win the pot. Is it a winning play to bet $1000 on the turn?

When considering whether a semi-bluff has positive EV, it is too fiddly to compare your odds ratio with your return/loss ratio. It is quicker and easier to work out the actual EV of the play and see if it is positive. You simply go through the three possible outcomes and multiply the probability of each outcome by your return or loss in each case. Adding these together will give you the total EV for the play.

Outcome 1: He folds. Probability: 35%. Return: the $1000 in the pot. EV = (0.35 × $1000) = $350.

Outcome 2: He calls and you hit on the river. Probability: (65% × 4/44). Return: the $1000 in the pot, the $1000 he calls on the turn and the $2500 he will call on the river = $4500. EV = (0.65 × 4/44) × $4500 = $265.91.

Outcome 3: He calls and you miss on the river. Probability: $(65\% \times 41/44)$. Loss: just the $1000 of your semi-bluff. EV = $(0.65 \times 41/44) \times -\$1000 = -\$605.68$

So your total EV = $350 + $265.91 - $605.68 = $10.23.

Making this play has a positive EV of $10.23 and is a winning play. It is easy to see that without the extra equity from hitting your hand and going on to win a big pot, this would have been a horrible play. If this were a pure bluff, you would simply win the $1000 in the pot 35% of the time and lose your $1000 bluff 65% of the time. The equity on this play is $(0.35 \times \$1000) - (0.65 \times \$1000) = -\$300$. Just having four miracle cards on the river is the difference between the bet here being a slightly winning play and the bet being a big losing play.

You must pick your opponents and timing for semi-bluffs carefully. The semi-bluff is a powerful weapon but if you routinely overestimate the likelihood of your opponent folding, or the amount you stand to win if you do hit, you will consistently be overestimating the EV of semi-bluffs and will often be making losing plays. The method is sound, but the conclusion will be accurate only if the data you input are themselves accurate.

Putting your opponent on a range of hands

When playing Texas Hold'em, you never know with 100% certainty what your opponent holds. In the calculations above, your opponent's hand was known to us, which made calculating the EV of the play a purely mathematical exercise. When you become adept at reading hands, you can often make predictions of your opponent's holding with a high degree of certainty; but you never know for sure what you are up against.

An experienced Hold'em player is able to appreciate that even though hand-reading skills point towards your opponent holding a certain hand, there is always a chance he will show down a surprising two cards – and you must adjust your play accordingly. Players sometimes pursue a course of action that is optimal against one possible holding, but disastrous against others. If their read was wrong and they lose a massive pot, they justify their actions by saying they 'put' their opponents on a specific hand. Their failure to pursue a compromise strategy that takes into account all possible holdings is the mark of a poor player.

In Examples 2 and 3 above, we saw that drawing to your flush against A-A was a winning play once you'd considered implied odds. We also saw that if you were up against a set, true outs and reverse implied odds could eat away at the value of your play, and turn the same call into a losing one. In a real Hold'em hand, you are never 100% sure of your read, so it is much more natural to assign a probability to each possible holding and find a compromise strategy. Now, we estimate that two-thirds of the time he holds A-A and the other third he holds top set. We know the EV of each play, so we can now work out the EV of calling against this range of hands.

$$EV = (2/3 \times \$62.50) - (1/3 \times -\$153.41) = -\$9.47.$$

Even though you believe he holds A-A, and if he does you should call, your uncertainty as to his holding has turned calling into a losing play.

Now that you understand expected value theory and its relevance to Texas Hold'em, you need to start looking at specific situations and ensuring you correctly apply the principles you have learnt. After all, your fundamental goal is to develop a sound basic strategy, and to use all the weapons available to you to make positive EV plays, and to prevent them being made against you.

4

In Practice

Pre- and Post-Flop Play

Pre-flop strategy

When to call, raise or fold

It is fundamental to your pre-flop strategy to understand that consistently playing stronger hands than your opponents will put you in positions to make positive EV plays on the flop and beyond. The strongest pre-flop hand is the one that figures to win the pot most often. Your first thought when you hold the strongest hand should be to raise or reraise, to get as much money into the pot as possible. Because you will be winning the pot more often than your opponents, the more money they commit to the pot pre-flop, the more will end up in your stack in the long run.

It sometimes makes sense to play even if you do not believe that your hand is currently the strongest. A hand that has a good enough chance of improving to win, and will earn you enough money if it does, can still be played for value.

Some hands are so weak, in comparison to the likely hands your opponents hold, that you should just fold. Even seeing the flop with the hope of improving to win the hand isn't worth the price of the call.

To make the above decisions correctly, you need to know the power of your own hand, the likely hands your opponents may hold, and how these hands will interact on the flop and beyond.

Absolute pre-flop power

Some hands lack intrinsic power, but have a slim chance of turning into a monster. Some have a decent chance of connecting with the flop, and make a solid holding when they do. Others are simply powerhouses in their own right. Understanding the merits of each type of holding is the first step to a solid pre-flop strategy. To evaluate pre-flop holdings, you need to know what kind of hands they make when they hit the flop and the probability that they will do so.

Big pairs: A-A, K-K, Q-Q and J-J. Most starting hands in Hold'em need to improve to stand a good chance of winning the pot. Big pairs are the exception. Even without improvement, these hands will be an overpair on the flop much of the time. Overpairs are often powerful enough to win a sizable pot without help. If big pairs do connect, and make a high set or full house, you hold a hand that will very rarely fail to win you the pot.

Medium pairs: T-T, 9-9, 8-8, 7-7. These are rarely strong enough to win a pot without improving – certainly not a pot that sees big action on the flop, turn and river. The true value of these hands lies in their chance of winning a huge pot when they hit a set. Few flops, particularly in multi-way or raised pots, are checked all the way around. A medium pocket pair that misses on the flop will usually have to be folded. The relevant odds when considering playing a medium pair are therefore the odds of flopping a set rather than making one by the river.

Small pairs: 6-6, 5-5, 4-4, 3-3, 2-2. Small pairs play very similarly to medium pairs in no limit Hold'em. Any unpaired holding will still need to improve to beat a pocket pair, no matter how small the pair. A flopped set is almost always strong enough that you are not going to fold, even if it is a set of deuces. If two players flop a set, of course, it is the one entering the pot with the bigger pocket pair that will win the day, but these things don't happen too often – and you still made the right play.

Big suited aces: A-Ks, A-Qs, A-Js and A-Ts. When these cards hit one pair, it will either be top pair of aces with a solid kicker or a big pair with top kicker. These hands are far from invulnerable but solid enough that, if played well after the flop, they should return you a positive EV. They can also make a nut flush or a 'Broadway' (ace-to-ten straight). The majority of the time these hands will be the nuts, so you don't have to fear reverse implied odds of losing a big pot when these holdings turn into a made hand. A-K has the special property of *always* making top pair-top kicker when it hits once, which elevates this hand significantly above any other big ace.

Big off-suit aces: A-Ko, A-Qo, A-Jo and A-To. Suited cards wind up making a flush only about 4% of the time, so big off-suit aces are only marginally less powerful than their suited cousins. Unfortunately, these hands can make a flush only if there are four cards of that suit on board. This is not only unlikely, but a situation where opponents will not lose a big pot. These holdings therefore lack the implied odds that big suited aces have from the huge pots that often result from making a two-card nut flush.

Big suited cards: K-Qs, K-Js, K-Ts and J-Qs. As soon as your hand does not contain an ace, you lose two very important properties. First, you can no longer make top pair-top kicker.

Every time you hit one pair, there is a chance that your opponents hold the same pair with a higher kicker. Not only are you behind here, but you are holding a fairly solid hand and stand to lose a sizeable pot. Secondly, some of the draws you hit will not be the nuts. Unless the ace of your suit is on board when you make a flush, you will always fear the nut flush. You can end up losing a huge pot with a second-best flush; and even when you *are* good, you will not always have the confidence to extract maximum value by betting hard into your opponents. These hands suffer pre-flop reverse implied odds and decreased implied odds. They are significantly weaker than big suited aces as a result. Fortunately, any straights using both hole cards made by these holdings will be the nuts. You do not have to worry about making a straight and losing to a higher one.

Big off-suit cards: K-Qo, K-Jo, K-To and J-Qo. These hands are just as dangerous as suited big cards and lack the implied odds from making a two-card flush. They can occasionally be played for value, but are a lot more dangerous than a learner player realises. They are too likely to make a second-best hand to be considered strong pre-flop holdings.

Little suited aces: A-9s through A-2s. These hands can be played for the implied odds of making a nut flush but nevertheless their value is often overestimated. They flop a made flush only 0.84% of the time, and a draw 10.9% of the time. Even flopping a draw is only part-way to making the hand. A far greater concern is the high probability that you will hit a one-pair hand and be out-kicked. If you are going to play a little suited ace for the implied odds, you must be able to get away from a second-best, one-pair hand cheaply. Otherwise the reverse implied odds from the times you hit and are out-kicked are going to kill any implied odds from making a nut flush.

Medium suited connectors: Hands like 5-4s and J-Ts lack any real ability to win by pairing once, so the majority of their value lies in the implied odds of hitting trips, two pair or a made hand. These pre-flop holdings are speculative. The majority of the time, they miss the flop and will have to be folded. On the rare occasions that these holdings make a powerful hand on the flop, they must win a big enough pot to pay for the cost of all your pre-flop calls. Consecutive cards that are not between 5-4s and J-Ts are limited in the number of straights they can make. The hole cards 3-2s can make only two straights: A to 5 and 2 to 6. Likewise A-Ks can make only one straight: the Broadway. They lack the 'stretch' of medium suited connectors, and as such are not included in this group.

Off-suit connectors / suited 1-gappers / suited 2-gappers and off-suit 1-gappers: Hands like 9-7o and 8-5s really are the weakest hands you should consider playing. They are speculative hands, but are less likely to make made hands than suited connectors. Also, when they *do* hit straights, they are probably not nut straights. They suffer lower implied odds than suited connectors, and greater reverse implied odds. They should be played only if the situation is perfect.

The table opposite shows the probabilities of certain types of hands hitting on the flop. To determine the relative pre-flop power of holdings, combine the probability of the holdings improving on the flop with the strength of the hands they make.

Pre-flop hand	Example	Flopped hand	Example flop	Probability
Pocket pair	Ah-Ad	Quads	As-Ac-5c	0.2%
Pocket pair	Ah-Ad	Full house	As-5c-5d	0.7%
Pocket pair	Ah-Ad	Set	As-8c-3d	10.8%
Pocket pair	Ah-Ad	Set or better	As-8c-8s	11.8%
Pocket kings	Kh-Kd	Overpair	Qs-8h-7d	79.3%
Pocket queens	Qh-Qd	Overpair	8c-2s-9h	67.6%
Pocket jacks	Jh-Jd	Overpair	7s-4c-4h	43.0%
Unpaired cards	Ah-Kd	One pair	As-6d-3c	29.0%
Unpaired cards	Ah-Kd	Two pair	As-Kh-4c	2.0%
Unpaired cards	Ah-Kd	Trips	As-Ac-6s	1.35%
Unpaired cards	Ah-Kd	Quads	Kh-Kc-Ks	0.01%
Suited cards	5s-Qs	Flush	As-9s-3s	0.84%
Suited cards	5s-Qs	Flush draw	As-9s-3h	10.9%
Connected cards	5s-6d	Straight	4c-7h-8h	1.3%
Connected cards	5s-6d	Open-ender	3c-4s-Kd	9.80%
Suited connectors	4s-5s	Straight or flush	As-9s-3s	2.1%
Suited connectors	4s-5s	Open-ender or flush draw	3d-6c-Qs	20.3%

Position

Your position relative to the dealer is a crucial concept in Texas Hold'em. Apart from pre-flop (where the small and big blinds are the last two people to act), the nearer to the button's right you are, the later in the betting rounds you will act.

When pre-flop in late position you have seen the majority of the other players act. Assuming that nobody has showed significant strength before you, you have to worry only about the small number of players behind you with unknown holdings. It is statistically less likely in this spot that there is a hand among your opponents that can stand up to a raise. Because the odds of a raise winning the pot are higher from late position, you can afford to sacrifice some post-flop EV by raising with slightly weaker hands.

Playing from the button, you know you will get to act last on every subsequent betting round. If you do have the best hand on and after the flop, your opponents will be forced to act before you have revealed the strength of your holding. In these cases, you can extract more profit post-flop than if you had been in early position. If you come up against an opponent with a stronger hand than yours after the flop, he will struggle not to reveal this when he acts first. You can get away more cheaply from a beaten hand in position after the flop than out of position. These two points are the equivalent of saying that in late position you have greater pre-flop implied odds and lower pre-flop reverse implied odds. Every type of hand benefits in these ways and is more valuable in later positions before the flop.

Because the advantage of acting last on the post-flop streets is so valuable, it often makes sense to try to drive out any players between you and the button. If you are in late position, and a raise succeeds in making the players between you and the button (button included) fold, you are now by default the last player to act each round after the flop. 'Buying the button' like this carries its own special value. You can afford to give up some EV on the pre-flop play by offsetting this against the advantage of position over every opponent after the flop.

Conversely, playing hands pre-flop from early position is a dangerous game. All the advantages I have mentioned of playing from late position become advantages your opponents have over you. Your implied odds go down, your reverse implied odds go up, and the chance of a raise picking up the pot decreases. There is such an EV loss associated with playing out of position that you need to restrict yourself to playing only those hands that have the greatest absolute pre-flop power. This should mitigate the EV loss from your positional disadvantage.

When you raise out of position, the need for a premium holding is even greater. Your raise indicates real strength, so the only hands your opponents will play against you are themselves powerful. Because there has been a raise and calls, the pot will already be building to a size uncomfortable for the first to act post-flop. Also, you will be out of position on every betting round after the flop.

How speculative hands play beyond the flop

With only one or two opponents, a solid one-pair hand such as top pair and top kicker is often strong enough to win the pot. In multi-way pots, there is a greater chance that someone has flopped a two-pair hand or better, and hands such as top pair-top kicker are less likely to win. Because of this, holdings that make solid one-pair hands fare well in heads-up or three-handed pots, but struggle to win if the pot gets multi-way. A much more valuable holding in a multi-way pot is one that has a chance of flopping a really strong hand – a set, a straight or a flush. If you do flop a powerful hand in a multi-way pot, there are plenty of players to extract bets from. Your implied odds are high. Accordingly, the value of big-card hands decreases in multi-way pots, and the value of speculative hands like suited connectors and medium/small pairs increases.

This impacts on your pre-flop strategy. When a pot is going to be multi-way, calling with a speculative hand is often correct even though you would have folded if the pot were heads-up. It is correct to fold suited connectors on the big blind facing a raise heads-up, but if the pot is four- or five-handed, this is now a good call. If you hold two big cards, especially in middle or late position, and it seems like the flop is shaping up to be multi-way, consider raising to thin the field. If your raise restricts the pot to one or two opponents, the one-pair hand you are hoping to hit has a greater chance of holding up.

Pocket pairs and suited connectors are both examples of speculative holdings, but they make hands on the flop that behave very differently. When you call with small and medium pairs, you are looking to hit on the flop or release the hand. Flopping a set or a full house with a pocket pair is such a strong hand that you hope to be facing big bets and raises on the flop and turn. Suited aces and suited connectors, on the other hand, will often flop draws. These hands require you to stick around till the turn or river in the hope of making your hand. When you flop a draw, you hope to be able to see the turn and river cheaply – that is, without facing big bets and raises.

Playing with lots of aggressive opponents means that there will tend to be lots of bets and raises on the flop and turn. Pocket pairs make hands that fare best in these types of games. If the game is passive, lots of flops and turns will be checked around, allowing draws to take free cards. Suited connectors and suited aces fare better here. If you don't base your pre-flop hand selection at least in part on how aggressive the play will be post-flop, you will be missing opportunities to further maximise the EV of your pre-flop decisions.

Isolating poor players

If there is a particularly poor player at the table, you can rely on him to allow you to make positive EV plays against him on the flop and beyond. If you have the advantage of position you can play almost any two cards against him for positive EV. If this is the case, you should do everything in your power to end up heads-up in a pot with this poor player. If you have position and he makes a raise, consider whether reraising will shut out the rest of the solid players at the table. This play can be made with holdings that lack the absolute pre-flop power usually required for a reraise. The huge EV advantage of playing a pot in position against a poor player more than makes up for weak starting cards.

If in doubt, raise

When uncertain of how to act pre-flop, err on the side of aggression, especially in late position. If you call, you have only the equity of hitting your hand on the flop and going on to win the pot. If you raise, however, the play is rather like a pre-flop semi-bluff. You can win the pot there and then; or, if you do get called, you can still hit a strong hand on the flop and win the pot. Additionally, raising pre-flop allows you to lead the action on the flop and beyond – which, as we will see, is an advantage in itself.

The 'squeeze' play

If one player opens for a raise and another calls, making a solid reraise with a non-premium holding is called a 'squeeze' play. The original raiser is now squeezed between your reraise and the first caller. He cannot know for sure whether the pot will be heads-up or three-way. He cannot know if the other caller might decide to push all-in and make a play for the pot. He also knows that you would reraise here with a premium holding, so must find a strategy that takes all these things into account. In general he will have to fold. The third player called the original raise but didn't reraise, so he probably holds a mediocre or spec-ulative hand. It might have been good enough to play in position against a single raiser, but will rarely be strong enough for him to call a solid reraise out of position.

Squeeze plays are most valuable when they have a high probability of winning the pot. They will win the pot only when the original raiser does not have a premium hand of his own. A tight player will raise under the gun with premium holdings only, so attempting a squeeze play here is foolish. He will often hold A-A or K-K, and your play will backfire. Your reraise must be respected, and will be only if you have the appropriate table image. If you have not made a pre-flop reraise for an hour or more, your opponents will believe that you have been waiting for a premium hand and should fold almost all the time. If you have been making lots of reraises, and been showing down mediocre hands, your opponents have no reason to believe that this reraise indicates a premium holding. They are more likely to call or reraise the squeeze play, so the play goes down in value.

Bringing it all together

You now have the information to put together a complete pre-flop strategy. You understand what makes a hand valuable, and how hand values vary in position and in different situations. You understand what you are trying to achieve when you raise, and the value of calling. The tables on pages 300–3 offer suggestions for how to act with certain hands based on the action before you. But they are no more than an initial guide, based to some extent on my own idiosyncratic style. To develop a sophisticated pre-flop strategy it is crucial to learn how to evaluate pre-flop hands, given the specifics of the situation. The tables are based on the tight-aggressive quadrant of playing styles (see page 113). As you develop your own playing style, you should not be afraid to diverge from the suggested courses of action.

Reading your opponents' cards pre-flop

When you accurately read your opponents' cards before the flop, it is much easier to choose the right play consistently. This is fundamental to playing winning poker. Understand that your opponents' pre-flop strategies are based on all the same concerns as your own, and their play reflects this. Whenever an opponent makes a pre-flop play, consider what would have led you to make that play in his position. This allows you to deduce his likely cards, assuming he is a competent player, and make sophisticated pre-flop plays. If you suspect your opponent to be holding a big pair, you know you have good implied odds (he will lose a lot if you hit). You also don't have to worry about reverse implied odds (if you hit only once, you are not going to lose any more money). Knowing this allows you to call with speculative hands, even heads-up. This is a far more profitable situation than playing a speculative hand against an unknown holding. You could end up leaking chips with a second-best hand, and might not even get paid off when you do hit big.

Mixing up your play

A complete pre-flop strategy contains elements that prevent your opponents reading your own cards. While the guidelines above are the main determinant of your pre-flop strategy, you should consider introducing an element of unpredictability. Playing a hand differently from what common sense dictates may carry a negative EV. In the long run, however, you will recoup more than enough equity by keeping your opponents unsure of your hands. An occasional raise from early position with substandard hands is the best way to achieve this.

The knowledge that you occasionally raise from early position with suited connectors causes your opponents to make two systematic mistakes. First, they can no longer fold knowing you hold a premium hand every time you raise from early position. Second, it prevents them from playing optimally on the flop and beyond in future hands. Suited connectors make strong hands on flops that otherwise look innocuous. The constant threat that you have raised with a suited connector prevents your opponents from confidently attacking you when you have raised and the flop is low.

These plays made for the sake of unpredictability must be only a small part of your pre-flop strategy. We have said already that, when raising from early position, you usually need a hand that has strong absolute pre-flop power to make up for the disadvantage of playing out of position. Raising with a suited connector under the gun is probably a negative EV play when viewed in isolation. You must not overuse this play, or you will be costing yourself too much in the name of deception. To keep yourself in check, it is a good idea to pre-select one or two suited connectors and include them in your mix of raising hands. You may choose 8-7s and T-9s. There are eight ways you can be dealt these two hands and 24 ways you can be dealt J-J, Q-Q, K-K or A-A. Including these two suited connectors in your list of early position raising hands means that one-quarter (8/32) of the times you raise from early position, it will be for deception. More often than this, and you are probably sacrificing too much short-term equity in the name of deception.

A subtle advantage of pre-selecting hands in live play is psychological. When you *are* dealt 8-7s or T-9s, you can't help but feel the rush that you have been dealt an early position raising hand. Your subconscious will respond exactly the same as if you had been dealt a big pair – and your opponents will read you accordingly.

Domination; or pre-flop reverse implied odds and slow-playing monsters

If two pre-flop hands contain a card of the same rank, the stronger hand is said to dominate the other. For example, A-Ko dominates A-Qo. Getting involved in pots with dominated hands can be disastrous. Hitting the shared card on the flop will not make a winning hand. If A-Ko and A-Qo both make top pair of aces, the dominated A-Qo is out-kicked. The situation is particularly bleak since the hand that A-Qo has hit is itself quite powerful. It is the kind of hand that loses a lot of money before you realise you are behind. You must do everything in your power to avoid this. A-Qo is a strong pre-flop hand but performs terribly against A-Ko. If your read suggests A-Ko as a likely holding for your opponent, you must be disciplined enough to fold.

Big pairs also play disastrously against even bigger pairs on the flop and beyond. Although not strictly falling under 'domination', according to the above definition, a bigger pocket pair stands to win a big pot most of the time. An overpair to the flop is a strong hand; when your opponent also holds an overpair, and you have him beaten with a bigger overpair, you can expect to extract plenty of chips from him. So you should do everything you can to give him the opportunity to play big pairs against your even bigger ones. If you raise from early position with A-A, and get reraised by a player from middle position, common sense dictates that he is also holding a big pair, probably K-K, Q-Q or J-J. It is certainly not a losing play to reraise here, but doing so would allow him to get a firm read on your hand, and he may fold his big pair. A better long-term play may be just to call and hope the flop comes out small enough for you both to be holding overpairs. If it does, you can use your post-flop weaponry to target his whole stack. You should be even more inclined to avoid the third raise if you are in late position, facing a raise and a reraise. Being in position after the flop will make it easier for you to extract chips on the flop, turn and river.

Flat-calling with aces is a powerful but dangerous play. Your opponents will flop a top set occasionally with their big pairs. Unless you are able to recognise these situations and make good folds (or 'laydowns'), simply pushing all-in pre-flop is probably the better play. Flat-calling a reraise with aces should also be done only against predictable players. If your opponent has reraised with a suited connector, the play loses all of its appeal. Your stack is the one in jeopardy. He will cripple you if he hits two pair or better on the flop, and will get away from his hand if he misses.

All-in before the flop

Facing a pre-flop all-in is rather a simple, if intimidating, decision. Usually, a lot of your mental energy pre-flop goes into thinking about how your hand will play on the flop and beyond. If you are considering an all-in bet before the flop, this is of no concern. All you need to assess is whether you will win the hand often enough to make the play positive EV. It is a simple pot-odds calculation. As we have noted, to make pot-odds calculations, you need an accurate figure for the probability of winning the pot. Pre-flop match-ups fall into broad categories. By learning the probabilities of these match-ups, you have all the information you need.

The following table shows the percentage of times that hands win in common pre-flop match-ups. Some pre-flop all-ins result in a split pot. When the two hands contain low cards, this is particularly common.

Hand A	Hand B	Summary	Hand A win	Hand B win
Ah-Ad	2h-2d	Best-case pair vs pair	82.9%	17.1%
3h-3d	2h-2d	Worst-case pair vs pair	81.1%	18.9%
Qh-Qd	Ah-Kd	Best-case pair vs 2 overcards	56.4%	43.6%
2h-2d	Js-Ts	Worst-case pair vs 2 overcards	46.0%	54.0%
Kh-Kd	Ac-Js	Pair vs 1 overcard 1 undercard	71.2%	28.8%
Ah-Ad	2h-7d	Best-case pair vs 2 undercards	89.0%	11.0%
Th-Td	4s-5s	Worst-case premium pair vs 2 suited undercards	77.3%	22.7%
Ad-Ah	Ac-6h	Best-case pair vs shared card and undercard	93.9%	6.1%
3d-3h	3c-2s	Worst-case pair vs shared card and undercard	84.2%	15.8%
Kh-Kd	Ad-Kc	Best-case pair vs shared card and overcard	69.8%	30.2%
4h-4d	4s-5s	Worst-case pair vs shared card and suited overcard	60.0%	40.0%
Ad-Kd	2d-7d	Best-case 2 suited overcards vs 2 suited undercards	68.7%	31.3%
As-Tc	4d-5d	Worst-case 2 overcards vs 2 suited undercards	58.7%	41.3%
Ac-Qh	Kh-Jd	High and 3rd card vs 2nd and 4th	62.6%	37.4%
Ac-6s	9h-Th	High and low cards vs two suited middle cards	51.6%	48.4%
As-Ks	Ac-6d	Best-case shared high card	75.2%	24.8%
Ad-3c	As-2s	Worst-case shared high card	49.9%	50.1%
As-Ks	Kc-2s	Best-case shared low card	78.2%	21.8%
2h-4d	2s-3s	Worst-case shared low card	50.1%	49.8%

Simply compare the pot odds with the probability of winning the hand and you call if the play is positive EV.

Example 12: You hold Ac-Js. There is $1000 in the pot (including any previous calls and raises) and an opponent pushes all-in, making it $600 more for you to call. Everyone else at the table folds, so it is just you and him. You know that he is holding Q-Q or K-K. Should you call?

Pot odds here are $1600:$600 = 2.67-1. For your hand odds, consult the table and convert the percentage figure into an odds ratio using the method in Chapter 1:

$(1/0.288)–1:1 = 2.47-1$

Your pot odds exceed the odds of your winning the hand, and so you should make the call.

As always, an aggressive play has the added benefit of folding equity. This adds significant EV to the play compared with calling, so you should be far more inclined to make an all-in raise than call, all else considered. If you get called, you know how to figure out if you will end up winning money overall. If you opponent docs not choose to call all-in, you win the pot 100% of the time.

When the flop comes down

The arrival of the flop is the defining moment in any hand of Hold'em. More than half the communal cards are exposed at once. The flop can turn an innocuous pre-flop hand into a powerhouse and can turn some pre-flop powerhouses into garbage. Let's look at the how the pre-flop hand types match up with certain flops.

Big pairs: Your first concern with a big pair is to see no overcards on the flop so as to be sure you are holding an overpair. If an overcard comes down, any of your opponents can beat you just by having paired one hole card. Top set is extremely powerful, and when you hold top set you will almost always gladly get all-in. Generally you are looking for innocuous flops that do not allow for flopped flushes and straights. It is not a disaster to see a suited flop as long as it is in one of the suits that you hold. You are still beating most hands, and only against a flopped flush are you a serious underdog.

Big aces (suited or not): The primary goal of a big suited ace is to flop top pair and top kicker. This beats any other one-pair hand apart from an overpair, and most of the time will be ahead. Top pair-top kicker is a stronger hand than top pair of aces with second or third kicker, even though in the second example the pair you have hit is higher. With top pair-top kicker, you are losing only to an overpair. With a pair of aces and second or third kicker, you are losing to any ace with a higher kicker. Your opponents will hold a big ace more often than a big pocket pair, so the pair of aces is more vulnerable than the lower top pair. A flush draw is part of the way to a made hand but still needs the turn or river to improve. They can be played for value, but opponents will know that a flush draw is a likely holding and may make you pay to see the next two cards. A flopped big pair *and* a flush draw is unlikely to be a serious underdog against any other hand, and is perfect for a big post-flop semi-bluff.

Big cards (suited or not): A perfect flop for two big cards is one that makes a straight. The hand will be the nuts, and the board will contain big cards that are likely to have made an opponent a second-best hand. More dangerous is top pair with second or third kicker. As we have seen, these hands are in danger of being out-kicked and losing a solid pot. Two big cards flop a lot of draws, and it is preferable to flop a straight draw than a flush draw. This is the case even though a flush draw will usually have more outs. Any straight draws these hands make will be to the nuts, but most flush draws will not be. Also, straights tend to make more money than flushes. For reasons best known to themselves, opponents fear the third of a suit on the turn or river a lot more than they do a card that completes a straight, so you can extract bigger bets with a straight than a flush.

Little suited aces: Hitting one pair with a little suited ace (or 'small ace') is not often a profitable flop. Pairing the ace or hitting trip aces will often see you lose a big pot when you are out-kicked. What you are really looking for is to flop a flush draw and to make positive EV calls on the flop and turn. When little aces hit two pair, it is often top two pair and can win big. Holding A-7s on a flop of 3-7-A beats any big ace hand and can expect to get rewarded handsomely. Flopping trips with the low card will be trips with top kicker, which is a powerful hand, losing only to a full house.

Suited connectors / suited gappers / off-suit connectors: Perfect flops for these hands add up to a made hand – a straight or a flush. This will almost always be a strong enough hand to get all-in there and then. When these hands flop a draw, as with any draw, you are only part of the way to the made hand. All you can hope for is to make positive EV calls on the turn or river, or to spot a chance for a positive EV semi-bluff. Suited connectors can also flop two pair on innocuous-looking flops and win big from over-pairs or top pairs with big kickers.

Flop texture

Your next concern is whether the flop is likely to connect with your opponents' probable holdings. Flops that contain two cards next to each other in rank allow for suited connectors to have hit two pair. Any time a flop already has a possible flush or straight, your opponent may have made his hand. Paired boards allow for your opponents to have flopped trips, and your read is rarely going to be so strong that you can rule out any hand containing a specific rank. Only if you have a strong read on your opponent from his pre-flop play can you rule out trips. In a reraised pot with A-A, you would rather see a 5-5-7 flop than a Q-J-T flop. Even though the board is paired, your opponent is extremely unlikely to be in a reraised pot with a hand containing a five. There is always a danger of running into a set, but this danger is equally present on any board. Your opponents make the same pre-flop plays with any of the small or medium pairs, so any three cards on the flop could have made his set.

Your post-flop play is determined by the combination of the strength of your hand on the flop and the texture of the flop with respect to your opponents' hands.

Broadly speaking, if your opponents are unlikely to feel confident in the strength of their hands based on what the flop contains, you should be more inclined to go for an aggressive play. Regardless of whether you believe you have the best hand, the texture of the flop can often indicate that a pure bluff is value. If you suspect your opponent holds a pocket pair J-J to A-A, and an ace flops, he is six times more likely to hold K-K, Q-Q or J-J and be scared of the overcard ace than to hold top set. This would be a perfect time to try a speculative pure bluff.

The texture of the flop also influences how deceptive you can afford to be when you think you are ahead. Slow-playing (see below) is suicidal when the texture of the flop allows your opponents to hold strong draws. Flops like 5h-6s-Th or Kc-Tc-8s combine with many playable pre-flop hands to make a big draw. If you suspect that you hold the strongest hand in a spot like this, your primary concern should be to charge your opponents for the right to draw against you. You save deceptive plays for those spots when the chance of their costing you the pot is slim.

Turn and river concerns – counterfeiting

Some hands are very likely to be ahead on the flop but vulnerable to a lot of turns and rivers. Top and bottom pair or bottom two pair on the flop are beating all one-pair-type hands and will be ahead the vast majority of the time. Unfortunately, not only can your opponents improve to trips or a higher two pair of their own, but your hand can be counterfeited. Another card on the board can pair, meaning that the lower part of your two pair no longer plays. For example, holding 5c-8s on 5d-8c-Jd is a solid hand. If the turn is another jack, however, your paired five is now irrelevant. Your hand is now jacks and 8s with a five kicker. Your hand is suddenly losing to any hand on the flop that contains a pair higher than 8s. On the turn with two pair, there are even more cards that counterfeit the hand on the river. So although these hands are strong, they are terrible hands to slow-play. A better play is to get as much money in the pot as you can when you know you are ahead. A big check-raise will do nicely.

After the flop

Slow-playing

When you hold a stronger hand than your opponent pre-flop, or on the flop, your first impulse should be to bet or raise strongly and get him to commit money to the pot when he is behind. If waiting until later in the hand to reveal your strength does not risk losing you the pot, you can consider slow-playing for deception. If you are first to speak, check and just call if your opponent bets. If you are last to speak, check if he has checked and just call if he has bet. The benefits of slow-playing are twofold. First, it conceals the strength of your hand and may trap your opponent into losing more money on later streets. Second, it allows your opponent to improve on the turn or river to a second-best hand that can lose a big pot against you.

If your opponent can only improve to a hand that is better than yours, the second benefit of slow-playing evaporates and the play becomes dangerous. The play may still be correct if two conditions are met. The chance of your opponent improving needs to be slim. The advantage you gain from concealing the strength of your hand needs to be large. If you hold 7-7 and call a raise against a likely big pair, a flop of 2-3-7 is perfect. When your opponent bets out strongly, you become even more certain that he holds a big pair. You know that if he improves on the turn, it will be to a higher set than yours. If this happens, you will lose your whole stack. The rest of the time, however, your deception will confuse him and he will lose more money than if you had raised. Since he hits on the turn only about 1 in 22 times, just calling may still be worth the risk. You stand to lose a big pot once in 22 times, but the other 21 times your deception will earn you more money than if you had raised straight away.

Check-raising

Checking your hand with the intention of raising (or reraising) in the same round after someone has bet is called check-raising. Obviously it can be deployed only when you act before the person you believe is likely to bet. One of the disadvantages of being out of position after the flop is that you have to reveal if you are holding a strong hand by acting aggressively. Check-raising is one way of forcing your opponent to commit a bet before you reveal that you have a strong hand. It is also useful to protect your hand against multiple opponents. If you have a solid hand out of position in a multi-way pot, simply betting might start off a calling chain where each subsequent person is getting more and more favourable odds to call you. A successful check-raise will mean that all players between you and the bettor face two bets rather than one. Check-raising is often the best way of preventing multiple opponents from making positive EV calls when drawing.

Check-raising is such an indicator of strength that your opponents often fold in this spot. You can use this to your advantage and start to include check-raise bluffs from time to time. These bluffs will make you money when they are successful. They also set up your opponents to make a stand against one of your check-raises in the future. As long as you ensure you have a legitimate hand when your opponents finally make a stand, your bluffs have set you up to win a big pot. The only major downside to this is that check-raising commits a serious proportion of your stack. When a check-raise bluff fails, it is costly.

Check-raising with a legitimate hand is a particularly powerful play when you are first of three to speak, and the person you expect to bet is second. If the second player bets, the third player will have to act before it gets back to you. He may call, in which case your deception has earned you two extra bets before you have revealed the strength of your hand. He may even raise, at which point the pot will be large enough for you to move all-in and be happy to win the pot right there.

Buying a free card

When you flop a draw, you want to give yourself the best chance of completing your draw and pay the cheapest price for this chance. This involves seeing the turn and river, but somehow avoiding paying full price. Strangely, this can often be achieved by committing *more* money than usual on the flop, with the intention of scaring your opponent into passive play on the turn. With a draw on the flop, consider raising or even check-raising. Not only could you pick up the pot right there (folding equity), but when you hit on the turn you have already begun to build a big pot (semi-bluffing equity). Crucially, your aggression on the flop will often scare your opponents into checking on the turn when you miss. You can now take the river for free, and will have seen the turn *and* the river for the price of a bet and a raise

on the flop. This is often a lower total price than calling on the
turn and again on the river.

Blocking bets

On the river, your hand may not be strong enough to bet for
value but strong enough to call if your opponent bets after you
check. A blocking bet is a bet in this spot designed to prevent
your opponent from dictating the size of the river bet. Blocking
bets work if your opponent holds a strong hand but fears you
may have the nuts. His hand is strong enough that he will probably bet for value if you check. If you bet into him, even a small
amount, he will be forced just to call. He cannot risk raising and
running into the nuts. If your bet is smaller than the bet your
opponent would have made, you have forced a showdown
cheaply.

An example may be when you have entered a pot with a little
suited ace and flopped trips with top kicker. The play on the flop
and turn suggests that your opponent has a big pair, but may
have a nut-flush draw. If the river brings the third of that suit,
your hand is probably still strong enough to check and call his
bet – he won't have the flush 100% of the time. If you check
and he holds a big pair, he will check behind on the river and
you won't win any more money. If you check and he has the
flush, he will value-bet and you will call and lose whatever
amount he bets. If you bet and he has a big pair, he will be
forced to call and lose more money. If you bet and he *does* have
the flush, the threat of your holding a full house will scare him
into just calling – and you have lost less than if you had checked
and called.

Blocking bets can also be used to force your opponent into
letting you see the next card cheaply. The intention of your bet
here is to scare your opponent into just calling a small bet rather
than making a large one. The result is that you get to see the
next card cheaper by betting than by checking and calling. This

play is dangerous against a smart or tricky player. Betting to buy a cheap turn or river is a well-known play and telegraphs your hand. Against a tricky player you might find yourself facing a big raise after betting here, and will often be forced to fold. This play should be used only against a passive, predictable player.

Stop/go plays

When an opponent raises pre-flop from late position, he will often hold a far from premium starting hand. Reraising from the blinds is often a correct play. A smart player will know that your reraise does not always indicate a premium holding, and may choose to call the reraise with any two playable cards. The advantage of position will allow him to outplay you on the flop and beyond. If the money is deep and your opponent is really skilled, he is probably correct to take a flop here. In this case, better than reraising is often just calling the raise with the intention of firing a bet on practically any flop. If the flop misses your opponent (which will happen two-thirds of the time if he starts out with unpaired cards), he will no longer have the same incentives to call a bet. You have a better chance if you wait for the flop to come before playing back at your opponent than by reraising pre-flop. This play is particularly powerful if the reraise you are considering making pre-flop would put either you or your opponent all-in, and one of you is short-stacked (holding, say, three times the amount of the initial raise). Rarely is a hand so big an underdog pre-flop as to make this a poor call on his part, so seldom will your opponent fold to the all-in in this spot. Waiting for the flop to come out will often let your opponent know that he is now a serious dog, and give him a chance to fold.

Delayed bluffs

When you bluff you want to have two boxes ticked. First, you want to have a good indication that your opponent is weak; and second, to have your bet credibly indicate a legitimate hand.

Bluff-raising on the flop is definitely a play you should be making from time to time, but you have had only one post-flop betting round to give you clues to your opponent's holding. Also, your opponent knows as much about slow-playing as you do – he knows that a lot of the time you hold a powerhouse, you would just call on the flop. If you have missed the flop completely in position and are thinking of a bluff, consider just calling on the flop. Your opponent will have to act first again on the turn – and if he checks, the evidence is starting to point towards his being weak. You can then make a bluff bet on the turn with more confidence of his folding than if you had raised on the flop. Further, your play is more consistent with your holding a powerful hand. You may even be lucky enough to make your opponent fold a medium-strength hand here.

This play is particularly powerful as a delayed semi-bluff. This involves calling on the flop with a draw that would not normally seem like value. You are obviously hoping to hit your miracle card(s). A lot of the value from this play comes from the times your opponent is forced to check on the turn when you miss. This reveals a weak holding and you can pick up the pot with a bluff. The beauty of this play is that your opponent is either weak (in which case he will probably check and fold on the turn), or he is strong (in which case you have great implied odds if you hit your miracle draw).

Controlling pot size

Big pots usually mean that there are big hands involved. If you hold a mediocre hand after the flop, such as top pair with a decent kicker, you are not exactly delighted to see the pot building to such a size that your whole stack is on the line. The majority of the time this happens, you will be going broke. Some of the time it follows that you should consider tailoring your post-flop play to keep the pot at a size commensurate with the strength of your hand.

For example, holding top pair-top kicker or an overpair in position as the pre-flop raiser, you should consider risking giving a free card in order to stop the pot from reaching uncomfortable levels. If there are no obvious draws, you should consider checking on the turn. You are either solidly behind against a hand such as a set, or solidly ahead against a one pair hand. If you *are* up against a set, checking on the turn stops the pot from building out of control, and saves you money. If you are against a second-best one-pair hand, your check on the turn might entice him to call rather than fold to your value-bet on the river, earning you an extra bet. If you are up against a complete miss, your check may entice a bluff on the river. The most outs a one-pair hand can have against you is five, often only two or three. Even though giving a free card that costs you the pot is a disaster, it is unlikely and should be offset against the fact that your check makes you more money in every other situation.

Reading hands post-flop

The principles behind reading your opponents' hands after the flop are the same as those before the flop. You watch their actions and consider what cards would have led you yourself to make that move in their position. Before the flop you always have to appreciate that your opponents might be making an unusual play for the sake of deception, but their play after the flop often allows you to rule out certain holdings completely. The equity loss from an unconventional play post-flop is often so high that no player would ever consider playing for deception in some situations. In a multi-way pot with the flop texture allowing for many draws, the equity loss in giving cheap or free cards is so great that you can be almost certain a player will not slow-play a monster hand here.

Your opponents know as well as you do the value of deception. They will be using semi-bluffs, delayed bluffs, slow-playing and all sorts of other fiendish tactics against you. This often means that their play on later streets is in conflict with the read you had from the flop. They might meekly check or just call on the flop and turn, then make a big raise on the river. They might play aggressively on the turn, then check the river. Any deceptive plays they make are designed to confuse you into making a big mistake on a later street, so you should trust the implications of their late-street actions. They will disguise the strength of their hand on the flop and turn to try to get you to make an incorrect call on the river. By the river, generally, they will revert back to making the play that is based on the actual strength of their hand, and hope that their deception has misled you into an incorrect read. Also, more cards are out by the river and there is a chance that the strength of your opponent's hand has changed considerably. If he plays meekly on the turn, checking behind you, but raises you when you bet on the river, he could have hit a miracle two-outer and made a set. If he check-raised you on the turn, but failed to bet on the river, he could have been semi-bluffing on the turn and know by the river that he has not made his hand. Players often use an opponent's play on an earlier street to justify a big call with a mediocre hand on the river, and the majority of the time this is exactly what the play on the earlier street was designed to achieve.

Mixing it up

A lot of post-flop situations will demand that you play your hand in a straightforward way. But you should still be looking for opportunities to introduce an element of unpredictability. If you always check-raise with powerful hands, always bet out solid one-pair hands, and always check and fold when you miss, you may think you are maximising your EV on each play, but in the long run your opponents will be able to take you apart. Occasionally, you *must* bet out with a monster hand. This will stop your opponents knowing with 100% certainty that whenever you bet out you have a solid but not powerful holding. You may lose an extra bet on the hand in question, but it will save you facing raises every time you bet out with a medium-strength hand. Likewise you *must* semi-bluff occasionally, even if it doesn't fit with your overall game plan. If you never semi-bluff, your opponents can put you to a very tough decision by making a big raise every time a draw hits after you've been betting. The individual plays may not be optimal, but as part of your long-term game, they are essential.

Changing gears

Related to but subtly distinct from 'mixing up' your play is the concept of 'changing gears'. It involves a shift of playing style not for the purpose of keeping your opponent guessing in the long run (though it does have this as a secondary advantage), but by deliberately exploiting the read your opponents have on you. In Chapter 5 we will learn that there are certain types of player with distinct styles. Once your opponents have observed your play for an hour or so, the better ones will be beginning to pigeon-hole you as a certain type of player, and adjusting their strategy accordingly. As they do so, if you are aware of what conclusions they are drawing, you can switch to a different style yourself and thwart their plans.

If you decide to play aggressively for an hour, and make lots of semi-bluff and bluff raises, you may very well pick up plenty of medium-sized pots without showing down a hand. Your opponents' responses will be to adjust their strategy to counter your style. Believing that you are a player who commits plenty of chips with non-premium holdings, they will plan to wait for a solid hand of their own, and then make a stand against you for all their chips. In anticipation of this, you 'change gear' and rein in your aggression. You suddenly tighten up your play and enter pots only with premium hands. When an opponent picks up a solid hand and decides it is time to make a stand for all his chips, you are ready for this counter-attack and have a premium hand with which to relieve him of his stack.

Conversely, if you have been dealt such an ugly run of cards that you have barely entered a pot for an hour, your opponents will figure you for a 'rock' and believe that you play only the very best of hands. An example of changing gear here may be to wait for a pre-flop raise with several callers and then reraise solidly with any two cards. Rather than realising that you have changed gears, your opponents are more likely to figure that you are indeed a rock, and that you have just been dealt K-K or A-A. You should pick up the pot uncontested nearly every time.

Post-flop when you raised pre-flop

When you miss

When you raise before the flop and miss completely, you have a decision to make. You can choose to continue aggressively, and try to pick up the pot on the flop, or you may accept that you have missed your hand and allow your opponent(s) to make a play for the pot. This is such a common situation that finding the right proportion of times to make a play, and the correct times to do so, will make a huge impact on your long-term profit/loss.

In position

In position after the flop, and facing a bet, you are in a tough spot. Folding your hand and waiting for a better situation is not strictly wrong. You are unlikely to have the correct pot and implied odds to call (situations where you flop a draw are dealt with below). In specific spots, however, you might be right to raise. If an aggressive player bets into you, he will often be holding a mediocre, one-pair hand. His bets will often be 'feeler' bets to test if you have connected with the flop. He is looking for you to fold your hand; but if you raise, he should give you credit for a big pair, and fold. This play should be made rarely, though, and only against the right type of player, such as an aggressive player whom you know to be capable of making that sort of move. Generally, in this spot, you know you are beaten and should fold and wait for a better time.

Out of position

First to speak or in position when checked to, you consider making a continuation bet. Your primary concern is the texture of the flop. Is it such that your opponents are unlikely to have flopped a strong enough hand to call or raise if you bet? Is the texture of the flop such that it is credible for you to have made a solid hand? If the answer to both these questions is yes, then the situation is perfect for a continuation bet. One exception is if you have a slim draw on the flop, such as a gutshot to a nut Broadway. Here, you should be more inclined just to take a free shot at the turn. The worst case here is making a continuation bet and getting raised out of the pot without having a chance to hit your slim draw. Once you have decided to make a continuation bet, you should be looking to bet somewhere between half and three-quarters of the pot   enough to drive out your opponent if he has nothing, but not too much to cost you dearly if you get raised.

Unconnected flops with all low cards generally do not connect with your opponents' likely hands if the pot is raised. Assuming your opponents understand pre-flop strategy, however, they will probably assume that your pre-flop raise was made with two big cards or a big pair. If the flop comes out with all low cards, they will know that you are happy with your hand only if you started out with a big pair. This type of flop supports continuation bets only if your opponents play in a straightforward way. In this case, they may *suspect* that you have not connected with the flop, but as they tend to make plays based only on the strength of their own cards, they will generally fold. Making a continuation bet on a low flop against tricky players is dangerous, though; they will raise on the bluff enough for you to be wise to avoid betting here.

A better flop to bet at is one that contains at least one big card. In this case, your opponents cannot be sure that you have missed if you started with two big cards, and will be less willing to put you to the test with a call or raise. But when you have missed and the flop is ace-high, you should be careful. Although it is credible that you have hit your hand, the second condition is not met; it is likely that your opponents have hit a hand that can stand up to a continuation bet. Many hands with which your opponents call a pre-flop raise contain an ace. If they have made top pair on the flop, your continuation bet is unlikely to pick up the pot for you.

Even flops containing at least one big card and no ace can sometimes fail to meet the criteria for continuation betting. Sometimes it is credible that you have hit a solid hand, but the texture of the flop makes it far too likely that your opponents have anyway hit a hand strong enough to beat you. If the flop is suited, or offers good straight and two-pair opportunities for suited connectors, you should be less inclined to make a continuation bet. Not only are you likely to run into a flopped two pair, but you are also going to get called any time your opponent holds a strong draw. Even though you are notionally ahead against a draw, it is going to be very tough for you to know how to play on the turn and river. You will often have to telegraph your weakness with a check, and your opponent can take the pot away from you. Even if you hit on the turn here, you could still not be good if you started out against two pair or if your opponent made his draw as you make a solid one pair. You should generally avoid making continuation bets into this type of flop.

A pair on the flop means that your opponent may have

flopped trips, but more importantly it means that there are fewer hands that can have paired up on the flop. An unpaired flop contains three cards, each of which has three other cards of that rank that may be in your opponent's hand. A paired board leaves only two of the rank of the pair, and three of the other card, that connect with the flop. Assuming he doesn't hold a pocket pair, it is almost half as likely that your opponent has hit one of his hole cards if the board is paired. You should be more inclined to bet out and try to pick up the pot on a paired board.

Examples of good flops for the continuation bet:

Kd-8h-3s
Js-Jd-3d
Qs-5c-8s

Examples of bad flops for the continuation bet:

As-Kc-Tc
8s-9s-Tc
Qc-Tc-6c

Once you have determined if the flop is favourable, you should consider the number and playing style of your opponents. The more players in the pot with you, the more chance one of them has hit a reasonable hand and will call or raise your continuation bet. In general, you should be looking to make a continuation bet more often than not when heads-up – probably close to three-quarters of the time. Adjust this depending on the style of your opponents. Against super-tight players, it is profitable to make a continuation bet 100% of the time; but against a 'maniac', or loose-aggressive player (see pages 114–15), a continuation bet is suicide. In a regular ring game with average players, two-thirds to three-quarters of the time is probably about right.

If you make a continuation bet and get raised, you generally have to fold. If you are called, deciding whether to fire a second barrel comes down a lot more to the playing style of your opponent than any practical criteria. When you sit at a table, whether online or live, one of the most important things to notice is how your opponents respond to a bet on the turn after calling a continuation bet on the flop. Some players will call a continuation bet with any one-pair hand, hoping that the pre-flop raiser has missed, but will readily fold if the second barrel is fired. Other opponents will tend to raise on the flop with a one-pair hand, and only smooth-call with a draw or powerhouse. Some are 'look-up artists' and will call a pre-flop raiser on all three streets with the hope of winning the pot in a showdown against unpaired high cards. Knowing which category your opponents fit into is by far the greatest determinant of the value of the second barrel.

Some turns obviously make a second barrel more likely to succeed, all things considered. Another high card that doesn't make a straight or flush will give your opponents even more reason to believe that you now hold a solid hand, and you should be more inclined to fire a second barrel here. If the top card on the board pairs on the turn, never fire the second barrel. Your opponent will often have made a mediocre top pair hand and will call once on the flop. If he has now made trips, there is no way a second barrel is going to pick you up the pot.

When you have a solid one-pair hand
If your two big cards make top pair or your big pocket pair remains an overpair on the flop, you are beating most one-pair hands and losing only if your opponent has connected hard with the flop. Post-flop with a solid hand, you have four goals. First, to make your opponent call you with second-best hands. Second, to charge him an appropriate price for his draws. Third, you want to minimise the damage to your stack if your opponent holds a

big hand. Finally, you want to give an opponent the chance to make a pure bluff if he has no hand whatsoever. The first two goals suggest continued aggression; the third and fourth suggest passivity. The playing style of your opponents and the texture of the board dictate which course of action is optimal.

Out of position

If your opponent plays in a passive, straightforward way, you should generally continue betting on the flop, turn and river. Looking at the four goals above:

1 If he has a second-best hand, a loose-passive player will call your bet and a tight-passive player will either call or fold. Because your opponent is passive, you cannot guarantee that he will bet the hand for you if you check. You will fail to extract money from him when he checks behind you, and you are giving him a free shot to improve and win the pot.

2 If he has a draw, you must bet out to make him pay. He does not semi-bluff enough for you to go for a check-raise. He would check behind and take a free shot – a disastrous outcome for you.

3 When a passive player has a monster, you can often find this out by betting. If he raises, it is usually because he can beat a one-pair hand, and you can make a good fold. But checking would not allow you to make a good fold. You have not defined the strength of your hand clearly enough to interpret his bet as a really powerful hand, and you would probably end up checking and calling bets on each street rather than making a good fold after one.

4 Finally, if he has absolutely no hand or draw, he will fold to your bet. Unfortunately, you can do no better than this by checking. A passive player is so unlikely to make a pure bluff that your deceptive check is of little or no value.

In all cases, betting is either superior or equivalent to checking, so you should look to bet into passive players with a solid holding on the flop.

If your opponent is aggressive, however, you would be more inclined to check. Considering each goal again:

1   If he holds a mediocre one-pair hand, an aggressive player is still inclined to bet for value, and you can check and call. You even have the option of check-raising if your read is strong enough. Betting into an aggressive player will not get any more money into the pot than if you check and allow him to bet the hand for you. It might even allow him to make a good fold if he is a tight-aggressive player.

2   Holding a draw, aggressive opponents are inclined to bet on the semi-bluff when checked to. If the flop contains a lot of draws, you can check-raise their semi-bluff and force them either to fold their draw or to make a bad call. But you must beware of quality aggressive players. These players are aware that their style can be exploited, and may take the free card from time to time.

3   If your aggressive foe holds a truly powerful hand, you are going to lose a big pot regardless of how you play – the exception being if he is aggressive but extremely tight, in which case you may be able to make a good fold. You cannot respect his aggression enough to fold a solid one-pair hand, whether you check to him or you bet out and he raises. Nothing you do can save you when you hold a solid hand against an aggressive player's monster.

4   Finally, if the aggressive player has no hand at all, you gain a bet by checking to him and allowing him to make a pure bluff. You can either raise here and win the pot, or consider smooth-calling and allowing him to bluff again on

the turn. Either of these moves is better than betting out and having him fold his terrible hand.

Although it may not be as clear as your decision when up against a passive player, there is something to be gained in each case by checking to the aggressive player. Betting out with a strong hand is probably safer, especially if there are draws possible. It removes his chance to countershift and take a free card with his draw. Checking to him will often make you extra bets when you are ahead – so if the flop texture permits, a check here can be preferable.

In position

If you are bet into with a solid hand, you will find that the majority of the time your opponent has a mediocre hand and is putting you to the test. On these occasions the correct play is to evaluate the texture of the flop, and either raise immediately to win the pot, or consider calling once and raising to win the pot on the turn. The second play is greedy, and risks your opponent improving on the turn. It should therefore be considered only if the texture of the flop does not allow for draws.

Your concerns if checked to with a solid hand are similar to those when you are first to speak. You have not gained much information about your opponent's holdings because he would check to you here with such a wide range of hands. Your hand is strong enough to expect to be ahead, so you should bet here almost all the time. You are looking to bet for value on all three streets here, and will continue to do so unless the turn or river is a scare card.

On the turn against an aggressive player, the board may allow for you to check in position. You are controlling the size of the pot to match the strength of your hand and as long as there are no draws, you are risking only a slim chance of losing the pot. Your deception will probably induce a bluff on the river if he has no hand, and may entice him to call you with a second-best hand. If he does have a monster, you will have saved yourself the bet on the turn. Checking here is the preferable play, no matter what your aggressive opponent holds. Against a passive player, however, you should probably go ahead and bet on the turn. This time your deception is unlikely to induce a bluff on the river, and he will probably call two bets with a second-best hand.

When you flop a big draw

A pair and flush draw, a nut-flush draw with overcards, or a flush draw with straight draw-outs are considered 'big' draws. Flopping a big draw as a pre-flop raiser means that you are unlikely to be ahead in the hand, but are also unlikely to be much of an underdog if all-in on the flop. You are happy to pick up the pot on the flop, and not too concerned at ending up all-in. If this intimidates you, you are probably playing for stakes that are too high.

Stack size is important when playing a big draw. When choosing your play on the flop, you should always consider what your stack will be in comparison to the pot on the turn. If a bet and a raise on the flop will leave you roughly the same amount as will be in the pot, you could be in trouble. If you get called on the flop and miss, you will most probably be facing an all-in bet offering you 2-1 on the turn. With only one card to come, your hand will almost certainly not warrant a call. You have blown half your stack on your flop play, and not even managed to see two cards for your trouble. A much better strategy would be to play your hand in a straightforward way. Take a free card if you get the chance or, if bet into, just call for value. If a semi-bluff leaves you with a stack much greater than the amount in the pot on the turn, implied odds may mean that you can still make a positive EV call. At least if you do fold on the turn, you have cost yourself only one bet.

Out of position

Betting out with a big draw is powerful. It has all the advantages of a continuation bet, and also has a good chance to go on to make a powerful hand when you are called. If your opponent has a mediocre hand and decides to raise, you can move all-in over the top. You might make a mediocre hand fold or snap off a bluff. Making your opponent commit a bet and a raise and then fold is perfect. Even if he does call you, your EV in the hand is only slightly negative.

As in the case where you had a solid one-pair hand, you would be more inclined to go for a big check-raise against an aggressive player. You know that he will be bluffing often in this spot, and will have to fold. You also know that he will make semi-bluffs when checked to and, crucially, your hand now crushes his semi-bluff. If you have a nut-flush draw and he has a lower flush draw, you are around an 80% favourite. If he has an open-ended straight draw against your flush draw, you are a 71% favourite. Big draws play very well when all-in on the flop against aggressive players. They are not too far behind legitimate hands, and big favourites when he has been semi-bluffing.

In position

When bet into as pre-flop raiser, you most often find yourself up against a feeler bet from a mediocre hand. With a big draw, you should again be inclined to raise. This will pick you up the pot much of the time. Even if your opponent has been betting a truly powerful hand, and moves all-in over the top, you can quickly call, knowing your draw is strong enough not to be too far behind. When checked to, you should also be inclined to bet. You would often bet with no hand when checked to in position as pre-flop raiser, and the fact that you now have a big draw has only made you stronger. If check-raised, you often face the decision of going all-in or folding. Calling here will leave you in the worst possible position with a big draw: lots of money committed to the pot, but only one card to come.

When you hit big

When you hold a monster hand such as top set or a flopped straight or flush, many of the concerns from hitting just once still apply. You still want to charge your opponent to draw against you, and should be inclined to bet out if the texture of the flop supports a lot of draws. The exception is when your opponent is hyper-aggressive and you can almost guarantee that he will fall for a check-raise. In all other cases, and against all styles of opponent, you should be far more inclined to check.

Out of position

Checking into an aggressive player when you have a decent hand is always profitable because it allows him to bluff and semi-bluff into you. Now, however, you should be inclined to check even into a passive player as a slow-play. You are no longer afraid of your opponent taking a free card with a one-pair hand and improving. This will result in him, not you, going broke. He may even read your check as weakness, and make poor calls with a one-pair hand on the turn or river. If the flop does not permit your opponent to hold a draw to a better hand than yourself, a check here is correct.

In position

If checked to with a monster hand, it is usually correct to check. Betting here will scare off your opponents too often. Checking may allow your opponents to catch up to a second-best hand, may induce a bluff on the turn or river, and may convince them to call with a second-best hand. When you are bet into, you should usually just call for the same reasons. The exception comes when there are big draws on the board. First, you must be wary of your opponents betting their draws, and a raise here will charge them appropriately. Second, if your opponent has a solid hand of his own, he will be afraid that you have the draw. If you slow-play in this spot, and the draw gets there on the turn, it may scare your opponent into folding. It is easier to get an opponent with a strong hand to commit money on the flop before a flush or straight card arrives on the turn.

Post-flop when someone else raised pre-flop

When you miss

When you call with a speculative hand, and miss the flop completely, you should generally be content to let the pot go and wait for a more profitable situation. You know from your own experience as pre-flop raiser, however, that many flops don't connect with a raiser's hand. Much of the time your opponent will be holding two big cards and will have missed the flop. If the texture of the flop does not connect with the usual raising hands, you should consider making a play. The presence of other players in the pot makes this dangerous. With many players in the pot, it is likely that someone holds a legitimate hand. Only if you think the situation is perfect should you consider making a play for the pot.

Out of position

Making a play from this position is dangerous. Betting into a pre-flop raiser usually signals a medium-strength hand, and you may get raised. The best chance to pick up the pot from here will be a check-raise. This commits a lot of chips, and is costly if it fails. You should make this play only when the texture of the flop makes it unlikely that your opponent is happy with his hand. This can be either because he has big cards and has missed the flop, or because it is so scary for him that you can hope he folds a solid one-pair hand. You also must choose your opponents for this play carefully. You should check-raise only players that make a continuation bet a high proportion of the time. Passive players are happier to check when they miss, so their bet here indicates a solid hand. The perfect time to make a play for the pot from out of position is against a fairly aggressive player when the texture of the flop meets either of the two conditions above.

You probably shouldn't make a play for the pot if there are more than two players involved. The exception comes if the pot is three-way, and you are first to speak with a tight-passive pre-flop raiser second. If you bet out here, your opponent has to fear not only your hand but also the player behind. He will almost certainly release unless he has hit a solid hand. The third player will also often have missed the flop and will have to respect your bet; after all, you bet from out of position into a pre-flop raiser and another player. Of course, if you run into a big hand, you are going to get raised. The power of this play comes from the fact that if it is made when both players have missed the flop, it will almost certainly take down the pot.

In position

It is unusual for a pre-flop raiser to check with a solid one-pair hand (unless he has you pegged as an aggressive player). Against a standard opponent, a bet here is certainly the right play. You may run into a slow-played monster from time to time, but usually your opponent will have missed and for whatever reason elected not to make a continuation bet. You can be even more certain of your read if the texture of the flop makes it unlikely that he would check a solid or monster hand. If the flop permits lots of draws, your opponent would feel obliged to bet with a solid hand or better, so his check almost certainly indicates weakness. A bet here is very likely to pick up the pot.

If you are bet into, much of the time this will be a continuation bet and your opponent will not be holding a genuine hand.

If your opponent is known to make continuation bets much of the time, you should consider raising here if the texture of the flop does not connect with typical pre-flop raising hands. If your opponent is passive post-flop, and will generally check when he has missed, you should fold and wait for a better time to make a stand.

Most of the time, you simply do not know if your opponent has raised with a big pair or if he has big cards and has missed the flop. You would be allowing him to walk all over you if you folded every time he bet out. If you raise every time, you become pegged as a maniac; he will adjust his play and take you apart. If the flop is suited to picking off a continuation bet, a raise here about one in four times will keep your opponent on his toes without making your aggression exploitable.

When you hit one pair

Your thought process when holding a pocket pair or pairing one of your small cards in a raised pot is actually very similar to that when you have missed. If your opponent has a big pair, or has connected with the flop, you are behind. If he has missed, instead of bluffing to pick up the pot, you can bet or raise for value with the best hand and pick up the pot. The difference is that having at least something of a hand does allow you to consider playing more passively on the flop.

Out of position

Instead of betting out here, and risking being forced to fold either by a bluff or by a value-raise, it may be correct to check and call. If you are up against an aggressive player, you may be able to check and call bluffs all the way to the river and pick up a decent pot. If your opponent holds a solid one-pair hand, you may improve to two pair or trips on the turn. If you are ahead, on the other hand, you are risking the turn improving his hand to beat you. But this is not a slow-play. It is a cautious play designed to exploit an over-aggressive opponent. Once he bets again on the turn, the pot may well be big enough for you to raise and be happy to pick up the pot there and then.

In position

Playing passively with a one-pair hand in position has advantages beyond checking and calling. For the price of a call rather than a bet and a raise, you will often find out if you are ahead. Most players will concede the pot if their first continuation bet is called. If you are checked to on the turn, you have learnt that you are ahead for the price of just a call on the flop. If you are bet into on the turn, you are beginning to suspect that your opponent has a solid one-pair hand and will probably fold. However, the turn can always give you the best hand. Of course you are risking your opponents improving on the turn, which will cost you the pot. If you believe that your opponent has made a continuation bet, and that you have the best hand, your first impulse should be to raise and protect your hand; but just calling here certainly has its merits.

When you flop a draw

The most straightforward way to play a draw in a raised pot is to consider pot odds, implied odds and phantom outs, and figure if your draw is strong enough to warrant a call. Only after you have considered this play should you try to figure if a semi-bluff is preferable. Semi-bluffing is essentially a greedy play, and players whose first impulse is aggression with every draw will be exploited.

Out of position

If you decide to play your draw aggressively, you can either lead out or you can check-raise. Check-raising traps your opponent for an extra bet if he is making a continuation bet, but it also commits more of your stack to the pot. The main thing to consider when deciding whether to lead out or to check-raise is stack size. Again, what you cannot afford to do is find yourself on the turn having committed half your stack. You need either to commit your whole stack on the flop, or leave yourself enough to call for value on the turn.

In position

Again, your first impulse should be just to call if you believe you have the odds to do so. To make a semi-bluff correct here, your opponent should be the type who makes lots of continuation bets. This will give you a good chance to pick up the pot. If the texture of the flop is such that it is highly likely your opponent has connected, and will be happy to get all-in, there is little point in making a semi-bluff. If you know you are going to be called or set in, there is no folding equity and you are essentially committing more money to a draw than you need to.

When you hit big

Hitting a monster hand against a pre-flop raiser is the most exciting situation in no limit Hold'em. It is your best chance to double up. You should be playing in a way that gives you the best chance to take his whole stack from him. Slow-playing can disguise the strength of your hand, but it also restricts the number of betting rounds and may allow your opponent to get away from a second-best hand cheaply.

Out of position

You should check here most of the time against all types of opponent. If they have missed, you are not risking the pot by allowing them to take a free card, and you are giving them a chance to make a continuation bet. The decision is whether to check-raise on the flop or check and call and go for the check-raise on the turn. Check-raising on the flop is often the better option. If you check and call on the flop, a good player will make a pot-controlling check behind you on the turn, and your intended check-raise will have failed.

Also, once a player has had one continuation bet check-called, he is unlikely to fire the second barrel. Raising on the flop has the best chance of separating your opponent from his whole stack in the event that he holds a genuine hand, and doesn't cost you anything if he has missed. Also, if you check and call on the flop, the turn may be such a scare card (the top card on the flop pairing, for example) that it kills any action on the turn and river. You should be particularly inclined to check-raise here if there are big draws possible. Not only will you need to protect your hand in case your opponent has the draw, but you also need to get him to commit his money to the pot before a scare card on the turn may kill the action.

In position

If your opponent checks and you hold a monster, you should check. It is unusual to raise pre-flop and then check a solid hand, so your opponent has almost certainly missed the flop. Betting here will end the pot, and not give your opponents a chance to make a second-best hand. If you check, your opponent can either improve on the turn or decide to fire a bluff. Either way, you will have earned yourself an extra bet. If your opponent checks a second time on the turn, he probably wants no further part in the pot. You may as well bet here.

Picking off reraisers on ace-high flops

When a tight player reraises pre-flop, he usually holds a big pair, Q-Q, K-K or A-A. If the flop comes out ace-high, it is far more likely that he started with Q-Q or K-K, and you should consider making a play for the pot. Given that you can see one ace on the flop, there are only three ways your opponents can hold A-A in his hand, but there are six ways he can hold each of Q-Q and K-K. When the flop is ace-high, it is therefore four times more likely that he holds Q-Q or K-K than A-A. Making a modest bet into the reraiser (or making a modest raise if he bets into you) will pick up the pot most of the time. Of course, if your opponent also reraises with A-K, you cannot be so certain that he is scared of the ace on the board. This play should be made only if you know your opponent is tight and reraises only with big pairs.

Post-flop in unraised pots

In unraised pots you are often up against multiple opponents, and you don't have as strong a read on their cards as when you are in a raised pot. You cannot make as many plays based solely on the texture of the flop and your opponents' likely hands. There are also too many players to risk many of your deceptive plays. You are forced to play in a much more straightforward way. When you have a hand that you figure is ahead, you bet it for value. When you have missed the flop, you are more inclined to release the hand and wait for a more profitable situation.

Thinning the field

When you hold a solid hand against multiple opponents, you cannot risk allowing too many of them to see a turn. Whenever an opponent gets to see another card, there is a chance he will improve to beat you. Allowing multiple opponents to see the turn compounds this risk. If you are in position facing a bet, you should very rarely smooth-call. If you are out of position, you should bet your hand for value unless the dynamic of the game suggests you will succeed with a check-raise. The exception is if your hand is so strong, and the flop so innocuous, that the turn can't really improve anyone to beat you. If you flop an overfull, or a top full house with unpaired cards, you can afford to allow multiple opponents to see the turn. The value of deception here is offset against practically no risk of losing the pot, so the play becomes viable.

Picking up unwanted flops

Sometimes your opponents make it clear that they are uninterested in the pot. You know that people play less deceptively in multi-way unraised pots, so when a hand is checked around on the flop it generally means that nobody has a piece of it. Once you have learnt that nobody has a piece of the flop, you can bet two-thirds of the pot and try to pick it up.

If the flop allows many draws, your bet is less likely to pick up the pot. Perfect flops for picking up unwanted pots are unrelated cards, preferably queen- or king-high. This last factor makes it unlikely that your opponents hold two overcards. If your opponents have not connected with the flop, and do not hold a draw or two overcards, they will almost certainly fold.

You are in danger of being check-raised from one of the blinds holding a strong but vulnerable hand such as bottom two pair, but unfortunately you can never rule this out. The big blind holds a totally random two cards, so you cannot rule out his having two pair. This happens rarely enough that you should still try to pick up seemingly unwanted pots most of the time.

Playing draws in multi-way pots

Playing a draw in a multi-way pot can be profitable but dangerous. Unless you are the last person to act in a given round, you risk calling for value and then facing a prohibitively large raise. If the call is marginal, all else considered, the presence of players behind will make a fold correct.

If you hold a non-nut draw in a multi-way pot you must be careful that you are not drawing dead. The more opponents in the hand, the more likely it is that the nut draw is out there. Even if you make your draw, and are not up against a higher draw, you may be wary of betting your hand fully for value. For you to call in a multi-way pot with a non-nut draw, the other conditions need to be perfect. You should be in position, and getting at least close to the correct pot odds, before you even think about implied odds.

Conversely, drawing to the nuts in a multi-way pot is highly profitable. There are lots of opponents for you to extract money from, and a good chance that one of them has a lower draw than you. You can afford to factor in decent implied odds with a nut draw in a multi-way pot.

5

Advanced Play

Tight/Loose/Passive/Aggressive

Playing styles

Considering what would have led you yourself to make a play in a given spot is an imperfect method for deducing your opponent's cards, since they do not play exactly the same game as you do. Yet understanding your opponents' playing styles is key to your success and permits you to make accurate reads on their two hole cards. This in turn allows you to tailor your play to extract the maximum EV in any given situation.

The tight/loose axis and the passive/aggressive axis
Before the flop, players are often torn between knowing that they give up EV every time they enter a pot with a substandard holding, and knowing that position, aggression and post-flop skill can mitigate this EV loss. Loose players enter pots with hands that lack absolute pre-flop power with the hope of recouping enough after the flop to pay for their expensive pre-flop strategy. Tight players like to enter pots only with powerful holdings. They may have to wait an hour for a premium holding, and they win only a small pot when they do pick one

up; but they will have paid so little in pre-flop calls and raises that overall their stacks will grow slowly but surely. Some players play less than 10% of their pre-flop hands voluntarily, and some play more than half.

Post-flop, players often find themselves in situations where two very different plays each have their own merits, and choosing one over the other is usually a question of personal style. One play tends to be aggressive, the other conservative and passive. For example, when holding a strong draw after the flop, the aggressive action is to make big semi-bluffs. The conservative and passive play is simply to call for value if the odds allow it, or to fold and wait for a legitimate hand. The semi-bluff may have a slightly higher EV, but the passive play avoids putting your whole stack at risk time and again.

Playing styles can be summarised by determining where players sit on two axes: tight/loose and aggressive/passive. Every player is naturally either tight or loose and either passive or aggressive. This means that all players can be classified in one of four broad categories: TP, TA, LP and LA.

Aggressive plays have the value of folding equity over and above the passive alternative. Aggressive plays also extract the most money from opponents when you are ahead. Regardless of your tight/loose position, aggression is usually preferable. The optimal tight/loose position is less clearly defined. There are successful no limit Hold'em players in live games and tournaments at both ends of the scale.

You should take great care when choosing a style for yourself. A player will struggle when he tries to play a style that is in conflict with his true personality away from the table. Players who shy away from risk and conflict will find themselves uncomfortable trying to pull off a loose-aggressive style at a poker table. Loose-aggressive styles are very fashionable, but in order to make up for entering pots with substandard holdings, you *must* be a talented enough player to play the flop, turn and river excellently. Also, a loose-aggressive style will see you tangling in pot after huge pot. Even if you master this style, you will still be the victim of brutal day-to-day fluctuations in your bankroll. Starting with a tight-aggressive style is probably the most advisable: you have the advantage of the power of your holdings, and your bankroll will be more secure. Only later should you begin to experiment with a loose-aggressive style, and see if you have the skill and temperament to pull it off.

Adjusting to specific playing styles

TP: Tight-passive players play very few hands. When they do, you can assume they hold powerful hole cards. They don't make many bluffs or semi-bluffs, so when they show aggression after the flop, it is almost always because their hand is strong enough to bet for value. Clearly, when a tight-passive player is leading the action, you need only the very strongest hands to take him on. When a TP player enters a pot pre-flop, you should fold hands that are likely to be dominated by premium holdings, and you should even consider folding the more speculative hands. Even though he will often hold a premium hand, he is so passive that you cannot expect to win a huge pot against him by hitting your dream flop.

Passive players tend to play in a very straightforward way. If they miss a flop, they tend to telegraph this by checking. If you do decide to play a pot against a tight-passive player, you should be looking to bluff or semi-bluff almost every time he shows weakness. The odds of his folding to these plays are unusually high, and the value of aggressive plays increases accordingly.

A further benefit of playing against a tight-passive player is that he will often fail to extract the maximum value from you when you have a second-best hand. Unless he holds a true powerhouse, he will fear raises and reraises so much that he will seek to get to the showdown without being put to tough decisions. He will check with the best hand in situations where a better player would extract more money. His passive play allows you to make a lot of pot-controlling checks with mediocre hands. Overall, by letting you dictate the size of the pot, a TP player wins small pots from you while losing big pots to you.

TA: Tight-aggressive players also tend to enter pots with hands that have good absolute pre-flop power, but you cannot exploit this as easily if it is combined with selective aggression and a little deception from the flop onwards. When they do have the best hand on the flop and beyond, they extract the maximum value from you by betting it hard. Unfortunately, you can't simply fold every time they show strength, because you would be playing into the hands of their bluffs and semi-bluffs. Tight-aggressive is an effective style, and adjusting to it is hard.

If the tight-aggressive player enters the pot, you should consider just folding all but premium hands or pocket pairs. This strategy does not restrict your play too much. He is tight and enters the pot rarely, so you have to fold only the occasional hand. You should certainly avoid playing out of position against a tight-aggressive player. His style is perfectly suited to using the power of position against you. If you are forced to reveal weakness, he will attack mercilessly. If you hold a second-best hand, his value bets extract a lot of chips from you on the flop, the turn and the river. Calling a tight-aggressive player pre flop with a pocket pair is profitable because of his aggression. If you hit on the flop, you know you will be facing big bets and raises, so your implied odds are high.

LP: Loose-passive players are the ideal opponents to have in no limit Hold'em. They are as predictable and exploitable as tight-passive players, but enter pots with weaker hands and stick around longer than they should. Because of the large number of hands they play, they are involved in almost every pot, so your opportunities to exploit them are plentiful. They fail to extract value from you when they are ahead by not acting aggressively, and they allow you to extract value from them when the situation is reversed.

When you are lucky enough to find yourself up against a loose-passive player, you should adopt a very simple, value-based approach. You should play any hands that are on average stronger than theirs, and any hands that have a good chance of connecting strongly on the flop.

Loose-passive players are inclined to overpay for their draws. When you do have a solid hand, you should bet more than you would against a normal opponent. You can trap LP players into making calls with negative EV by betting strongly when they are drawing. Be reluctant to bluff or semi-bluff because the loose-passive player will not fold enough to make these plays valuable. You should simply stick around until you have a hand that you figure is ahead, then bet strongly all the way to a showdown. Much like the tight-passive player, the few times a loose-passive player *does* show aggression after the flop almost always indicates a legitimate hand. You should make a stand only with a power-house of your own.

LA: Loose-aggressive players are dangerous, but often exploitable. At the extreme, they are often referred to as 'maniacs'. If you are going to win lots of huge pots in quick succession from a certain type of player, it is likely to be a maniac. Because he is loose, he enters lots of pots, often with substandard pre-flop cards. If you wait for a solid pre-flop holding, the chances are that when one comes around, the maniac will be involved in the hand and you will have a chance to exploit him.

You can adjust your style to counter a maniac in one of two ways. The first is similar to the value-based approach you use against loose-passive players; enter pots with solid hands, or those that have a chance to connect with the flop in a big way. When you do have a strong post-flop hand, you can sit back and allow the maniac to fire huge bets into you. You don't have to concern yourself too much with deception or hand-reading. Even though maniacs occasionally do have big hands, your solid holding is usually good enough to win the pot.

The other way to adjust your style against a maniac is to counter his aggression with aggression of your own. You know that he will hold substandard cards much of the time. No matter how loose or aggressive a player is, he cannot *call* all-in without at least a solid hand or big draw. If you wait for a maniac to commit a decent amount of chips to a pot, and then move all-in over the top of him, he will be forced to fold the majority of the time. You should be even more inclined to do so with nut-flush draws as a semi-bluff. The reason for this is that the maniac himself will have been semi-bluffing much of the time. If he does elect to call when set all-in, your nut draw is a big favourite over his lower flush or straight draw. This method of countering the maniac is powerful but highly volatile. Maniacs are impossible to read, and if you pick the wrong times to make this play, you may find yourself being called by hidden two pairs, straights and other powerful holdings.

The countershift

Not all players with unusual playing styles are idiots. Many appreciate that they have a style that differs from the prescribed tight-aggressive standard, and are aware that other players at the table will be adjusting their games to exploit this. Once you have exploited their style a few times, they will know what you are up to and will not fall into the trap again. If you check-raise a loose-aggressive player on the flop with a medium holding, the chances are he will not have the strength to call you. If you use this play again, he probably still won't have the strength to call you. By now, he is aware that you are using the check-raise to exploit his style, and has come to expect it. When you check-raise him a third time, his hand is probably strong enough for him to be expecting – indeed hoping – that you check-raise. The third time you check-raise a loose-aggressive player, you had better have a powerhouse of your own and be in a position to call his all-in all too eagerly. One check-raise is a tragedy, two are suspicious and three amount to murder.

The third axis

Frustration affects everyone at the poker table. Losing a few big pots hurts, and will throw players off their usual game. It has many names, two of the most common being 'on tilt' and 'steaming'. Crucially, however, it pushes people in one of two directions.

Most people respond by getting angry and pugnacious. They also get desensitised to the pain of losing. When these emotions are combined, the result is a catastrophic change in their style. They look for every opportunity to play big pots. They stop respecting your aggression, and are too angry and fired up to fold *any* reasonable hand. They will take greater risks, and accept greater EV losses, for a chance to claw back their deficit. Crucially, they often fail to increase their own aggression, electing to insta-call huge bets with slim draws, and mediocre hands without sufficient thought. Frustration pushes this player right up into the loose-passive quadrant.

The minority of players respond to frustration by becoming defeatist and feeble. Instead of becoming desensitised to the pain of losing, they cannot bear the thought of getting 'stuck' even deeper. These players are so convinced that the world is out to get them that they are terrified of tangling in another big pot, and look for any opportunity to fold their hands. Frustration pushes this type of player down into the tight-passive quadrant.

In live games it is easy to see which way a person is responding to frustration. In the flesh, you can observe their emotional state. The first type of player can be seen visibly bristling. His voice will get louder and more aggressive, and he will begin to throw chips and cards around. The second type of player will whine, tut, moan and lament with everyone at the table. Every time a third flush card hits, he will roll his eyes. Every time an ace flops when he was holding a big pair, he will show the table. He is desperate for us to vindicate his theory that the poker gods are out to get him, which makes this syndrome very easy to spot, and a joy to play against. Online, you have only betting patterns to go on. When you see someone lose a couple of big pots, you should keep an eye on their play. Next time they make a big call on the river, check the hand history and see if the call was justified. If he called a big bet with middle pair or ace-high, the chances are he is the first type of 'tilter'.

Position relative to the maniac

If you have a choice of seat in a game, you should take a little time to determine the playing style of the players at the table. You should then consider where those open seats are relative to any loose-aggressive players.

When you have position on a maniac, you can see whether he is going to be in the pot before you make your pre-flop decisions, and can adjust your hand selection accordingly. Post-flop, you will almost always be facing a bet before you have acted. You can snap off bluffs or elect to raise if you have the goods, and get away cheaply if you have missed. If you choose to sit to the maniac's right, you can win more when you have a strong hand. You can trap the rest of the table between him and you. This makes limp-reraising before the flop and check-raising after the flop particularly powerful. The maniac will almost always bet, and every other player at the table is forced to act before you reveal the strength of your hand. Because he is a maniac, his bets and raises won't be respected, so you will often pick up lots of calls before the action returns to you.

Either position has its advantages, but conventionally it is considered optimal to sit to the maniac's left. You can play a simple, low-risk game here, using the advantage of position to gradually call his bluffs and poor-value bets. Playing on a maniac's right is much more volatile. When you check-raise, you either win a big pot or run into a very strong hand and lose a big pot. You often limp into pots before the flop, and end up having to call a raise as well. If you hit a good run of cards to a maniac's right, you will be rewarded handsomely. If you miss all your flops and draws and run into the occasional big hand, it will be expensive.

Short-handed play

With less than a full table (or fewer than nine or ten players), you need to switch to a short-handed strategy. The main shifts you make are to increase your aggression, increase the number of hands you play, and increase your use of deceptive and aggressive post-flop strategies.

Pre-flop strategy
Aggression

Short-handed play calls for increased aggression pre-flop. With fewer players at the table, there is a lower probability that one of them has a premium holding before the flop. The situation is analogous to sitting in late position in a full ring game and the hand is folded to you. Any time you enter a pot in a short-handed game, you should be looking to raise. Your raises will pick up the pot much of the time. Also, there can never be many players between you and the button, so your raises always have a good chance of buying the button. Furthermore, the blinds pass through your stack with increased frequency. It is too expensive to sit patiently waiting for premium hands. Spend too long waiting for a premium holding, and you will have lost so much that even doubling up only puts you back to where you started. Unless you start making frequent raises pre-flop and picking up plenty of pots, your opponents' aggression will steadily eat away at your stack.

Power rankings

You should also be aware that your opponents are loosening up their own pre-flop raising standards. Their raises, even from early and middle position, no longer indicate as much strength as before. When they raise from late position or on the button, they could hold almost any two cards. This should have two effects on your pre-flop strategy. The first concerns big aces. In a ring game, you would generally fold A-Qo in the face of an under-the-gun raise, because you run into hands that dominate you (A-K or a big pair) so often. In a short-handed game, the quality of raising hands is so low that the reverse is true. Your A-Qo now dominates many of your opponents' raising hands. Instead of folding big aces to early position raises, you are now inclined to call or reraise.

The second adjustment is to make more reraises of your own on pure bluffs and with speculative hands. In short-handed games, your opponents will be raising before the flop with a wide range of hands. Many of these will be too weak to call a reraise. A steal reraise from the blinds or the button will take down the pot often enough to make it a big part of your pre-flop strategy.

Because your opponents are making the same adjustments, you know you will now be seeing many more reraises with non-premium hands. Unlike in full ring games, you will see lots of opponents reraising on the steal and reraising with big aces for value. Consequently hands like A-Ko and Q-Q are now so strong that you are often happy to get all-in. If you hold A-Ko on the big blind, and there is a raise and a reraise before you, an all-in here will pick up the pot much of the time; even when you are called, you will occasionally find yourself up against a dominated hand such as A-Q.

Pre-flop, short-handed games are very aggressive. This makes it dangerous for you to call raises with mediocre hands when there are players still to act behind you. You may be getting value to call one raiser, but your hand will not be strong enough to call a reraise. In short-handed games, you are more likely to find someone reraising from the blinds for value with a pair or big ace. You are also more likely to find people making squeeze plays. In a particularly aggressive short-handed game with people to act behind you, hands that can stand to call a raise but not a reraise should often be folded.

After the flop

Your opponents have looser pre-flop raising and reraising standards in short-handed games, so you know that they will be holding unpaired cards more often and will have missed the flop. This means you have ample opportunity for exploiting their continuation bets. A major factor in short-handed strategy is applying pressure on the flop in raised pots. If someone raises pre-flop, and the texture of the flop makes it unlikely that it has connected with their hand, you should raise any bet they make to take down the pot. This applies especially if you have a small piece of it or a solid draw. The exception is when you flop a very strong hand. Raising on the flop wins the pot so often that when you are inviting action, you need to slow-play a lot. Your opponent will have missed so often that you need to induce bluffs, and let them catch up to a second-best hand.

Short-handed, the game becomes much more psychological. You keep applying pressure on the flop, with raises and semi-bluffs picking up lots of small pots. Your intention is to goad your opponents into making a big play for a pot. The only chance your opponents have to counter your aggressive style is to muster some aggression of their own.

Once you have picked up plenty of small pots without showing down a hand, you should expect soon to face a big raise. Your opponent may have finally made a strong hand, or he may simply have tired of your running over the game and be attempting a big steal. If you can correctly read the situation, you can make the appropriate counter-play. This is why hand-reading and paying attention to table dynamic are so crucial in short-handed play.

6

Tournament Play

Everything you do in cash games is designed to maximise your expected profit over the medium to long term. This underpins your tournament strategy, too. After all, playing in a way that gives you the best chance of adding chips to your stack seems like the best way of ensuring that you get deep into the tournament and make it into the money. Tournaments are different from cash games in that you cannot usually bring out more chips if you lose your stack, and that chips do not correspond directly to monetary rewards. They determine the place you finish on the leader board, but during the tournament you cannot put a definitive cash-value on a given chip. For these reasons, tournament strategy is more complex and subtle than cash game strategy.

Protecting your stack

Assuming that you are playing at a level appropriate to your bankroll, in a cash game no positive EV play should be turned down. If you make a positive EV play and still lose, you pull out more chips and carry on with your game knowing you made a correct play. In a tournament, even though a play has a positive EV, it might be better to turn it down and pursue a strategy that gradually adds to your stack in smaller, less volatile pots.

For example, in the first round of the main event of a major tournament, you might be inclined to fold in a spot where you know you are a 55% favourite to win, if your entire stack is on the line. This play does, on average, add chips to your stack; but 45% of the time you will bust out of the tournament in the first round. Most tournament players would rather pick up lots of small pots – stealing blinds, picking off bluffs and picking up uncontested pots with well-timed steals – than stake everything on a marginally winning play.

Bluffing and semi-bluffing in tournaments

Tournament players' unwillingness to put their entire stack on the line opens up great opportunities to the savvy competitor. Any time your opponents are likely to favour folding in the face of aggression, the value of bluffs and semi-bluffs increases. Accordingly, if you can make an aggressive play that threatens an opponent's whole stack, you will find it wins you the pot almost all of the time. If you have managed to build a stack that makes you chip leader at your tournament table, these plays won't even put your whole stack at risk. In this case, you should be 'bullying', or looking to take almost every semi-bluffing opportunity that puts an opponent all-in. You will nearly always win the pot without risking a showdown. This tactic adds so much to your stack uncontested that you can afford to get called on the rare occasions you run into a powerful hand.

The gap concept

In tournaments – particularly in the early rounds, when the blinds are low – it is generally considered correct to play very tight. You do not want to be putting your stack at risk, and will usually avoid confrontation. This applies as much to your opponents as it does to you, so it leaves room for exploitation. You know that most of your opponents will be getting involved only if they have very solid hands. When you are facing a pre-flop raise, you need to give it a lot of respect. Even strong hands need to be folded in the face of a pre-flop raise, because you know that this signifies real strength from your opponents. You can put the same pressure back on your opponents, however, by making raises yourself. They are playing tight, and folding all but the best pre-flop hands to a raise. So you don't need the same pre-flop power to make a raise as you do to call one. The gap between the strength required to make a raise and to call one is at its largest in the early stages of a no limit Hold'em tournament. The best players exploit this by making lots of aggressive plays for the pot with marginal holdings, and folding all but the very best hands when facing aggression.

How stack size affects your play

The size of your stack in a tournament should have a big influence on the way you play. The key figure is not the actual number of chips in your stack, but the ratio of your stack size to the amount it costs each round in antes and blinds. This value is referred to as your 'M value' (as made famous among poker geeks by the manuals of Dan Harrington). M is the number of rounds you could last if you decided to fold every hand.

Playing with a big M

When your M value is high, say 20 and above, you have the luxury of a big stack and are not compelled to play any particular way. You can afford to play conservatively, and try to maximise your chance of making it into the money. Alternatively, you can decide to push the advantage of your big stack and play hyper-aggressively. You can put pressure on medium stacks by setting them all-in without risking your whole tournament. You can call with speculative hands and try to take down big pots. The correct style of game to play depends on how risk-averse you are in relation to the prize levels (see below, 'Playing to move up places or going for the win').

Playing with a medium M

When your M is between 10 and 20, you are certainly not in dire straits, but you no longer have the luxury of playing conservatively and moving steadily up the money finishes. You are safe for the moment, but the blinds and antes will start eating into your stack and soon you will find yourself short-stacked. With a medium M value, you must be aggressive with marginal hands. You must be prepared to make lots of raises pre-flop to try to add to your stack. If the first few moves go wrong, you find yourself with a short stack. This is worth the risk. After all, you were only a few rounds away from being short-stacked by playing conservatively. Also, you can no longer afford to call with speculative hands. You don't have a big enough stack to win a huge pot when these hands flop a powerful hand. Furthermore, the price of calling a few raises is going to push you down into short-stack territory.

Playing with a small M

An M of 6–10 is quite similar to one between 10 and 20. You are not critically short-stacked, but things are certainly getting worrying. You cannot afford to be speculative. You should be playing very aggressively, looking to add a few small pots to your stack without resistance and pull yourself up into the medium M zone. A 6–10 M stack is big enough to be feared by the medium and large stacks around the table, so fortunately you do still have folding equity. You can still steal pots by raising to 3.5 times the big blinds. At the top of the small M zone, you can even pull a squeeze play if the situation is perfect. There is no point in trying to wait for a premium hand when you have a small M. If you wait three rounds and drop to an M of 5 or below, and finally pick up a premium hand, doubling up will only take you back to where you were before. It is much better to be aggressive and try to pull yourself up into the medium M zone.

Playing when critically short-stacked

When your M is 5 or below, you have only one choice – fold, or go all-in before the flop. Even raising to three times the big blind will commit more than half your stack, and you will not be able to fold correctly if set all-in. Far better to make the all-in move yourself, and try to win the pot uncontested. The correct strategy for a stack this short is to go all-in with any pair, any ace, any two face cards and even any suited connectors.

As the bubble approaches

Tournament players are always reluctant to put their whole stack on the line, and never more so than in the period just before the bubble. Finishing just out of the money is the worst result possible in a tournament. You have put in the time and mental energy to last this far, only to fall at the final hurdle and fare no better financially than the player who busted out on the first hand. If you find people thinking this way at your table, it becomes correct to raise into them almost every hand before the flop. If they make a standard-sized raise pre-flop, you should almost always reraise – setting them all-in unless they have a big stack relative to yours. The majority of the time these players will fold and you will win the pot uncontested. Even if they call, you could still get lucky and win a big pot. When you have a stack large enough to survive a loss or two, hyper-aggressive play at this point in a tournament is essential.

Even if you have a small-to-average stack, you should be looking to play this way. When you play aggressively and bust out, you have cost yourself the value of a low-money finish. You could, perhaps, have folded every hand until you made it into the money. But the number of times this approach works will give you a good chance of not only getting into the money, but of going deep in the tournament – and moving into the big-money finishes. Tournament payout schemes tend to be top-heavy, with the majority of the money held back for the top few places. You will make more in the long run by maximising your chances to make it to the top few than by taking a guaranteed low-money finish every time you have the chance.

Multi-table tournaments often pay life-altering prizes, even in the lower tiers. Some satellite qualifiers will find that the lowest payout is more than you have ever won at a poker table. If a bottom-tier money finish would be life-changing to you, you should consider turning down plays that maximise long-term financial EV for a more conservative approach that guarantees a money finish. A player in this situation will not find himself approaching the money in a major tournament often enough to care only about EV. It is not irrational to choose a guaranteed lower EV option if it is a one-time chance.

Playing to move up places or going for the win

The same applies once you are in the money. A hardened tournament pro will be thinking only of what maximises his expected return. Mere mortals will have to consider whether the amounts at stake are so large that it is better to sacrifice EV to move steadily up the prize ladder.

Knowing how the prize money is structured is crucial. There is no point in playing conservatively to ensure that you move up five places if the next six places all get the same prize money. Here, you are not losing anything by putting your stack on the line, and you should be looking for chances to take a shot at doubling up. If you succeed, and now have enough chips to fold every hand and still make the next prize bracket, you can re-evaluate your decision.

When you are *by far* the short stack in a tournament, your best chance to move up the prize money is for two bigger stacks to play a pot against each other and for one to bust the other. Your stack is sometimes so small that even doubling up will leave you not much better placed than before. In these spots, allowing your opponents to get all-in against each other is your only hope.

Example: You are in the final three of the WSOP main event. You are in third place and on the big blind with 700,000 chips. The small blind and button are equal on about 40,000,000 chips. The button moves all-in and the small blind calls. What should you do?

Note that you don't even need to look at your cards here. By folding you are guaranteed second in the tournament (unless your opponents split the pot). Even if you call and treble up, you will be heads-up with so few chips that it is practically impossible to overcome the deficit and win the tournament. Far better to guarantee yourself second place than to risk a chance of busting out in third.

Single table tournaments (STTs)/Sit-and-gos

The strategy discussed so far has been tailored for playing in multi-table tournaments (MTTs). STTs are sufficiently similar to MTTs that all of this strategy applies equally well to them. In fact, an STT is analogous to an MTT final table where everybody starts on the same stack. The only difference is that in a standard STT, only the top three places receive prize money. Timid players in STTs cannot afford to play super-tight with the hope of moving up the leaderboard if the leaderboard only starts at third place! All the other concerns apply – your stack needs protecting, you raise with weaker hands than you call with, your play varies with M value and your opponents are bullyable – particularly as the bubble approaches.

The speed at which an STT progresses is determined by the ratio of starting stack to starting blind size, and the speed that the blinds increase. Even though each website alters the specifics, STTs the cyber-world over last roughly the same amount of time. If you are still seated after an hour, you will almost certainly be in the money. How that tournament progresses depends on the playing styles of the other eight or nine players. If you are lucky enough to find an STT with several loose-aggressive players, you may find yourself down to four or five players after only a few hands. Even if you have not entered a single pot, and find yourself fairly short-stacked, you have only one or two other players to outlast before you reach the money. At the other extreme, with eight or nine tight players at the table, you may find yourself still with plenty of players left as the blinds become large. In this case, the tournament becomes a series of pre-flop all-ins, with the result determined in the most part by your run of cards – and pure luck once you end up all-in.

A successful STT player need only apply the skills he has learnt from the rest of this section on tournament play, and try to develop an ability to determine the dynamic of the table as quickly as possible. A basic strategy would be to enter plenty of unraised pots with speculative hands in the early stages, when the blinds are small, while avoiding the bigger pots that put your whole stack at risk, and then loosen up and start to raise more when the blinds have increased. With luck, your tight image and the proximity of the bubble will allow you to pick up plenty of chips uncontested and build a stack to take you into the money.

Deals

Most poker players (particularly professionals) are risk-averse. All other things being equal, they seek to remove volatility from their annual profits. This is particularly so when there is a large amount at stake, and the luck factor is high. This is never truer than in a big tournament with a few people left. Here, the blinds are so large compared to the stacks that the tournament will be decided on the strength of cards dealt and one or two crucial all-ins. The difference in payout between places is huge.

It may be that every player left would prefer to a take a guaranteed figure that represents the value of their position rather than playing on. They may prefer to agree to split most of the remaining prize money and play on for the remainder and the title. If every player left in the tournament can agree on the figure that represents the value of their position, they can strike a deal. Unless every player at the table voluntarily agrees on the amounts offered, the tournament must continue. The more players remaining, the greater the chance that someone will object to a proposition, so it is usually impractical to discuss a deal until there are only two or three players remaining.

The value of your position in a tournament is somewhere between the lowest remaining payout and the first-place payout. Where it lies between these figures is a function of your chip stack and your playing skill. The better player you are, and the more chips you have, the more you should be demanding for your settlement.

Some televised tournaments have recently been trying to ban deals. Once a deal has been struck, there is often little or no prize money left to play for, so the thrill of the final table evaporates. This kills the excitement usually associated with the final hands of a big tournament. Those tournaments that do allow deals certainly won't make one explicit in the televised coverage. In many of the big tournaments seen on TV, the prize money has been carved up long before the final hand. Even some online sites now allow deals to be struck at the end of their big tournaments. It pays to find out if deals are allowed as you approach the final, and to understand how to calculate the value of your position in the endgame.

7

Limit and Pot Limit Hold'em

Limit Hold'em

Before the advent of the World Poker Tour on television in 2003, and the sudden rise of the no limit game, the vast majority of cash games found in US casinos were fixed limit Hold'em. They were popular, and in some places still are, because limit offers a safer, calmer and more mechanical game than big bet Hold'em. The notorious 'hours of boredom and moments of terror' experienced in no limit Hold'em are replaced by a steadier stream of decisions, each of which can have only a minimal impact on your long-term results. Bad players can play for longer without going broke, and good players can make their living without having an uncomfortable amount of money resting on the turn of one card.

Pre-flop hand selection

The fixed bet size in limit Hold'em makes it much harder for you to put real pressure on your opponents on the flop and beyond. Pre-flop, and on the flop, the bet is fixed at the size of the big blind. On the turn and river, a bet is always twice the size of the big blind. Compared to the huge bets you can make in pot and no limit, this is a very restrictive structure. Semi-bluffs and pure bluffs always offer your opponents very attractive odds on their call, and are successful much more rarely than in big bet Hold'em. You cannot pick up unwanted pots as often, because players will often be correct to call even with two overcards to a low flop. When you do have a solid hand, you cannot thin the field with big bets or big check-raises. In limit Hold'em, therefore, it is much more common to reach the showdown, where the pot is simply won by the best hand.

This has an impact, of course, on your pre-flop hand selection. Much of the time in big bet Hold'em you allow yourself to play hands without the prescribed pre-flop power. This playing style is defensible only because your tricky and aggressive post-flop play allows you to pick up enough pots on pure and semi-bluffs to make up for the cost of all those pre-flop calls. In limit Hold'em you are forced to play in a much more straightforward way after the flop. When you enter pots with substandard hands in limit Hold'em, you will simply not have the chance to make enough plays at the pot when you miss. Accordingly, you must be much more straightforward in your pre-flop hand selection. You should only be playing cards that have a good chance to win a pot in a showdown. Big cards and big pairs make solid hands much of the time. They are your bread-and-butter hands in most limit games.

In big bet Hold'em, it often makes sense to call with speculative hands that have a slim chance of connecting with the flop, but make a huge hand when they do. The main reason for playing these hands is the chance to target a player's whole stack and win a big pot. If you are up against a calling station in big bet Hold'em, you can fire three big bets on flop, turn and river, and force him into either committing his whole stack or folding. In limit Hold'em, with controlled betting sizes post-flop, you can no longer put such pressure on your opponents when you have a monster hand. The most you can force opponents to commit before a showdown is one small bet on the flop, plus one big bet on each of the turn and river. This amounts to five big blinds in the usual structure. This is in contrast to the hundred or more big blinds often at stake in a game of pot or no limit Hold'em. You do not win big enough pots in limit when your hands connect big with the flop to make calling pre-flop with speculative hands correct very often.

All the other concerns from big bet Hold'em apply to limit. You still play more hands from late position. You still raise to buy the button and to isolate poor players. But in general you cannot be as creative with your limit Hold'em pre-flop hand selection as you can in the big bet game. From most positions you can afford to play only hands with genuine pre-flop power. You can no longer limp in early position with small/medium pocket pairs, and you cannot call raises with pocket pairs or suited connectors unless the pot is extremely multi-way. Even if the bet size on post-flop streets is unusually small, the presence of multiple opponents means that you at least have the chance to recoup a large profit if your speculative hand connects with the flop.

Look-up calls

As mentioned, bluffs and semi-bluffs in limit Hold'em almost always offer very attractive odds to a call. This comes into play when you are facing a possible bluff, particularly on the river. You have to be very sure that you are beaten before you can make a correct fold. The more money in the pot, the more certain you have to be that you are losing before you can fold. Your 'break-even percentage' is the proportion of the time that calling here must win you the pot for it to be a break-even play over the long run. If the pot is offering you 9-1 on your call, you need to be right the same proportion of the time (1 in 10) to break even. If you call here ten times, nine times you will lose one bet and the other time will win nine bets.

In limit Hold'em, the pot odds offered by a river bet are often 9 or 10-1 or higher. In these cases, you need pick off a bluff only one in ten times for calling to be a winning play. If the betting patterns on previous streets indicate even a slim chance that your opponent is bluffing on the river, you are almost obliged to look him up.

Not only is calling here often an EV play on its own, but it also has a beneficial impact on the long-term table dynamic. Being seen as a player who is prepared to call on the river with mediocre hands prevents you being run over by your opponents the rest of the game. If you are not prepared to make look-up calls on the river, your opponents will be correct to bluff into you almost every time they have missed. Once you call them down with bottom pair or a good ace-high, they will have to think twice about bluffing you in future. This will actually benefit you by forcing your opponents to play in a more straightforward way against you from then on.

Choosing your post-flop weapons
In big bet Hold'em, deceptive plays often risk losing you the pot, but can reward you with an opponent's whole stack if success-ful. In limit, they often still risk losing you the pot, but you stand to gain only an extra bet or two. In limit Hold'em, you very rarely use plays that risk costing you the pot in the name of deception. Consider slow-playing and check-raising only if you have a complete lock on the hand. You don't have to worry about the size of bets you may face on later streets, so checking to control the size of the pot is not a concern. Overall, play a much more value-based game on the flop and beyond. If you believe you have the best hand, you should almost always bet it, or raise if you are bet into.

Unless you have a strong read that your opponent is aggres-sive and has no hand whatever, you should often still bet for value even with a complete lock. People are more inclined to

make look-up calls with really quite weak hands in limit
Hold'em – hands that they would not necessarily have bet for
value if checked to. They also are braver when considering raising for value with a solid hand. When you bet for value with a
monster, you usually win one bet, and often trap your opponent
for three. Going for a check-raise risks winning you nothing, and
nets you only two bets when successful.

Draws in limit Hold'em

The betting limit pulls the value of draws in both directions.
First, you can no longer put your opponents to a tough decision
for their whole stack once you have made your draw. You can
bet only the prescribed limit – or maybe go for a check-raise.
Implied odds are easier to calculate, but are lower and will play
a far less significant role in determining the correctness of calling with a draw. Conversely, your opponents are also restricted
in the amount they can charge you for your draw. Calculating
effective odds with more than one card to come is no longer
too tricky. You know that your opponent can bet only a small
fraction of the pot on the turn if you miss. A call on the flop
in limit Hold'em is correct in a place where the threat of a big
turn bet in pot or no limit Hold'em would have forced you
to fold.

The betting limit also removes your concern regarding
stack size when considering a semi-bluff. In big bet Hold'em
you often have to turn down an otherwise profitable semi-bluff
on the flop because it would leave you with an awkward stack
on the turn. In limit Hold'em, a serious player will have enough
chips at the table that he is effectively playing a bottomless
stack. If this is the case, you can always make a semi-bluff if it
seems like a profitable play. Further, you can make more multi-
barrelled semi-bluffs because a raise is not going to price you out
of the hand. If you bet your draw on the flop and get called, a
bet on the turn may have a good chance to win you the pot

because it is interpreted as representing a genuine hand. The betting limit has increased, and a lot of players are not brave enough to fire a second bet when still drawing. Even if the play backfires and you are raised, the raise will be offering you sufficient pot odds that you are not making an EV error to call. Incorporating a plan to fire a second barrel when you consider semi-bluffing on the flop can often make the play profitable.

If you hold a nut draw in a very multi-way pot, it can actually be correct to bet or raise *for value* in limit Hold'em. Up against five solid hands, such as top pairs and sets, a nut-flush draw is rarely less than a 30% favourite to win the pot. On the button in a loose-passive game, with a bet and four callers before you, you should raise. Everyone will call for one extra bet. Six bets will be committed to the pot (one of which is yours). You will win on average 30% of the money committed, or 1.8 bets. The play wins you more than it costs to make, so is a winning play.

One-pair hands as slim draws

Because the betting limit offers such favourable odds on bets after the flop, one-pair hands that don't figure to be ahead can actually be considered as playable draws. In the right situation (unless dominated), they have five outs. This equates to about a 20% chance of ending up with the best hand against other one-pair hands. Often, the pot is big enough that you should call here even in the knowledge that you are behind.

This is not, though, a play you should make every time you have any piece of the flop and are bet into. For the play to be correct, you need to be certain that your five outs are true outs. If your opponent has already got a two-pair hand or better, you are drawing very slim indeed, and your call here is incorrect. You will end up losing a big pot even if you do hit. Also, if there is a chance you are dominated (and share a kicker with one of your opponents), you don't have the true outs you thought you did. The only time this play is correct is when you are certain that your opponent has a one-pair hand, and that all five of your outs are true outs.

If you are in a raised pot against a tight player, you can often read him for a one-pair hand at best. If you hold 8c-7c, and defend your blind against a middle position raise, a flop of Ah-4s-8d is a good time to make a speculative call. You are unlikely to be up against a flopped two-pair or low set. The most common hand for your opponent to have is a big ace, meaning that all your outs are true outs, and you will win a decent pot if you improve on the turn. Holding Ah-5h on Qs-Jc-5d in the same situation is *not* a good time to call. You will too often find your-self up against A-J or A-Q here.

Short-handed limit Hold'em

When short-handed in a limit game, for all the same reasons as in short-handed, big bet Hold'em, you become more aggressive, looser and trickier. Further, on the flop and beyond, the pots are now often small enough in relation to the betting limit to take the chance to pick up unwanted pots and take people off their hands on pure and semi-bluffs. This means that you can afford to sacrifice some pre-flop power by playing in a tricky and aggressive style on the flop and beyond.

When short-handed, you are paying more in blinds per round than in a full ring game. You simply don't have the time to take the value-based approach you would normally employ. If you don't start making plays for the blinds, your stack will be eaten up by the blinds passing through it every few minutes. You should be inclined to raise into the blinds with any playable hand, even from early or middle position.

You also know that when a pot is short-handed, it is unlikely that any of your opponents holds a genuine hand whether pre-flop or on the flop. You should reraise frequently, to isolate players and try to put them to the test on the flop and beyond. They are raising as liberally as you are, and you need to reraise in position and keep firing on the flop and beyond. You also need to reraise from the blinds with many different hands to keep them from feeling confident in attacking your blinds.

The basic strategy in short-handed limit Hold'em is to counter your opponents' increased aggression with an even greater shift in your own aggression. You rely on the fact that they miss flops so often to pick off their bluffs and take them off their hands. Short-handed limit Hold'em is a psychological war relying on momentum, initiative and intimidation. You are looking to run over the table and dominate with your aggression. If this fails, and your opponents hit a run of good hands or manage to read you correctly every time, it is going to be expensive. Then again, when it pays off, running over a short-handed limit table is one of the most profitable and satisfying hours you can spend playing Texas Hold'em.

Pot limit Hold'em

In pot limit Hold'em, your maximum bet is the size of the pot, including any bets, raises or calls before the action gets to you. If you are raising, this includes the amount of the bet you are facing. If there is $1000 in the pot, for example, and someone bets $500, you match the $500, making $2000 in the pot, and this is the total you can then raise. So your biggest available raise can take the pot up to $4000.

Pot limit Hold'em plays out in a very similar way to no limit. When you are playing no limit Hold'em, you tend to raise to about 3.5 big blinds pre-flop, or bet between half and the full size of the pot on later streets. Both of these amounts are allowed in pot limit. It is only when you would like to make an overbet that the rules of pot limit rein you in.

Pre-flop

One of the best times to make an overbet in no limit Hold'em is before the flop. If you have a premium holding, and are facing a raise and a lot of calls or a reraise, you should often push all-in. This puts your opponents to the test, allowing them to make a big mistake by calling. In pot limit, you are restricted by the size of the pot, and may be allowed to raise only half your stack or so. The problem here is that hands like Q-Q or A-K tend to play very well pre-flop in aggressive games, but will often not be strong enough to call a pot-sized bet on the flop. Two-thirds of the time you see a flop with A-K you will miss, and you will often have to fold in the face of strength. It is catastrophic to commit half your stack with A-K pre-flop, and then miss. You might get taken off the hand by a bluff, or you might have to fold on the flop when the turn or river would have made you a winning hand. In no limit you can combat this by simply pushing pre-flop. In pot limit, however, you must consider how your hand plays on the flop, and whether a reraise will leave you in danger of committing half your stack and still having to fold. In this spot, it is often better just to see (or 'take off') a flop and make sure that it fits with your hand before you commit that much of your stack.

Building the pot

Sometimes it is a good move to overbet in no limit Hold'em when you have flopped a monster hand. If you believe your opponent has a big hand of his own, you can often force him to make a big mistake on the flop or turn by calling. You might be afraid that the turn will be scary enough to kill the action, whereas you can trap him for his whole stack on the flop by simply moving all-in. In pot limit, you can't just push all-in and force him to call off his whole stack or fold. You must rely on other techniques to target his whole stack. You might want to flat-call on one street and risk the scare card, so that by the time he bets again on the turn, your raise will set him all-in. You might want to make a suspiciously small raise, so that he decides to go to the third raise and you have trapped him for his whole stack. Either way, being unable to make an overbet here has meant that you need to come up with much more creative ways of targeting your opponent's whole stack.

Watching the pot size when drawing or semi-bluffing

In no limit Hold'em, as we have seen, you must avoid making a semi-bluff that will leave you about the size of the pot on the turn if called. This will often find you missing, and no longer having a strong enough draw to be willing to get all-in. In no limit, you have total control over the size of the semi-bluff that you make. If a standard check-raise leaves you the wrong amount in your stack, you can just go all-in right there on the flop. In pot limit, you do not have that luxury. This means that there are times when a semi-bluff would be the correct play in no limit, but in pot limit you cannot bet the correct amount. If you find yourself in this spot, you have to play in a much more straightforward way. You can either call for value if the pot and implied odds permit, or fold and wait for a better time to make a play for the pot.

8

Online Tools

As I've said all along, these poker-playing principles apply equally to online and 'real', bricks and mortar play across a good, old-fashioned green baize. Online play is faster, against opponents who can be read only by their playing style and their betting patterns (apart, of course, from their inanities in the chat boxes). But there are some extra tools available that can really add that extra edge to the game of the serious, dedicated player. Here is a quick guide to those tools, and how to use them. If you choose not to bother, just remember that the best of your opponents do!

Player notes

Every online site now has the option of storing your notes on the playing styles of your opponents. These notes are readily available any time you see that player at a table in the future. Some even allow you to attach coloured markers to a player's name or avatar as a quick visual reminder of their style. To get the most value from player notes, they should be as concise as possible and stick to a regular format. It is more use to have the player's tight/loose and passive/aggressive mix than long details of specific hands they have played. It is also valuable to note any specific plays that the opponent over- or under-uses, and adjust accordingly in the future.

The pool of online players is huge, and it is impossible to remember many individual players. However, on a given site and at a given size of game, you often do encounter the same players from day to day. Keeping detailed player notes is a simple and effective way of giving yourself an edge over the casual player. You can make much more sophisticated plays against a player when you know their style and how to exploit it. By storing notes on a player, you can begin adjusting to their style the moment they sit at the table.

Player notes are also of use when deciding which table to sit at. Most sites will have at least a handful of tables fitting exactly the size and style of game you wish to play. By quickly opening all the tables on offer and reading any notes you have on the players, you may be able to determine that one table contains more poor players than the others. Routinely playing in soft games will do wonders for your long term profit.

Probability calculators

Programs such as PokerProbe are available online as free downloads and every serious poker player should have one such program on his desktop. These allow you to input the details of a match-up and then run the hand through to completion hundreds of thousands of times. The more basic probability calculators simply allow you to enter your cards, your opponents' cards and the board cards and then return the probabilities of each hand winning. The more advanced programs allow you to give your opponents random unknown cards or a range of possible hands. They can also be set to return 'equity' figures for playing the hand rather than a simple probability figure.

These programs take too long to be of use during a hand. Their value comes from allowing you to analyse decisions you have previously made and accurately determine if you made the correct choice. It is particularly difficult to calculate winning probabilities of multi-way pots, and these programs will allow you to input the hands and quickly get the winning probabilities of each hand.

PokerTracker

PokerTracker is an incredibly powerful analysis program. Underneath or to the side of every hand that is played online, there is an accompanying text record. This text, often called 'dealer chat', contains a record of every card dealt and every action taken by each player at the table. Contained within this text is enough information to recreate every hand in perfect detail.

PokerTracker is stored on your computer and keeps a log of all of this dealer chat from every table you have open. You do not even have to be playing at a table for PokerTracker to gather its data. The software then allows you to carry out a wealth of analysis on your own and your opponents' play. You can filter for specific hands and see how much you have won or lost with these hands from early, middle and late position. You can see how often you raise pre-flop, how often you bet on the flop after raising pre-flop and whether these plays make you money in the long run. The same analysis can be carried out for any opponent who has played at a table PokerTracker has been observing.

The morality of using PokerTracker to observe a table when you are not currently playing is hotly debated. Proponents say that these tools are available to anyone choosing to play online, and failing to take full advantage is foolish. Opponents say that this 'data-mining' is not in the spirit of the game. Observing a player at the table and getting a *feel* for their style is one thing; but using automated programs to keep records of every action a player takes, even when you are not even in their game, is another.

PokerTracker's usefulness is twofold. First, at regular intervals in your career, it pays to spend a few hours analysing specific aspects of your play. PokerTracker will allow you to see if there are certain plays (for example, raising from late position with suited connectors) that lose you money in the long run. It can also be used to show whether you win more money by opening for a raise with medium pairs, or simply calling before the flop. Once you identify plays that lose you money in the long run, eliminating them from your game will increase your long-term profit.

Secondly, PokerTracker provides the data for heads-up displays (see below). At the time of writing it was available on a 30-day free trial, then for a small fee ($90).

Heads-up displays (HUDs)

Programs such as PokerAce use the data stored within your PokerTracker database and present this in an easily readable format on top of your actual poker table. The software places customisable data above each player at the table, showing vital statistics about their play. Common figures to have are BB/100 (number of big blinds per 100 hands won or lost), pre-flop aggression frequency (a measure of how often a player raises before the flop) and CBet frequency (how often a player bets at the pot on the flop after raising pre-flop). Users of HUDs can select as many other statistics as they deem manageable and have these displayed above their opponents' names.

Whenever you observe players' styles or make notes on them, you are trying to get a feel for how often they make certain types of play. The tight/loose and passive/aggressive axes are tools for making this process manageable. Using PokerTracker and an HUD is more accurate, more detailed and more comprehensive than observing and noting their style. With sufficient data on a player and an HUD displaying appropriate statistics you can choose the exact counter-strategy that is best to exploit their style.

SharkScope

SharkScope is an online database of tournament results and functions much like a simplified worldwide PokerTracker for tournament play. The software records (by observation) every tournament played on the major poker sites. It then allows you to look up your opponents in the database and check their results. The analysis possible on SharkScope is simpler than that from PokerTracker. It is possible only to check tournament-by-tournament performance figures and analyse players' profits at a given size of tournament. Although SharkScope cannot give details on opponents' playing styles, it is useful to know whether you are up against a winning or losing player. It is also useful for helping you choose between various tournaments on offer. As you see a sit-and-go filling up, you can look up the players on SharkScope. If the majority are poor players, it will be a soft tournament and well worth playing. If most of the players are winning tournament players it will be better to wait for the next one. SharkScope also has its own inbuilt HUD which at the time of writing was still in beta-testing. At present you are allowed five free searches a day (on a database containing the results of more than 100 million sit-and-gos); on top of this, you can sub-scribe for $11.99 per month, allowing up to 150 searches per day, or for a flat fee of $9.99, allowing a total of 200 searches over any period of time.

9

Bricks and Mortar

Knowing your way around a cardroom

Waiting lists

When you walk into a cardroom, your first decision is which game to play in. The list of games on offer and the waiting lists for them are usually displayed on big screens above the main desk. Once you have decided on a style and size of game that suits, ask the person behind the desk to add your name to those lists. When your seat is ready, your name will be called over the intercom or your beeper will go off if you have been given one. When this happens, you have only a few minutes to make yourself known to the staff and to take your seat before they call the next name on the list, so don't stray too far from the cardroom or you will lose your seat and go back to the end of the queue.

Buying chips

Some cardrooms prefer you to have bought your chips from the cage before sitting down. Others have chip runners who take cash from you at the table and return with your chips. Ask at the desk before you take your seat if you can get chips at the table. If you need to top up with more chips during a game, you can usually buy directly from the dealer or, if not, the dealer will call a chip runner for you.

Rulings

If there is a dispute at the table, and any player is unhappy with the decision of the dealer, that player is entitled to call a floor-person for a ruling. Often there is a lot of money at stake, and the decision can be rather subjective. When a floor-person comes over to give a ruling, it is the job of the dealer, not either of the players, to explain the situation and what is disputed. The floor-person should then check with both players that this is a fair representation of what happened, and rule accordingly. It will do you no favours to launch straight into your own take on the situation when the floor-person arrives.

Tipping

If tipping is legal where you are playing (in the US, for instance, but not in the UK), you are all but obliged to tip the dealer after winning a pot. After winning each pot, pass the dealer one of whatever is the smallest chip in play at the table (usually $1). If you take down a very large pot, you will be expected (but not obliged) to tip a bit more. It is also a nice touch to look after the other employees — chip runners, floor-people and cardroom managers. If you are going to be visiting a particular cardroom often, a $100 bill passed to the cardroom manager after your first solid win will prove money well spent. Once on familiar terms with the cardroom manager, you will begin to earn the $100 back with interest. You may be allowed to phone in and get on the waiting list before you even set off for the cardroom. This can save hours of sitting around killing time. If you are elsewhere when your seat is called, they will hold it a little longer for you. You may even get a heads-up from the cardroom manager when he is about to open a new game, and get your name put down before the list fills up. Most importantly of all, you may get tipped off about a particularly juicy game on one of the other tables, or a particularly poor player who is about to sit down to play. The value of information like this will make the $100 seem like a modest investment.

Comps

Most cardrooms offer some sort of player-reward scheme based on the number of hours you spend at the tables. If you intend to play in a particular club often, it is well worth the time to sign up for a player-reward card. Cardrooms tend to give back a proportion of the rake (or table-charge) in these reward schemes to the tune of about $1–$1.50 per hour. This may not sound like much; but over a long session, you will have earned a free buffet dinner or a round of drinks. If you are serious about making money at poker, you should not turn down *any* opportunity to make more money from your play. Taking five minutes to sign up for a player-reward card is a guaranteed way to be $10–$15 better off after a long session. You would be crazy not to take it.

Live play strategy and 'tells'

In a bricks and mortar cardroom, the basic strategy to employ is no different from that in the online game. You need to be aware of a few mechanical differences, but all you are really doing is trying to apply the same techniques. In a live game, the pace is slower, you have to make sure you don't physically telegraph your strength, and you should make sure you behave courteously.

When playing online, you have to rely on your opponents' betting patterns and an understanding of their playing styles to deduce their likely holdings. Playing live, you can also use tells – their body language, vocal patterns, hand movements and posture – to determine their cards. There are two categories of tells: deliberate and subconscious. Deliberate tells are the easier to spot. They tend to be overblown pieces of theatre designed to throw off other players at the table. Subconscious tells are subtler, involuntary bodily responses that a player either doesn't know about or is unable to control.

Mike Caro first coined the golden rule of deliberate tells: 'strong means weak'. An unusually deliberate and confident-sounding bet is usually a bluff. A disinterested shrug and look away, or a grimace as a bet is made, usually indicates real strength. Novice and amateur players tend to operate at the first order of deception. They cannot help but think that the best way to conceal the strength of their hand is to act in an overblown way and give off the opposite signals.

Sometimes a player will suddenly call over a cocktail waitress or start asking questions about the televised football game he has previously been ignoring. This is usually a transparent attempt to deflect the attention away from the hand, and to convince everyone at the table that his own hand is so weak he's all but forgotten he's still playing. Of course, if he really does have a lousy hand, he may decide it's time for a cocktail. Only if his actions appear theatrical and over the top should you be inclined to read this as a deliberate tell.

To exploit deliberate tells, all you really need to do is be aware of Caro's golden rule and to pay attention at the table. Deliberate tells are most exploitable against weak and mediocre players. Experts are aware of the folly of giving off deliberate tells, and will either act neutrally at all times or throw in the occasional 'reverse tell' and trap you into making incorrect deductions about their hands.

Subconscious tells are harder to spot but, once spotted, are firm indicators of strength. Deliberate tells may be thrown in for deception; but since a player is usually unaware of a subconscious tell, it comes straight from the part of the brain that deals with genuine response to fear or excitement.

Shaking hands and a faltering voice are indicators of strength. The shaking does not usually come from the fear of making a big bluff, but the excitement of holding a monster hand. If a player moves chips into the pot with a shaking hand and an unsteady voice, you can bet that he has the nuts, or close to it.

When a player calls a raise with a speculative hand, and the flop comes out perfectly for him, he will struggle to control the instant adrenaline rush. Many players can't help but glance down at their chip stacks for a fraction of a second before looking away. Their subconscious brain is already looking ahead to the giant pot it hopes to win. The look shows them thinking about how much to bet or raise, and considering how impressive their chip stack will look after this hand. Some players avoid looking down at their stack, but respond immediately to a perfect flop by looking up and away across to the other side of the cardroom. This is not a deliberate tell as such. It is more a desperate, subconscious attempt to look innocuous, and should be treated the same way as a glance down at a chip stack.

'Chirping' means a player suddenly becoming vocal at the table – often in a higher pitch and faster pace to his usual voice. This is usually a result of the adrenaline and excitement of holding a big hand. If you are facing a large bet, particularly an all-in, and your opponent starts chirping, it is usually a bad sign.

When facing an all-in bet, most players are subconsciously looking for a reason to call. They consider where they stand; and if they can't find a reason to call, they will eventually fold. If, during the thought process, they find anything that points towards a call, it may trigger their calling impulse; they may blurt out 'call' or shove chips forward without careful consideration. If you are considering an all-in and an opponent is chirping at you or needling you, he may be trying to trigger your calling impulse. You should be inclined to fold. A bluffing opponent in this spot will usually be sitting quietly, drawing no attention to himself, and willing you to arrive gradually at the decision to fold.

You will have a much better idea of how to handle the later stages of each hand if you've made the best possible start to it. So, to end at the beginning: when the hand is being dealt, don't be too impatient to look at your own cards. Depending on your position, you can watch the other players' reactions to their hole cards before checking out your own. This, you will find, can reveal as much as any subsequent tells in gauging the strength of their hands.

Cardroom etiquette

A player should act at all times in a way that allows the game to play out smoothly, quickly and as the rules intended. And he or she should treat all other players around the table with respect.

Acting out of turn

Some behaviour at the poker table may seem harmless enough, but can drastically alter the balance of power in a hand. It may even cost another player thousands of dollars or his life in a tournament. Acting out of turn gives information to players who are not entitled to it. When you act out of turn, every player yet to act has information that may change the way they would have played the hand. For example, Player A makes a bluff on the river. Player B is next to speak, and you are third. Player B suspects that Player A is bluffing but the threat of your calling behind means that he cannot risk the call, and intends to fold. Before he folds, you announce 'fold' out of turn. Player B now has only Player A to beat, and quietly elects to call. Player A may have made the bluff relying on your presence in the hand to scare out Player B. By folding out of turn, you have changed the way the hand should have been played, and you have cost Player A a big pot. Accidents do happen, and a normal poker game won't go more than an hour or so without somebody acting out of turn, but you should still pay attention at all times. Always knowing how many players are in a hand and who is next to act will help you avoid acting out of turn.

Revealing your cards after your have folded

Just as acting out of turn gives players information they shouldn't have, so does exposing your hole cards. When you fold, your cards should be carefully pushed forward rather than thrown carelessly into the middle of the table. If you routinely expose hole cards by throwing cards around, you will begin to irritate the dealer and the other players at the table. Nor should you act in a way that gives away what your hole cards were, even without exposing them. If a flop comes down 9s-9d-9c, and you sigh or thump the table, the message is clear – you held the 9h. This gives information to other players and again could cost someone at the table.

Keeping your cards on the table

For reasons of security, you should always keep your hole cards visible and on the playing surface. When looking at them, don't lift them off the table and hold them up to your chest. Simply bend the corners up while they are still lying on the playing surface in front of you. Likewise, during the rest of the hand, you should not hold your cards down in your lap or close to your chest. Players tend to keep track of the number of people in a hand by looking to see who still has hole cards in front of them on the playing surface. Hiding your cards can lead to players acting out of turn – and it will (rightly) be you that gets the blame. Furthermore, when you hold your cards to your chest or down in your lap, you could easily be switching cards with an ace from your pocket or sleeve. You will be firmly reprimanded, at the very least, for acting this way.

Protecting your cards

When your cards are on the table in front of you, you must protect them from being mucked. If any folded or discarded card touches yours, and they are not protected, your hand will be declared dead. If the dealer accidently sweeps up your cards and puts them into the muck pile, you cannot fish them out. To protect against this, place your two hole cards one on top of the other and place a chip or personalised card protector on top of them. This signals to the dealer that you have not folded, and will prevent your cards from being scooped into the muck. It also means that if an opponent throws in his cards to fold, and one touches your hole cards, the dealer will be able to retrieve it with no doubt as to which two cards are yours. You will be able to play on in the hand.

Hollywooding

Poker is an inherently manipulative game. When you play live, you seek to conceal strength in order to extract the maximum from your opponents. This can be taken too far and become unsportsmanlike. If you hold the mortal nuts, and a player bets into you on the river, you know you are going to raise. You are perfectly entitled to act in a neutral way, or even throw in a reverse tell and try to induce a call. What you should not do is put on a big theatrical performance designed to convince your opponents that you don't have the best hand. If you waited three to four minutes in this spot, with lots of sighing and tutting and comments like 'Hmm . . . I hope you don't have the flush' before you make your raise, when you show down your own nut flush it will be exposed as an elaborate act. Although not strictly against the rules, behaviour like this lowers the tone of the game. There is enough room for deception in betting patterns, and in concealing tells, to make 'Hollywooding' an unnecessary and unwelcome addition. The least you can expect after a performance like this is a dressing-down from the veterans at the table.

Slow-rolling

When it comes to a showdown on the river, the player to make the last aggressive action (a bet or a raise) is the one that is called on to show his cards first. Most people do not enjoy showing down a beaten hand, so if you hold the nuts or close to it, when your opponent has made the last aggressive action, it is courteous to show first and allow him to muck his hand unseen. Again, though not strictly against the rules, forcing your opponent to show his hand when you know he is beaten is less than courteous and will not go down well at the table.

Rules specific to live play

String betting

A bet or raise at the poker table must be in a single, deliberate motion or announced verbally prior to the physical act of moving chips. If these conditions are not met, the bet or raise will be called 'string' and will be disallowed. The string bet rule is there to stop a player gaining information before he has committed to a course of action. If you move into the pot only enough chips to call, and in doing so detect weakness from your opponent, you cannot decide that a raise would have been a better play and reach back for more chips. Only the call will be allowed. To avoid any ambiguity, bets and raises should be made in one of two ways. Announcing verbally your full intentions cannot be misinterpreted. If you face a bet of $500 and wish to raise another $1500 say 'Raise' or even 'Raise to $2000' before you start moving chips around. Alternatively, if you wish to remain silent, you *must* move all $2000 chips into the centre of the pot in one smooth movement. Also be aware that if you use a single large chip to make a raise, it could be that you just wanted to call but didn't have the correct change in chips. In the example above, if you had simply moved a $5000 chip into the middle without verbally announcing a raise, the dealer will rule that your action constitutes a call rather than a raise.

Moody

The 'moody' rule is upheld in only some cardrooms; but you should check the local rules before you sit down, as a mistake here can be extremely expensive. The moody rule prohibits a player who still has live cards from making comments that in any way refer to the specifics of the pot in play. You may not – even jokingly – talk about the cards on the flop or what you or your opponent might hold. If you do, you will be prohibited from taking any aggressive action in the pot from that moment on. You can still call if bet into, but you will not be allowed to bet if your opponent checks, and you will not be allowed to raise if your opponent bets. The moody rule can be strictly enforced. Comments like 'You better fold here, pal, I'm holding the nuts!' are obviously out of order, but referring to any aspect of the cards in play can result in your hand being killed. Even saying 'Wow – what a flop' may be deemed, by a particularly irritating opponent, a comment specific to the cards in play.

Absurdly, there is no standard international set of poker regulations. Different casinos, different countries, different competitions all have different rules. Always be sure you know the local rules before you sit down to play.

PART THREE

On the Road

Having mastered the precepts in Chapters 3–9, we
are now going to hit the road with the European
Poker Tour, to put what we've learnt into practice –
and to learn more from the play, on good days
and bad, of the top professionals

10

EPT London

Queen Vicky

Universally known as 'The Vic', the Victoria Casino in the London district of Paddington, amid the mideastern delights of the Edgware Road, has always held a special place in the hearts of British poker players. At some point in their poker lives, everyone has played there. Pretty much everyone who works in the game – OK, everyone of a certain age who works in the game – has at some time worked there. In the days before the internet – and strange as it may seem to younger readers, there actually *was* poker life before the advent of the world wide web – many people played their first hand of poker there.

The first time I myself played poker in public, as opposed to the Tuesday Night Game, was at the Vic in the mid-1970s. Throughout the 1990s, the club's Saturday-night Hold'em tournament was a regular fixture in my married life with Cindy Blake, the 'Moll' of *Big Deal*. My three sons even had their eighteenth birthday parties there, on becoming old enough to enter a casino. The winner of the £1m first prize in the first ever Poker Million, John Duthie, played his very first hand of poker at the Vic, where he soon became a regular. It was also the first venue to which Duthie came in 2003, when setting up the European Poker Tour (EPT), a European version of the televised tournament circuit that constitutes America's World Poker Tour. The Vic now hosts the EPT's London event each year.

Through various poker metamorphoses over the years, from a small, crowded room on the second floor to a small, crowded room on the first, the Vic has always been there, seeing off passing rivals – the Lyndhurst in St John's Wood, the Barracuda in Baker Street, the Gala Regency in Russell Square – like swatting so many upstart flies. Properly called the Grosvenor Victoria Casino these days, its cardroom enjoyed its latest makeover in 2007, moving back to the second floor in bigger and better shape, in the wake of the exciting events that are about to unfold. Thanks to sponsorship from PokerStars.com, we're embarking on a voyage round various venues on the 2006–7 circuit of 'EPT 3', in the hope of learning from some pivotal hands played by the European (and American) masters (and mistresses).

On Saturday, 23 September 2006, day three of the London event of the EPT's third season, the record 398 starters (at a buy-in of (€5000) had been whittled down to 40 survivors, 32 of whom would get a share of the prize pool of £1.4 million. I myself had been eliminated the day before, after a less than distinguished performance even by my standards. Other early victims included Phil Ivey, Barry Greenstein, Joe Hachem and Gus Hansen. As the TV coverage of day three began, it was dispiriting to see my own name crawl across the bottom of the screen, even in such illustrious company, among the defeated. On Brad ('Otis') Willis's blog, moreover, there came a less than earth-shaking newsflash:

Maestro Gone

Anthony Holden

Moments later it's Tony Holden who beats Andreas [Hagen] to the rail. He moved in with Ace-Queen, to be called with pocket nines. No help on the board and the author was confined to the bargain bin.

'It's the best hand I've seen all day,' he said. 'I didn't even catch a pair.'

Excuses, excuses.

The EPT's London leg had always been won by a Brit, and the crowds at the Vic were hoping for a repeat, despite the menacing profusion of top Scandinavians. As day three began, the chip leader was British pro Ashley Hayles with 460,000, followed by the Swedes Jonas Molander with 362,400 and Peter Hedlund on 307,500, American Chad Brown (305,200) and Australian Emad Tahtouh (237,700). Three Brits brought up the rear of the leaderboard: Vic veteran Barny Boatman of the Hendon Mob (129,400), Mike Ellis (126,700) and Tim Flanders (125,200).

Another British player, the writer and semi-pro poker player Victoria Coren, was at this stage on just 60,000. I mention this now because Vicky went on to win the tournament. The masterclass contained in this chapter will consist of watching how she did it.

Anything Moneymaker can do . . .

With 40 players left, the blinds are 2000–4000 with a rolling ante of 400. Six more players have departed – so the tourney is just two off the bubble, the worst place of all to go out – when Vicky Coren is dealt a pair of pocket eights. First to speak, with a huge stack of chips in front of him, Jonas Molander raises 12,000.

With one of the shorter stacks at the table, 72,000, Coren has little option but to put him on two face cards and go all-in, hoping her pair will stand up. Molander calls and rolls over pocket aces.

'Oh dear, bad timing,' mused John Duthie in the commentary box. A close friend of Coren's, well aware what a boost a female British victory would give his EPT, Duthie seems as dismayed as Coren to see those Swedish bullets. 'She's played so well, too,' he goes on. 'It will be a shame to see her go.'

Other players at the table, including her friends Andy Black and Barny Boatman, smile wryly at Vicky, whose face shows only a seen-it-all-before resignation. Until the flop comes 9-8-6, when it stays fixed, unsmiling, but with resignation now replaced by determination. Trip eights! Some people play long and hard enough to make their own luck, and this looks like one of those moments. Only a third ace can beat Coren now. Slowly, agonisingly, the turn brings a jack and the river a . . . four. At this comparatively early stage, alas, there is no crowd to cheer the local favourite; Vicky Coren spends so much time playing in the Vic that she calls it her second home. By the end of the weekend, some people will be joking that they named the joint after her.

She needed to make a move, and she got lucky. Vicky would be the first to admit it. At the time, Vicky gave Molander an apologetic sort of shrug, and hauled in a pot totalling 154,400. It had proved an eerie action replay of the famous hand when Chris Moneymaker's pocket eights beat Humberto Brenes' pocket rockets, the turning point of Moneymaker's unlikely progress to the 2003 world crown.

Know thy enemy

In the next hand, Andy Black (a.k.a. 'The Monk', so named after five years in a Buddhist retreat) makes a misread, and moves in with bottom pair, which sees him eliminated two off the money. Now we're on the bubble. Coren limps in with Qd-5d. So does Barny Boatman with 5h-7s, Sid Harris with Ks-Qc and Swede Shamir Shakhtoor with Jd-6h. The pot stands at 18,400 as the flop brings 9h-8c-6d, giving Boatman an unlikely straight. Coren checks to him, and he bets 5000.

Harris and Shakhtoor fold, leaving Vicky to think. After a while, she starts talking to her old pal Barny, in the seat behind her, trying to get a read from his reaction. 'You made that bet very insouciantly,' she says with a smile. Barny looks puzzled. 'In-sou-ci-ant-ly?' he repeats. 'What does that mean?' He's still wondering when Vicky finally, and sensibly, folds. At another table, Irish veteran Donnacha O'Dea goes out on the bubble. So now Coren is in the money, albeit with something less than the average chip stack of 124,375. While the cameras are elsewhere, she goes right back down to the felt before bouncing back enough to take on Barny Boatman again.

Sinking a Boatman

The pot is 13,800 before the flop. In late position, the cut-off seat, Vicky raises to 16,000 with Kd-Js, and Barny calls with Ah-Td. The flop comes 9s-Th-Kh. Vicky plays it cute with her top pair, and checks. With second pair, Barny bets 17,000. She calls, and again plays it canny by checking in the dark before the turn brings the 4h, giving Barny the nut-flush draw. He checks, too. With the odds 62-38 in Vicky's favour, the river is the 8s. Thinking she's winning, Vicky makes a value bet of 42,000. Barny replies by going all-in, to the tune of 115,000, building a pot of 236,800.

Vicky knows Barny well; she has played with him for years; and now she goes in for as much chat as if they were back in their home game. At first she mutters to herself, but loud enough for Barny to hear, so she can watch his reactions as she replays the hand in her head. 'He didn't bet the straight,' she says, and turns to stare at him. Barny, she can see, is not looking too comfortable. 'You're supposed to have called the sixteen? With two hearts in your hand. Which two? Which two hearts?' Boatman looks increasingly uneasy. 'You got a flush?' he asks her. 'No, I haven't got a flush,' she replies. 'But if you had a straight, or two pair, or a set or something you'd just call, would-n't you? You'd call and turn your hand over. So to go all-in, rather than just call, you've either got a flush, or I'm winning. You can't . . . you wouldn't . . . why would you, why would you make that raise with . . .'

Vicky is showing great powers of deduction. But it's still a tough call for her to make with just one pair, albeit the top pair. 'Sorry,' she says to the table, 'I just need a minute.' She leans back in her chair, throwing her head aloft for one last think. Then she makes up her mind. 'OK, then, come on, Barny,' she says suddenly, and calls.

It was a great move by Barny, but a better call by Coren, who hauls in a pot of 309,800 as Boatman takes his leave, eliminated in twenty-second place. John Duthie's verdict is that Boatman didn't think Coren 'had it in her' to make that call. 'She worked that out really, really well,' he says with genuine admiration. 'That was a really significant hand.' Says La Coren, as she stacks her chips: 'It's lovely to have the chips, but I wish they'd been someone else's.' 'Ah,' says a wiseacre on the rail, 'there are no friends at the felt, Vicky.'

Vicky's logic here is sound. When a player of Barny Boatman's quality makes a bet or raise, it is for a good reason. Barny has the option of just calling and proceeding to a showdown. Given that he in fact decides to raise, the intention must either be rais-ing for value or bluffing. As Vicky correctly deduces, with the vast majority of hands neither of these intentions is achieved with a raise. If he were sitting on a set or two pair, his raise would not be called by a worse hand, so there is no 'value'. Also, with a hand this strong, there is no need to bluff-raise. A bluff only makes a poor hand fold, and he could call here and defeat a poor hand without risking the rest of his stack. Vicky can now put Barny on one of two hands – a hand so powerful (a flush) that he must raise for value, or a hand so weak that he cannot win by calling and showing down. Which one is the case here is down to hand reading, physical tells and, who knows, maybe some female intuition. The pot stands at 236,800 and Vicky is facing a raise of 73,000. The pot odds are 3.25-1. As we know from Chapter 3, to make a call here correct in terms of EV, Barny must be the kind of player who would make a bluff at least one in 4.25 times (or 23.6% of the time). Vicky eventually decides this to be the case – and makes an excellent call.

The kicker plays

When the TV version of the event appears, the next signifi-cant hand is played 'blind with Vicky Coren'. In other words, the viewer sees it from her point of view, knowing only her hand – which happens to be Kh-Jh – and 'sweating it out' with Vicky as she tries to figure out what her opponents are holding. The pot is 16,800 when she flat-calls the big blind of 8000. Peter Hedlund and Jonas Molander also limp in before the flop brings 2s-3h-4h, giving Vicky the second nut-flush draw with two overcards.

Molander bets 16,000, and Coren decides just to call. The turn is the Ad. Now Molander bets 50,000. He can't have a five or an ace, she figures, or he wouldn't bet that much. She's get-ting pot odds of around 2-1, so she's got to call 50,000 to win a possible 111,000. This is the wrong price to make her flush, but she seems to be thinking he might also be on a draw, and won't dare 'fire' again – after two calls from her – if he misses it. 'I should really raise here,' she said later, 'because king-high isn't really good enough to keep someone honest. But I don't want him to move all-in and take me off the pot when I might still make a flush. I've got a good draw against a made hand, and I might be beating a draw, so I'm postponing the decision.' At the time she just says, 'I've made my decision, a very tight decision,' and calls. The river brings a blank. Both players check. Molander turns out to hold K-T to her K-J. Vicky wins a well-deserved pot of 160,800.

With hindsight, a raise on the turn would have been a nice play, which could have won the pot there and then. The ace is a scare card for Vicky to represent, in case Molander is sitting on a medium pocket pair (unlikely, given that he didn't raise pre-flop); but it may also have hit Molander, who could easily have been betting on the flop with an unpaired ace. Raising is, however, dangerous. If Molander *did* have a solid hand such as two pair on the turn, he would not be afraid to move all-in – as Vicky fears. There are not many hands containing a five that Vicky could have at this point, given that she voluntarily called pre-flop.

If Molander moves all-in, and Vicky is forced to fold, this is a disaster. She has committed a big chunk of her stack and not even had the chance to catch her flush. The only thing nagging at Vicky to raise here is that Molander could easily believe she is bluffing, but actually has a slightly better hand than Vicky's K-J. If the action goes check-check on the river, and Molander shows down K-Q or a low one-pair hand, Vicky would kick herself for not raising on the turn and picking up the pot. In the end, Coren chooses the safer option of just calling, and is fortunate that her second card out-kicks Molander by one, and not the other way around.

Down to 12

There are now 16 players left, two tables of eight. The blinds have gone up to 5000–10,000, with antes of 1000. With pocket fives, Jonas Molander bets 27,000 – more than the total pot of 22,000. With Ts-8s, Coren reraises to 60,000. Molander folds. That raise has proved creative. As Vicky is now one of the larger stacks at the table, she is one of the only players who can threaten Molander's own big stack. Knowing this, Vicky realises Molander will avoid tangling with her unless he holds a genuine powerhouse, and she uses the threat of her big stack to pick up a tidy pot.

It's time to sweat it with Coren again, as she makes it 25,000 to go, with Ad-Jc. Norway's Jan Sjavic calls, Peter Hedlund calls. The flop comes 3h-3d-8c. They check; Vicky checks. The turn is the Th. Hedlund bets 30,000 and Coren folds. And she turns out to be right – just; he is holding As-Qh.

On the next hand, the French player Michel Abecassis calls the 10,000 big blind under the gun with Jd-Qd. Two players fold before Vicky, with pocket sixes, decides to move in, boosting a 48,000 pot to 208,000. It's a heck of a reraise, as if she'd got some sort of read off Michel – who folds, justifying a very bold move on Vicky's part. But she had recently slipped down to 160,000, so had to start getting busy.

A few hands later, Coren limps in with a weak ace, Ah-4d. Michel Abecassis raises with Qh-5c. 'I should have raised,' she moans, and passes her ace. He flashes his queen, takes out a notebook, and jots down an aide-memoire about his opponent's play. Gus Hansen has also been making notes at the table, I am told, by talking into a Dictaphone.

Overnight, as they adjourn till the final day, there are twelve players left. Britain's Victoria Coren lies in eighth place, with the leaderboard looking like this:

Chad Brown (USA)	611,000
Peter Hedlund (Sweden)	523,500
Emad Tahtouh (Australia)	504,000
Michael Muldoon (N. Ireland)	422,000
Ashley Hayles (UK)	324,000
Jan Sjavic (Norway)	296,500
Michel Abecassis (France)	277,500
Victoria Coren (UK)	222,500

Next day Jonas Molander is the first to go, then Ashley Hayles, then Michel Abecassis. When the fourth player, Oscar Schweinebarth is eliminated, we have reached the final eight.

THE FINAL TABLE

In Seat 1: chip leader Chad Brown, with 795,000, cheered on from the bleachers by his glamorous, poker-playing girlfriend, Vanessa Rousso. A New Yorker, Brown is a well-known TV poker host in the US.

Seat 2: Emad Tahtouh, with 696,000. Emad is a close friend of Joe Hachem – indeed, the man who persuaded him to play in the 2005 World Series of Poker, where Hachem won the world title.

Seat 3: veteran English player Sid 'El Sid' Harris, with 277,000. An amateur player who doubles as a writer.

Seat 4: Irishman Michael Muldoon, with 550,000.

Seat 5: the respected Norwegian Jan Sjavic, with 440,000, an ex-IT manager of 42.

Seat 6: the excitable, talkative Swede Peter Hedlund, with 387,000.

Seat 7: another Swedish pro, Jules Kuusik, with 240,000.

Seat 8: the UK's Victoria Coren, with 632,000. Thirty-three years old, she started playing when just 15: 'My brother used to play, and it was a way for me to hang out with the boys. I got bored with them in two weeks, but totally hooked on poker.' The internet, she believes, has been an especially radical poker revolution for women. 'Across a real table all that face-to-face combat, staring people down, bullying them, pushing them around, etc., is really a guy thing. But, as a woman on the internet, it's just brilliant – you can do all that bullying, but from behind the safety of a screen-name.'

As battle recommences, the chips are fairly evenly spread. Anyone can win this thing. Second place secures £285,900, third £168,600, fourth £110,000, fifth £58,600, sixth £44,000, seventh £36,600 and eighth £29,300.

The blinds are now 8000–16,000, with antes of 2000, so there's 40,000 in each pot before play begins. A misdeal on the first hand winds up giving Peter Hedlund pocket sixes; he bets 50,000 and wins it uncontested. The final table seems unusually relaxed, given how much money is at stake. There is a lot of chat. They all look very comfortable, considering they're playing for a half-million-pound first prize.

Talking your way to a pot

Vicky is dealt pocket jacks. With the blinds at 8000–16,000, and antes of 2000, she raises the pot by 40,000 to 80,000. It's folded around to short-stacked Sid Harris, who has pocket nines; he goes all-in to the tune of 238,000, making a total pot of 318,000. 'It's not easy to get dealt a pair in this game,' says a gnomic railbird, as Vicky ponders Harris's raise. Harris probably thinks he's winning – up against A-Q or A-J. Vicky's well aware of this, so she starts talking to him to see if he's got a higher pair than jacks.

With a percentage advantage of 82-18, though she doesn't yet know it, Vicky says: 'Sidney, you old troublemaker! Why such a big raise? Why not a nice, small raise? I've got a hand . . .'

and so on. It's a third of her chip stack at stake here. But surely she's got to call?

'Oh, go on then,' she says eventually, and does so. No more betting; cards on their backs. The flop brings Kd-4d-Tc, which makes no difference as neither player has a diamond. The turn is the Kh, the river the Js. Coren's full house wins her a big hand, shooting her up to chip leader on nearly 900,000.

More table talk – maybe too much?

There are a couple of interesting hands for Vicky to watch before she needs to get involved again. Peter Hedlund raises with As-3s, and Chad Brown calls with Jd-Qc. The flop of 8s-Kc-Ts gives them both big drawing hands, Brown to a straight, Hedlund to a flush. Hedlund bets again, and Brown calls, building the pot to 200,000. The turn is a blank, 5d. Again Hedlund bets; now Brown doesn't look too comfortable, but he makes him sweat awhile before calling. The river is an irrelevant 8h. With the pot at 462,000, Brown bluffs to the tune of 120,000 – and Hedlund folds. 'I put you on J-Q,' he says, without having seen Brown's cards. 'I should have backraised. I would have won a big pot.' Yeah, sure, but you didn't.

Upset with himself, Hedlund now seems to go on tilt. Under the gun, he goes all-in with Kh-Qc, only to find himself called by Michael Muldoon with Ah-Kd. With a pot totalling 723,000, the odds are 3-1 in Muldoon's favour. This was a very reckless play by Hedlund. He really didn't need to do it; with the blinds at 8000–16,000, and his stack at 275,000, there is still a lot of play left in the tournament. With a flop of 8s-2d-7h, Js on the turn and 4h on the river, Hedlund goes out, kicking himself, in seventh place.

Now Vicky Coren gets pocket sixes. Under the gun, she doubles a pot of 36,000. 'Don't raise too much,' she begs Emad

Tahtouh as he fingers his chips. 'Make it small!' As a result, perhaps, Tahtouh just calls with K-Q, building the pot to 106,000.
The flop of 9s-Qc-Qh is a great one for Emad. Vicky checks, and
he bets 50,000 – a smart bet, because he knows Vicky knows he
probably wouldn't have bet that much if he had a queen. While
thinking it over, she says as much: 'That would be silly if you had
a queen. No one's that lucky. Make it two hundred.'

Oops – she's fallen into Tahtouh's trap. 'If you've got a
queen, you're winning, I'll tell you that for nothing,' she adds
with disarming honesty. Does Tahtouh believe her? Of course
he does. He calls – smarter, if she's going to make this sort of
play, than raising. 'Why are you calling?' asks Vicky.

'Because I don't know what you have, and I'm scared,' he
replies coolly. The turn brings the 10d.

First to act, and so out of position, Vicky says, 'I think you
probably have two jacks, which means if I check that gives you
a free chance to make a straight. That would be bad.' She
pauses. 'But what if I go all-in and you do have a queen? That
would be terrible.' Eventually she makes her decision. 'OK,' she
says, checking, 'do your worst.'

'What the hell's going on?' asks Tahtouh.

'I've no idea, honestly, I've really no idea,' responds Vicky,
perhaps too quickly.

'Now I'm confused,' suggests Tahtouh, fingering his chips
while scratching the back of his head. Vicky laughs. The badi-
nage continues as he appears to be trying to think, with Coren
saying, 'I think you'd probably pass if I bet, but then if you've
got a full house you'd probably win and I'd feel like an idiot, so
I'm just checking to see what you do. Honestly.'

Tahtouh responds by going all-in.

'Are you all-in?' asks Vicky. 'Now the thing about this is . . .'

'Can I leave?' asks Emad. 'I really don't want to listen to
this . . .'

'. . . Now the thing about that', Coren continues, 'is you can't do that with two jacks, that would just be silly. Now maybe you've got nothing at all.'

'Does anyone have an iPod?' asks Emad, turning away from Coren and covering his ears.

'That's a very confusing thing for you to do,' says Vicky. 'I was thinking I was behind, but now you do that, now I'm thinking maybe I'm not.' She gets really into his face. 'I thought I was losing but now, hmmm, why would you do that with a good hand?'

'Very simple,' he replies, 'just fold and let's move on to the next hand.'

'But no,' she counters, 'it's like – but what if I've got a better hand than you? Then I would feel silly.'

'I'll make you feel better by showing you when you muck,' he says, 'and then you won't have any hard feelings.'

'No, you won't,' she goes on, 'you'll show me like an A-K and you'll laugh and laugh – and I'd *hate* that.'

'Why would I call you pre-flop with that?' asks Tahtouh.

'That's true,' replies Coren.

Then Chad Brown decides to get involved: 'Maybe he's got two eights?'

'Can he *beat* two eights?' responds Vicky. Finally, to universal relief, she says, 'Go on, then, have it,' and folds. 'And this hand better be good.' Coren is clearly expecting Tahtouh to honour his promise of showing her his hand if she mucked. But he just throws it in. 'You said you'd show it!' shrieks Vicky.

'Oh, come on,' says Emad, with a grin.

It's as if Coren were playing in some enormous home game rather than the final table of a big-money tournament. Still the chat goes on. 'I was seriously terrified when you raised me,' says Tahtouh, a 25-year-old from Melbourne. 'She's put on this massive performance, and if she's sitting there with nines full or A-Q you're going to go through the roof.' That sets Vicky off again, and the consensus is that she has certainly taken over from Peter Hedlund as the noisy one at table.

Soon she is dealt two black jacks. But just limps in. As Tahtouh thinks, Vicky says: 'I'm planning to limp and reraise, so careful what you do.'

'That so?' asks Tahtouh, who raises the pot to 122,000, holding two black eights. She reraises him by 186,000. Now they go quiet and stare at each other. 'I'm pretty sure', he says, 'I know what you've got. Ninety per cent sure it's A-K. Looks and smells like A-K. I'm gonna let you have it.' He shows her his eights, she shows him her jacks. 'I would never limp with A-K,' says Vicky. 'I can't believe you'd limp under the gun with two jacks,' says Emad. 'I'm limp-reraising,' she explains earnestly. 'Seriously!'

'Ah, shut up,' he replies, not altogether jokily.

With six players still left, the blinds now go up to 10,000–20,000, with 2000 antes. There is 42,000 in each pot before the flop. They can't sit waiting for big hands now; these pots are too worth picking up. Tahtouh limps in with Td-Jd in late position, on the button. In the big blind, Jan Sjavic checks with 6d-8c, and the flop comes 9c-9s-Js. Tahtouh plays it cute, checks as well. The turn is the 8d, giving Jan a pair; he checks. Tahtouh bets the pot, 60,000; Jan thinks awhile, then raises to 222,000. Tahtouh goes all-in, making the pot nearly a million – 989,000. This is very strong poker; he has top pair and an open-ended straight draw. Jan now knows he has to fold, and duly does so; but it was clever of Emad to suspect that Jan didn't have a nine. Power poker by Emad makes him chip leader with 989,000, against Brown's 729,000, Muldoon's 696,000, Coren's 562,000, Sjavic's 435,000 and Kuusik's 399,000.

Checking in the dark

The next hand is folded round to Vicky Coren, who plays a weak ace aggressively, raising 50,000 with Ah-4h. Chad Brown calls with Ks-Js, bringing the pot to 132,000. After a flop of

2h-Th-5h, giving her the nut flush, Vicky fingers her chips. It would be orthodox to check here, but she bets, 60,000, clearly hoping Chad has some sort of hand. He doesn't know, of course, that he's drawing dead, so he throws in an exploratory raise of another 60,000, bringing the pot up to 312,000.

Maybe Vicky's bet wasn't so dumb, after all; Brown clearly thinks her hand is weak or she wouldn't have made it. Now what to do? She just calls, for all the world as if she had only, perhaps, the ace of hearts. Craftily, also, she checks in the dark, to give Brown more to think about, before the turn brings the 9d. It looks, as she hoped, as if she's missed the nut flush; but Brown is too smart to fall into her trap, and checks as well. The river is the 3s – a queen would have made it interesting, given straight draw – and now Vicky has to bet. She does so, 100,000, bringing the pot to 472,000. Chad folds. Vicky grins at him enigmatically.

Thinning the field

An actor as well as a TV poker host in the States, Chad Brown has been in such Hollywood 'classics' as *Basket Case 2*; he is also proud to play at the top level of America's amateur baseball league. Now he sits out the next hand as Michael Muldoon makes a bet from the button with Ah-Jh. Jules Kuusik, who hasn't played a hand in a while, finds himself with a weak, unsuited ace, Ac-5s, and comes over the top – going all-in with 220,000 to make the pot 327,000. Muldoon calls, of course; he is 73-27 ahead before the board brings overkill: 2h-Tc-Js-Jc-8s. Sweden's Kuusik is out in sixth place. It is unusual by EPT standards for both Swedes at the final table to have gone out so early.

Michael Muldoon and Jan Sjavic have been the quiet ones at an unusually noisy final table. Coren and Tahtouh have got some sort of verbal sparring match going. But Vicky folds quietly enough as Sjavic bets 80,000 with pocket sixes. Holding Ad-Qh, Chad Brown asks for a chip count, then goes all-in with 450,000, pushing the pot up to 570,000. Jan has to call; it's pretty much a coinflip, but he's technically 55-45 ahead. If Jan weren't the short stack going into this hand, it would be a pretty dodgy call. At best he can only be a slight favourite, as indeed he turns out to be; but he could easily run into a larger pair and be a serious underdog. He might have done better to fold, and wait for the chance to make an aggressive all-in.

Before the flop, Chad says he's lost the last three times he's played A-Q at final tables. And now does so again, as the board comes 3d-6c-7s-Qs-3h, giving the fortunate Jan a boat, and doubling him up. Soon after, Sjavic gets pocket nines and raises the pot by 70,000 to 110,000. With Qs-8s the short-stacked Chad Brown moves all-in, taking the pot to 266,000; there is an instant call from Jan, who's ahead by 68% to 32%. The flop of Tc-2d-6h brings Brown no help; despite a turn of 8h, offering him some hope with a lesser pair, the river comes the Js. Having come to the table as chip leader, Chad Brown is out in fifth place.

Never surrender

So now we're down to four players, and nearing the dinner break. With Ad-9s – a strong holding, four-handed – Vicky Coren raises 40,000. Tahtouh and Muldoon fold, but Jan Sjavic raises another 100,000 from the big blind. Vicky doesn't know it, but he's got pocket rockets, Ah-As. She quickly calls. After an irrelevant flop, Sjavic moves in, taking the pot to 867,000.

A check by Sjavic might have been better here. As he holds such a strong hand on the flop, Coren is unlikely to have many outs against him. If she decides to make a play for the pot, it will have to be with all her chips. By moving all-in, Sjavic is giving Vicky the chance to make a fairly easy fold.

As it is she thinks for a while, but she knows Jan doesn't reraise with rubbish. Well known to be a tight player, he's been living up to his reputation all day. With only 400,000 left, Coren may have to call, thinks the gallery. But she folds, dejected, and heads off to regroup over dinner with a bunch of pals led by Neil 'Bad Beat' Channing.

They've all played in the tournament, and they've all swapped slices of each other, so these guys have an interest in Vicky winning this thing. The last few hands have dented her morale as much as her stack, so they sternly tell her to stop drinking red wine. 'We'd all swapped shares,' she said later, 'so they all had an interest. No wonder they were advising me to get off the wine!'

Coren knows liquor has no place at an EPT final table. 'Switch to tea' is one of many pieces of technical advice she is given over dinner – which she subsequently did, earning the nickname 'Teacup', after her famous victory. 'It's a name I actually like,' she says now, 'because it's quite sweet and British. On the internet, unfortunately, it soon became D-cup . . . [sigh]'

As the final session begins, the chip standings are as follows:

Emad Tahtouh 1,996,000
Jan Sjavic 1,230,000
Victoria Coren 404,000
Michael Muldoon 350,000

Now the blinds are up to 15,000–30,000, with 3000 antes, making the pot 57,000 before play commences. On the first hand, Jan Sjavic bets 110,000 with Kh-9s, and Vicky moves in with Ah-Jh. Four-handed, she knows that the value of A-J is much higher than usual, and with an M of less than ten, her stack is not large enough to leave any room for tricky play on the flop and beyond.

Sjavic folds, and Coren's stack rises to 553,000.

Running good

On the very next hand, from the dealer button, Vicky moves in again. This time she's holding another strongly suited ace, Ah-Th. The pot leaps from 57,000 to 597,000. Tahtouh folds his 9h-5h, but Muldoon calls with 7s-7d. Sjavic folds 4h-2h.

With the pot now at 987,000, Muldoon is slightly ahead in the coinflip, 52–48. But the first card up is an ace, as the flop brings Ad-8d-5c. Vicky's face is unmoved – she may even be feeling some rueful guilt, as she's been on the receiving end of so many such beats herself. The turn is the Qd, the river a third ace. Coren shakes her head in disbelief, closes her eyes as if thanking the poker gods. Muldoon goes out in fourth position. Despite winning a pot of 987,000, Vicky still has less than Tahtouh and Sjavic. She may still be in third place, but she's back on terms. She grins, and beats the table as if to say let's get on with it, I'm back in the game – and I'm running good.

On the button on the next hand, Coren gets 6h-7h – and starts talking again. She's relaxed, re-energised. 'Now I'm going to make, like, a small raise,' she says, building the pot from 54,000 to 129,000. Her raise is 45k, so it's 75,000 to play for Tahtouh, who holds Ac-7d, which would put him ahead by 66–34. He calls, and Sjavic folds Jh-Td. With the pot at 189,000, the flop helps neither player by bringing 2s-Ks-Jc. Tahtouh checks, and Coren bets a brave 90,000. There are cries of 'Go Vicky' from the rails. Tahtouh folds, saying, 'Nice hand, Vicky.' She replies with a demure 'Thanks', as if she actually had one.

This flop lent itself well to Coren's continuation bet. The king made it credible that her probable big cards made top pair, and the lack of two cards of a suit mean that Tahtouh could not hold a flush draw and get curious. A continuation bet was definitely called for, and Vicky was not slow to make the correct play.

On the next hand, with 54,000 in the pot before the flop, Tahtouh raises 65,000 with 6h-7c on the button. Sjavic folds Qc-2s. With a weak ace, Ah-6c, Vicky can only raise or fold; the crowd wants her to raise, but she folds.

Now Sjavic is on the button. With 3h-3c, he raises the pot to 80,000. With Ad-Jc in the small blind, Vicky reraises to 369,000. Tahtouh folds his 9-T, and Sjavic – a narrow favourite at 53–47, though of course he doesn't know that – goes into the tank. If he were to move in, would Coren call? He decides just to come along for the ride, to call and look for a low flop. It comes 9s-Ts-Th. Coren quickly says, 'all-in', building the pot to 1,317,000. Sjavic knows she could be making this play with two overcards; but she has more chips than him, so his tournament life is at stake. Calling all-in with a pair of threes is a tough move at this stage. He probably thinks he's winning, but spends some time trying to get a read on Vicky. She, for once, stays silent, her face suitably impassive.

Sjavic stays frozen in indecision. After a while it is Tahtouh, not Coren, who puts the clock on him – a most unusual move, to say the least, for a player who is not in the hand. Sjavic now has sixty seconds to make his decision, or his hand will be dead. Tournament director Thomas Kremser counts all the way down to seven-six-five before, finally, he calls. They roll the cards over, and Vicky sees she's losing. But the situation is not too bad; she had expected him to pass, but she can still hit an ace, a jack, a nine or a running pair, so she's only about a 40% underdog to make the winning hand.

As she thinks all this through, Vicky shakes her head. When the turn brings the Jh, there's a roar from the crowd – but a pensive Vicky just rubs her nose. The river is an irrelevant 8c. It was a great call from Jan, correct in the circumstances, but it sees him go out in third place. Vicky shakes his hand almost apologetically. He had really put her through the wringer there, and shown a lot of courage. 'Looking over at her,' he says later, 'I picked up a couple of things. She didn't really want a call. She was nervous. That's what tipped the scale for me.'

HEADS-UP

Coren vs Tahtouh

So Coren is now heads-up with Tahtouh, and they're about equal in chips. Sjavic says he thinks Tahtouh has the edge, that Tahtouh will win. John Duthie thinks otherwise. 'This is her casino. This is her destiny. I believe in destiny.' Besides, she is playing aggressively, and she seems to be hitting cards.

The head-to-head lasts only two hands. On the first, Tahtouh pulls Jd-8h on the button (the small blind) and calls. Coren, with Qc-Tc (a 67–33 advantage before the flop) pumps it up from 130 to 200k. He calls, and the flop comes 5d-8d-Ts, giving Vicky top pair.

It's perfect for Coren: she's hit her ten, he's hit his eight. She bets 100,000, and he quickly calls. The turn brings an irrelevant 2c. Coren keeps firing, another 300,000. Tahtouh calls immediately. The pot has now reached a million. With the 9d, the river brings straight and flush possibilities. Tahtouh could have two pairs. After Coren checks, he bets 600k. Vicky wonders aloud what that nine means to him. 'I got a total blank on the end there,' she turns round and tells the crowd, full of her poker pals. 'Would he bet that big with two pair? Probably less.' She thinks while counting her chips – then calls. And an inspired call it proves. Coren's top pair is good, winning her a pot of 2.2 million.

That first hand of heads-up has given Coren a big chip lead. Now the late-night crowd, who've been rooting for the local girl all evening, really believe that she's about to win. Tahtouh is still hurting about the last hand. On the big blind, he is dealt 8c-6h, Vicky 6c-7d. She calls the blind, and he checks. The flop, amazingly, brings 5c-3c-4d, giving Vicky a straight. Tahtouh checks, and she bets 100k. With an open-ended straight draw, he raises 450k. She calls for a count – is he pot-committed? Cleverly, she just calls. The turn card is the Td. Tahtouh declares all-in, and of course Coren calls immediately.

Both stand up, and he sees the bad news. There are more cheers from the crowd for the local favourite. Tahtouh is gutted: he needs a seven to make a higher straight, and one of them is in Vicky's hand; so he has only two outs among 44 cards. Touchingly, they embrace before the river, which comes the Js. Victoria Coren has won.

She is visibly in a daze. Strangely calm, she shakes hands with Emad Tahtouh, and takes a kiss from Thomas Kremser. When Natalie Pinkham presents her with the trophy – the EPT's first female winner, and in her home town of London, her very own cardroom – Vicky Coren is unusually lost for words. She can only say: 'It's in London, in my little home casino, with all the Vic players . . . I cant really speak, but . . .'

The trophy is so heavy she all but drops it. Hours later, even PokerStars' intrepid blogger, Brad 'Otis' Willis, is still choking up: 'Vicky's win here feels like some old English fairy tale with a happy ending, with our "English Rose" princess taking the top prize. Of course I know it's poker, and so there's nothing fairy tale about it all, not really; but humour me a little with this happy whimsy please . . .'

All week, after Coren's victory, people kept saying to me: 'You must be jealous!'

Yes, sure, I replied, but Vicky . . . well, far more than me, especially at the Vic, Vicky has 'put in the hours'. She played well, and she deserves it.

Later, she herself would say: 'I found the right cards. When I flopped a straight, all I had to do was bet it weakly, and Tahtouh could not resist the temptation to shovel in his chips and try to bully this nervous girl out of the pot. Three hands later, blinking and speechless with disbelief, I was clutching the trophy and one of those ridiculous giant cheques you see on Comic Relief.'

Coren's win reminded the world that women compete with men at poker on completely equal terms; but it didn't seem to change her life overnight. Only coyly did she mention the £500,000 win in her next *Guardian* column, and then only (she said) at the behest of her editor. She really had no idea, she went on, how she'd done it. 'I can't really explain it at all, except via two big, general factors in tournament poker. Being "in the zone" is being focused, making the right decisions, and knowing the reason for every bet that you make. Being "on form" is hitting lucky cards at the right time. Either of these can get you a long way in a tournament; when both happen together, you're unbeatable . . .

'For me, it could be ten years before the two come together again. That's why, after the madness of the past five days, I think I will spend the next week just staring in disbelief at the trophy.' Sensibly, she didn't get carried away and give up her regular, extra-poker sources of income: the *Guardian* column, another in the *Observer*, her TV poker commentary work.

Not until a year later, in a long article for the *Guardian*, did Coren finally admit publicly that the win had been 'life-changing'. At the World Series of Poker's London event, its first bracelet event to be held outside Las Vegas, she counted herself the short stack in career winnings at a table featuring Gus Hansen ($5m), Jennifer Harman ($2m), Ram Vaswani ($3.1m), Swedish veteran Chris Bjorin ($3.2m), a teenage internet pro ($Godknowshowmany) and 2004 world champ Greg Raymer ($5.9m). At $2.1m, Vicky's own tournament profits – 'most of them collected in one life-changing poker competition, over four incredible days, exactly one year ago' – were 'dwarfed' by the bankrolls around her.

The WSOP London event was won by an 18-year-old Norwegian, Annette Obrestad, whose £1 million first prize merely doubled her online winnings over the previous 12 months. At thirty-three, said Coren, she had until recently felt like 'a freakishly young poker player in a world of elderly men'; compared with Obrestad, however, she felt like 'an ancient dowager of the baize'.

The money she could 'take or leave'. As it happened, she left it. 'That £500,000 stayed on deposit at the casino for a good month, until I finally took it out and deposited it in a building society account, where it still is today. I haven't bought a flat, a car, new breasts or a ticket round the world.'

Eighteen months later, after an unprecedented degree of discussion and thought, Coren signed a sponsorship deal with PokerStars Team Pro. But the most significant result of winning the EPT event, for her, was still 'the confidence and self-belief that comes from winning a major tournament outright'. The experience had made her 'a braver person, as well as a better player. The bankroll is there, in my heart, to allow me to keep buying into the big tournaments for years to come, and protect me against any serious runs of bad luck. When you are a gambler, there is always a rainy day.'

You either feel it or you don't, Vicky concludes enigmatically. 'If you don't, perhaps you will find all this obscene. I have had days, walking into a Las Vegas tournament room where 3000 people have paid $5000 each to play a game that might end for them in five minutes, when I've felt pretty unsettled myself. The feeling passes soon enough. It is madness, but it is a wonderful madness.'

11

Copenhagen

Very clever, Mr Bond . . .

In Ian Fleming's first James Bond book, *Casino Royale*, 007 visits the eponymous casino in Monte Carlo to play cards against his sadistic enemy, Le Chiffre. Like all seasoned card players, Bond has a well-worn personal routine as he sits down at the table:

> Bond lit a cigarette and settled himself in his chair. The long game was launched and the sequence of these gestures and the reiteration of this subdued litany would continue until the end came and the players dispersed. Then the enigmatic cards would be burnt or defaced, a shroud would be draped over the table and the grass-green baize battlefield would soak up the blood of its victims and refresh itself.

When Daniel Craig donned Bond's tuxedo for the first time in the 2006 film version of *Casino Royale*, however, the 'long game launched' was no longer baccarat – as was Bond's wont, from Sean Connery via Roger Moore to Pierce Brosnan – but the poker game yet to reach Europe when the novel was first published in 1953, Texas Hold'em.

Fleming could rest assured, none the less, that the 'grass-green baize battlefield' would be just as bloodied. In the 1953 novel, Bond risks a whopping 32 million francs; in the movie, Craig's Bond plays for a massive $10-million buy-in, with $5-million rebuy. The stakes had never been higher – literally. I know of no real game of no limit Hold'em in poker history that has ever even approached such a scale.

Fleming's Bond displays a pragmatic approach to cards that well becomes a Hold'em player. His demeanour suggests that the choice of Hold'em – which is, after all, less a gambling game than one of skill – might in fact have received Fleming's approval. In the novel, Bond refuses to join his friends Felix Leiter and Vesper Lynd at the roulette table. 'I have no lucky numbers,' he tells them unsmilingly. 'I only bet on even chances, or as near them as I can get.'

But it is not the same tight-lipped hero who returns to the poker table in the recent film adaptation. Having just taken a serum in the parking lot, to prevent certain death from the poison a femme fatale has slipped into his martini, Bond quips suavely: 'That last hand nearly killed me.' Many dapper poker players have indeed passed away at the baize, notably Jack 'Treetops' Straus and the British writer David Spanier; but Fleming would have cringed at such cheesy table talk.

He may also have winced at the hands that the screenwriters gave Bond. Cinema has always, for dramatic effect, exaggerated the hands that appear in celluloid depictions of high-stakes poker, from *Big Hand for a Little Lady* (a.k.a. *Big Deal in Dodge City*) to *The Cincinnati Kid*, and even in the better recent Hold'em movies from *Rounders* to *Lucky You*. The remake of *Casino Royale* is no exception.

The first significant hand between Bond and Le Chiffre shows a flop of 5h-8h-9h. The blinds are at $5000–$10,000. Le Chiffre bets $50,000 after the flop. There is an icy stare between the two players before Bond calls.

The turn brings the 9c. The straight possibilities now look very remote. This being the movies, we're surely looking at a flush (possibly even a straight flush) versus a full house. Le Chiffre bets a further $100,000. Bond's girl, Vesper, gives him a very public kiss, and he decides to call. He does so rather non-chalantly, apparently distracted by his moll.

The river brings the 2h. So the flush is very much on. Le Chiffre ups his bet to $200,000. Again, Bond just calls. On their backs! Le Chiffre shows the full house – deuces full of nines. He was not flushing, after all; his underpair on the flop didn't improve on the turn, but made a fluky boat on the river. Bond mucks his cards. Had he been holding the flush all the way? We don't get to know. It doesn't appear to affect him – but of course not – as he signals for the barman and smiles.

Bond takes a moment to reassure Vesper that the last hand was worth it. 'The odds against when he made his first raise were 23-1 . . . winning was blind luck . . .' He is wrong, of course. On the flop Le Chiffre is only about 10-1; on the turn he is 22-1 (1/23 translates as 22-1, not 23-1).

But maybe this movie poker is not quite so silly, after all? Losing all those chips was worth it, claims Bond, to have discovered Le Chiffre's tell – a habit of nervously flipping his chips in his right hand. Many poker players would disagree; $350,000 is a pretty expensive way to figure that out. Then again, perhaps Bond knows he played the hand badly, but is maintaining his poker face to reassure the lovely Vesper, who is not just his moll but is also bankrolling him – with taxpayers' dough! We should all get so lucky . . .

The next big clash between our hero and his nemesis involves a third player, Bond's CIA friend Felix Leiter. We join the action after the turn. The communal cards are: Jh-Ks-Ac . . . Jd. The American bets $300,000. Bond and Le Chiffre both call. The straight is very much on, but surely, again, one of them now has the full house?

The river brings the Kd. Now the house is a really strong bet to win. But how will whoever has it play it?

Leiter checks. We see Bond's hand: he has the king, with an ace kicker. Big slick, big boat. But of course he does! He's 007!

As Leiter has checked, Bond could slow-play by checking, too. This would open the door for Le Chiffre to bet big, allowing Bond to follow up with a hefty check-raise. But what if Le Chiffre also checks? Then Bond would have wasted a powerful hand. No, a strong bet here is called for; after all, the other two players must have something, or why were they throwing chips into the pot on the turn?

And that's exactly what we get, as Bond – after some cool deliberation – places a chunky $500,000 chip into the pot. The moody music swells on the soundtrack. Le Chiffre displays his tell again, flicking those chips in his right hand. This hand must be Bond's for the taking. But, wait, Le Chiffre raises Bond's bet by all of $1,000,000. Leiter wisely folds. Bond, cool as a cucumber, reraises $2,000,000. Le Chiffre goes all-in, to the tune of no less than $40,500,000 . . .

Bond calls his bluff, and confidently turns over his house, kings full of aces. Le Chiffre shrugs defeatedly, and turns over the jack of clubs. He pauses before turning over his second card – to reveal the jack of spades. Le Chiffre breaks into a cocky smile and throws a little jab at Bond's expense: 'You must have thought I was bluffing, Mr Bond!'

Such crowing is rare at the poker table – and not good etiquette. Nor is slow-rolling the nuts. But etiquette has never been Le Chiffre's strong point.

The table breaks again. Le Chiffre waltzes away, leaving Bond to rue his costly misread. Vesper tells Bond that he let his ego get in the way of his play. This is an acute read from the moll, and a cardinal sin for any player. A furious Bond grabs a knife and hurries after Le Chiffre, intending to kill him. (That's not good etiquette either, by the way. Most normal players would hit another cash game or slink off home. But then most normal players don't use their winnings to fund terrorism.) Leiter stops Bond on the staircase and talks him out of it, by staking him the $5-million rebuy. The CIA, it seems, has deeper pockets than MI6.

Back at the table, Bond begins building his stack with some aggressive play. After that pause to avoid death by poison, which his opponent arranged to be administered (more poor etiquette), the big blind is raised to a massive million bucks.

Soon Bond and Le Chiffre are in a pot that has mounted to a whopping $24 million. The communal cards are Ah-8s-6s, with a turn of the 4s. Two other players are also in the hand. All check before the river, which comes up the As. Once again, there are strong flush possibilities up against potential full houses. Or even quads again.

The two other players take the pot up to $35 million. Le Chiffre raises by another $12 million, leaving Bond to consider his options. Le Chiffre twiddles his chips again. But 007 now knows this is not a reliable tell. Bond's blue eyes stare across the table into his enemy's, which have been known to weep blood. Bond goes all-in – to the same tune as Le Chiffre's earlier $40,500,000. The pot now stands at $87,500,000.

Le Chiffre smiles and looks again at his cards: Ac-6h. He has the house. There are only two hands that could beat him, A-8 for a higher house, or an unlikely straight flush. Cockily, Le Chiffre calls, apparently forgetting that he is an arch villain in a Bond movie playing against the hero. The pot now totals $115 million. Player One reveals a flush (Ks-Qs). Player Two grins as he turns over a pair of eights, giving him a house, eights full of aces. He thinks he has it in the bag. Le Chiffre takes his own sweet time before revealing his higher full house.

Now it is Monsieur Bond to show. And, of course, he has 5s-7s. The straight flush. Naturally. Game over.

The chances of Bond making that hand on the turn were a mere 46-1 against.

All of which means that one table in particular must have quaked into its martinis as they took their seats in the Casino Copenhagen, as the 2006 EPT tour reached Denmark. Forget former world champion Tom McEvoy and poker legend T. J. Cloutier (more than $9 million in lifetime winnings between them), who had crossed the Atlantic for the occasion. Also taking his seat on day one was none other than Le Chiffre himself!

But there were no $115 million hands this time around. Nor were there to be any tears of blood. This was not in fact Bond's arms-dealing nemesis, but the actor behind the tuxedo, Danish movie star Mads Mikkelsen, back on home turf after his trip to the Montenegro location of *Casino Royale*.

In Hold'em, however, as some wisecracker cruelly pointed out, you only live once (which this is the chance I have waited for so long to correct to You Live Only Once). No full houses or straight flushes were involved as Mikkelsen made an early exit, his pair of tens seen off by Big Slick, A-K, on a king-high board.

But there is still a representative of *Casino Royale* on hand here in Denmark. The expert adviser for the film's poker sequences was none other than . . . yes, the EPT's own founder-director, John Duthie. At least, that was the word on the circuit all year. When I asked the man himself, he flatly denied it: 'To be honest, Tony, there is no truth to the rumour that I was adviser to the Bond film. I wish I had been!' So how come his official bio as a member of Team PokerStars says, *inter alia*: 'Duthie was brought in to coach the new James Bond, Daniel Craig, in *Casino Royale*, where poker plays an integral part'? Online sources from the ever reliable Wikipedia to the even more authoritative CommanderBond.com say that Duthie was flown out to the set to advise on the poker scenes; it quotes the *Daily Express* quoting him talking about the cast and crew staking their wages on 'extra-curricular' poker games. Maybe he's in a state of denial after seeing the movie? Deciding that this is a case of 'Very clever, Mr D., but *not* clever enough . . .', I raise the subject with him again, only to be told: 'I think that the *Sun* originally published my name as adviser, but have no idea where they got that from. Your guess is as good as mine as to how it spread across the internet. Eventually I got so fed up with denying it that I decided to have some fun with it, and almost always say "I couldn't possibly comment" whenever asked. The PokerStars profile really shouldn't have it in, and I will ask them to take it out.'

Enough said, Mr D.

During the early twenty-first-century internet boom, poker has grown more significantly in Scandinavia than – as yet – in any other global region. The area has 90% internet penetration. GDP is high there, and the dark seasons for these countries are also longer than most. Which helps explain the veritable army of formidable Scandinavian players currently on the professional poker circuit. In Copenhagen 70% of the 400 starters, at a €5,000 entry fee, were Scandinavian. With many high-profile Scandinavian exits on day one, however, would the crown leave the region this time around?

The EPT Season Two winner in Copenhagen had been Denmark's own Mads Andersen, who beat Sweden's Edgar Skjervold to first place and €413,442. Andersen would be knocked out on day one of Season Three's Scandinavian tournament, where the first prize had risen to €711,842. Norway's Johnny Lodden, renowned and feared on the internet, also went to the rail on the first day. He was in good company: former world champ Tom McEvoy made a day one exit, too.

Don't show your hand unless you have to

With the blinds at 1500–3000, the USA's Brian Williams is dealt Ad-3h. On the button, he plays his position to make a raise of 5000. The pot rises to 14,900.

The big blind is 38-year-old Welshman Iwan Jones, a former TV producer and winner of the $750,000 first prize in the 2005 London Open. With 8s-9s, his suited connectors make a tempting hand with which to go after Williams, whose stack is beginning to run low. At a discount rate, thanks to his 3000 big blind, Jones calls.

The flop falls As-Th-7c. Williams has made top pair. But Jones is sitting relatively pretty. There's a decent range of cards that could help him to victory; this was a good flop for his suited connectors. He has open-ended straight and back-door flush draws.

Williams is a strong favourite, but he needs to bet big to bully his opponent out of this hand. So he bets 15,000. Jones can well afford to call him and see the next card, but he chooses to throw in his hand. 'Can't change that seven for a spade, can you?' he chortles as he mucks. Williams looks relieved and surprised by the laydown.

It was quite unnecessary for Jones to reveal his hand. This was a very conservative play; with opponents as smart as T. J. Cloutier at his table, subterfuge and secrecy would have been the smarter move. He's given them all useful information.

Scandinavian position play

Just before the bubble, with the blinds at 2000–4000, two Scandinavians tangle. Their positions tell a simple story. Ingmar Jonsson, a Swede, is on the button. He understandably tries to steal the blinds with an 8000 raise, on a decent enough holding of Tc-Js.

But the small blind, Theo Jorgensen of Denmark, reraises 30,000, taking the pot to 60,800. Jonsson doesn't know it, of course, but Jorgensen has him dominated, with Kd-Td. Jonsson has previously been raising with weaker hands, so Jorgensen has reason to be suspicious of his button play. The Swede folds, and the Dane is pleased to see off the challenge before a flop came along to complicate matters.

Blowing the bubble

One place off the bubble, the average player's instinct is to fold, unless he's short-stacked enough to be in dire straits. He's come this far, why not hang on to get in the money? But that's no excuse for cagey play. Brit John Shipley sees a good chance to steal some blinds, still at 2000–4000. His holding, As-Kd, demands a pre-flop bet, if not raise, so Shipley wades in with a healthy 8000.

All players fold round to the big blind, Theo Jorgensen, who sighs and contemplates his 7h-7c for a moment before calling. He wants to see the flop, and put Shipley to the test. It comes 5h-9c-Jd. Jorgensen to bet. Will he dip his toe in the water? Throw a rocket Shipley's way, or at least give him something to think about? Or will he allow the Brit another free card?

Both players check. Fatal mistake by Jorgensen. This flop would not have connected with Shipley's most likely hands (two big cards) so it would be natural for Jorgensen to bet out, making Shipley pay for the chance to draw to his overcards. Perhaps he expected Shipley to make a continuation bet and was going for the check-raise? Either way, Shipley plays the flop correctly and takes his free card.

Sure enough, the turn brings the Ad. Shipley is now equipped to see off Jorgensen, which he duly does with a bet of 15,000.

THE FINAL TABLE

With the two biggest names in the tournament, Americans McEvoy and Cloutier, out of the running, the final table is left to the Europeans. More than half the last eight are Scandinavian. Perhaps the crown will, after all, remain in their part of the world? But France's Bertrand Grospellier is chip leader going into the home straight, with a daunting 1,086,000. Better known by his online screen-name, 'ElkY', the 25-year-old has been playing online for three years, and has now turned pro. Like they say, it's a tough way to make an easy living. The blinds are up to 6000–12,000 as the final eight take their seats.

Giving up the ghost

Thomas Holm, representing Denmark on home soil, lies in fourth place with 409,000. In second place, from Hungary, is Richard Toth with 814,000. When Holm looks down to see Jc-Qc, he has to call Toth's pre-flop raise of 21,000. The big blind, Holm fancies his suited connectors and wants to see a flop. Which brings Th-9d-3h.

The flush is not going to happen, but Holm has an open-ended straight draw. It's him to speak. Will he check and allow Toth to set the pace? Or will he fancy his straight and overcard chances, and test the water with a bet? Holm thinks long and hard. Toth waits, with the silent satisfaction of knowing that his T-x gives him top pair. Eventually Holm bets 42,000. He seems to want to send Toth a message.

The Hungarian reaches for his chips and raises 68,000. Holm calls, taking the pot up to a round 300,000. What does Holm figure Toth is holding? If this looks like an optimistic, cavalier call, it ain't necessarily so. Toth has been bet into as the pre-flop raiser, and has now elected to raise. Holm can be fairly sure that Toth has a solid hand – probably top pair or even an overpair. The Dane has six outs to the nuts, and another eight possible outs to a pretty strong hand. The raise he is facing is small, only 1.5 times his bet of 42,000, so this call is probably a winning play.

When fourth street brings a second nine, Holm checks. Toth immediately sets his opponent in, to the tune of 725,000. With the pot now over a million, Holm has to acknowledge that discretion is often the better part of valour – and limp out. A 2-1 dog, he is right to put the hand down.

Even with four players left and millions at stake, beware of the big bluffer

With only four players left, Richard Toth is well ahead of his opponents on 1,783,000. Bertrand Grospellier has fallen behind, in second place with 1,135,000. Playing catch-up is Magnus Petersson, lying third with 588,000. The Swede will have to hope that one of those above him makes a rash play soon, to build him an opening. His conservative play will not win him the big bucks he needs, so he's got to make a move at some point in the near future. If his opponents choose to tear each other apart, however, at no expense to himself, so much the better. He can just sit back and watch. How Petersson must have enjoyed doing just that, as the following hand unfolded.

On the button, with 7h-5c, Grospellier decides to try stealing some blinds. He bets 29,000. Toth, the big blind, likes what he sees with Ah-Jh in the hole, and reraises 71,000. Grospellier's bluff has been called.

Rather than limp out, however, he decides to up the stakes with a reraise of 169,000. What can he be thinking? Something like this: with the increased aggression that accompanies short-handed games, a raise from the button is far from a strong indicator of strength. When Toth reraises from the blind, Grospellier knows there is a good chance that this is simply a re-steal designed to pick off his own steal from the button. So instead of meekly folding, ElkY decides to put Toth to the test with a solid reraise. Much of the time, Toth won't have the cards to call out of position. These third raises on the steal are a major ingredient of short-handed play. Perhaps ElkY just likes 7-5 unsuited? Either way, Toth calls – and the pot has swollen to 586,000 as the flop brings 4s-3s-Jd.

Toth, who has now made top pair, is first to speak. He taps a crafty check, willing Grospellier to reveal more about his hand. Now on an inside-straight draw, with an 11-1 chance that the six should fall, the Frenchman checks, too.

Toth can now rule out the likelihood of Grospellier holding a high pair, as ElkY would no doubt have bet big to take the hand down right there. Or can he? When fourth street brings the Qs, Toth meekly checks again. Grospellier's straight remains a pipedream – but he delves into his chips without a flicker of the eyelid, and boldly pushes 250,000 into the pot. It's a super-aggressive play, designed to scare his opponent into thinking he's made a flush.

Clearly unimpressed, the Hungarian immediately calls. The pot is now a whopping 1,086,000. Going to the river, Grospellier knows he has only a 10-1 shot of making his straight. Surely he won't throw more good chips after bad once the river lets him down? But Lady Luck has a habit of turning fickle. The dealer turns . . . the 6c! Grospellier's crazy risk has been rewarded with the gutshot. Now he has not only made his straight; he has his opponent by the cojones.

Toth checks. Grospellier goes all-in, eagerly pushing his

598,000 to the middle of the table. Only a flush can beat him. But he can be confident it's not out there, after Toth's rap on the river. The Hungarian looks over the board, and fiddles with his chips. Grospellier takes a deep breath and stares his opponent down from behind his trademark Oakley sunglasses. Then, amazingly, Toth calls! Grospellier's unpredictable play has clearly bamboozled the tournament's chip leader, who now looks on with disbelief as the Frenchman flips over his straight.

ElkY has coaxed Toth into the pot. The young Frenchman's racy play has paid off big-time. But he's a very lucky boy. Forty times out of 44, or ten times out of eleven, it wouldn't have.

Trusting your instincts

Soon afterwards, still sore from his big loss to ElkY, Toth is asked to make another tough read of an opponent's bold play. With Qh-9h, Toth deliberates whether to call Theo Jorgensen's all-in, pre-flop bet of 251,000. After thinking long and hard, to the point where his opponent puts the clock on him, Toth turns to the Dane and says: 'Theo, I have to trust in my instincts' – he wiggles his nose and shakes his head while Jorgensen remains impassive – 'and they tell me you've got nothing.' He calls the quarter-million.

No sooner has he done so, than the Dane flips over pocket rockets. The home crowd cheer. This hand is in the bag. Toth smiles. Jorgensen smiles back, saying: 'Wrong instincts this time!'

The players are still grinning, resigned to their fates, as the flop brings Tc-4h-7d. But the relaxed smiles suddenly slip as the turn then brings the Jh. Suddenly Jorgensen looks seasick as Toth makes the first half of both a back-door flush draw and a back-door straight draw. From 3-1 down, Toth now has both straight and flush possibilities. An eight, a king or any heart will save him and be a fatally bad beat for the Dane.

The river comes the 10h. Jorgensen takes off his trademark hat, in mourning for his aces. With a back-door flush on the river, Toth is one mightily relieved survivor. He should never have played that hand. But what do we analysts know?

Worst hand wins the day

With three players left, it's double-or-nothing time for the short-stacked Magnus Petersson. Grospellier is back in the lead, with 2,216,000 – largely thanks to that straight he made on the river. Toth is now in second place, with about half ElkY's stack, 1,117,000. Petersson has half as much as Toth, a mere 542,000.

The Swede still needs to make that big-hand break for the border if he is to win anything more than bronze for Scandinavia. With the big blind now at 20,000, Petersson knows he must soon make a move. So now he does, reraising Toth's pre-flop raise of 55,000 by a whopping all-in 520,000. And what's he holding? Only 7d-2h. This is clearly a bluff designed to capitalise on Petersson's conservative play thus far.

Toth is holding Ad-9s, a strong hand with just three players. Strong enough to call what turns out to be Petersson's bluff. The pot now stands at 1,096,000. Snorts of laughter at the Swede's audacity greet Petersson's cards as he flips them on their backs. Toth is proved right to trust his instincts again. He's a 2-1 favourite to win the hand.

But the flop brings a deuce, giving Petersson bottom pair, and transforming him into a 3-1 favourite. There follow a king and a jack – but no ace or nine. The pair of deuces proves enough to take a pot of well over a million dollars.

How often does a 7-2 effect such a transformation? Now Petersson is right back in the game. Later, he explained: 'I decided at that time to be more aggressive when we were down to three players and to use my tight image. Toth raised on the button, and as I needed to get chips I wanted to get them off him. ElkY would have called me, and I thought Toth would fold a lot of hands to my bluff. Unfortunately he called!'

Déjà vu

With Ah-9s before the flop, Toth raises 35,000. This was the hand that let him down against Petersson; but, hey, it's still strong three-handed. ElkY folds. Petersson calls. This time there's no need to go all-in – even though his hand is a tad more respectable: suited connectors, 5d-4d.

The flop comes Qd-7h-5h. Petersson checks. He has bottom pair again; this time he'll let Toth make the play. The Hungarian bets 70,000. Petersson calls.

The turn brings the 3d. Now Petersson has flush and inside-straight possibilities. Can he ride his luck again, inflicting another brutal beat on Toth's A-9? He checks. Which seems to force Toth's hand. Feeling the need to set the pace, and kill this hand off, the Hungarian bets 120,000.

With a pair made, and flush and straight possibilities, Petersson check-raises all-in – to a total of 1,079,000.

Toth can only fold. Petersson's comeback has been achieved in the most cheeky but effective – and fortunate – manner. He got lucky when he needed to, winning two huge hands against the odds. Poor, demoralised Toth is soon knocked out by chip-leader Grospellier.

HEADS-UP

Grospellier vs Petersson

As the last two players go heads-up, the blinds stand at
10,000–20,000, with antes of 2000.

A classic check-raise

With Qd-2h, Grospellier raises before the flop to the tune of
80,000. Petersson calls with Th-6h. The flop brings Tc-6c-4h.
Petersson calmly checks his top two pair. Grospellier falls into
the trap, betting 120,000 in the hope of pushing his opponent
out of the hand. But when Petersson raises 200,000, he knows
he is a goner. The Swede is taking no chances, and is happy to
kill off the hand there and then. Grospellier recognises immediately that he has fallen for another classic check-raise from the
Swede, and folds.

The river wild

The blinds are now up to 15,000–30,000. The flop brings 7h-
Ts-2s. It's Petersson to act first. With pocket threes, he decides to
check. Grospellier has a deuce, with an ace kicker, and is also
happy to check.

Fourth street brings another deuce, giving Grospellier the
unlikeliest trips. Petersson checks again, but not this time the
Frenchman, who throws in a modest bet of 50,000. Petersson
calls.

Then the river shows a miraculous three, turning Petersson's
pocket pair into a house. He bets 80,000 into Grospellier, who raises

to 200,000. Petersson mulls it over before going all-in, for a total of 1,425,000. Grospellier calls, perhaps remembering the earlier 7-2 bluff from the Swede. With a whoop, Petersson signals his excitement at winning this turnaround hand. Grospellier holds his head, knowing that his long-held chip lead has finally gone. Now it's the Frenchman playing catch-up, with 800,000 to Petersson's 3.2m.

Could Grospellier have played it differently and saved some chips? Should he have bet more on the turn and made Petersson fold? Trips with an ace kicker is a powerhouse in a heads-up game. A lot of the time, Petersson will be drawing dead here, so betting modestly is a sensible play. If he does have a pair, Petersson is drawing to two outs, so only one time in 22 will the river cost Grospellier the pot. The bet is designed to trap Petersson into calling when he is way behind – and indeed he does call. Unfortunately for Grospellier, this was just a cold deck. He knows that he may have just received a killer blow. The Swede's softly-softly approach has paid off.

An eye for the ladies

Grospellier is dealt Ah-Jh. He raises 55,000 before the flop. Petersson looks down to see Qc-6c, and calls. The pot is now 176,000.

The flop brings Qc-7h-6h.

Petersson's tactical checks have stood him in good stead in the big hands during the Copenhagen EPT, building him many big chances. Again, he checks his two pairs. And again Grospellier falls for the bait, though he must fancy his flushing chances as he decides to go all-in. Petersson calls immediately.

In time-honoured fashion, seeing that he's losing, Grospellier stands up. The odds are 2-1 against him. Petersson's amazing climb up the final table is all but complete. But the Frenchman has quite a few outs, not least the nut-flush draw. Any heart will do. Or running aces. Or running jacks. Or running A-J or J-A . . .

The turn does indeed show a jack. But the odds don't look good for ElkY. Only another jack or an ace or a heart can save him. He glares at the deck, willing the river to bring a heart. But the river comes the ten of clubs. Petersson yells in delight: 'Y-E-S!' He has won the Danish title, and the €711,842 first prize.

'I played tight all day and my purpose was to change gear and get aggressive,' he says later. His slow-burn tactics worked and saw off ElkY, who had been nothing but bold from the first hand.

For all the excitement, Petersson said that he would not be giving up the day job to become a pro-poker player: 'I am a financial adviser, so I will now advise myself to invest in some stocks and bonds.' The Scandinavians had won on home soil yet again.

Postscript: Don't feel too bad for young ElkY. In January 2008 he beat 1136 other players to win the PokerStars Caribbean Adventure, and a first-place prize of $2,000,000.

12

Barcelona

Ivey meets his match

One of the modern poker greats, Phil 'Phenomenon' Ivey, made his first EPT appearance of the 2006–7 season at Barcelona. Though the likes of Joe Hachem and Isabelle Mercier also made the trip to Barcelona Casino, at the foot of Frank Gehry's twin towers in the Port Olympic, 30-year-old Ivey went in with the most formidable reputation of all. Although primarily a cash-game player – once known as 'No Home Jerome', after the moniker he gave himself on the fake ID card with which he served an under-age poker apprentice-ship in Atlantic City – Ivey had amassed $7 million in tournament winnings before arriving in Catalonia. He was also the proud owner of five World Series bracelets (if none for Hold'em). Three of these were won in 2002, tying him with Phil Hellmuth and Ted Forrest as the record holder for most bracelet wins in a single year.

EPT Barcelona started with 480 players putting up the €5000 entry fee. As the penultimate-day players took their seats, Ivey declined to reveal the secrets of his success to the TV cameras, but did offer one piece of pithy advice: "The key to poker is not what you have, it's what the other person has.'

We shall see.

A perilous Ivey all-in

Dan Pedersen, from Sweden, who has just been moved on to Ivey's table, is immediately given a nice welcome with Ah-Kh. With the blinds at 1500–3000 and 300 antes, he raises 8500. The next player up is Philip Can, from Sweden. He also has A-K, but not suited. Can goes all in, to the tune of 32,000. He would be unlucky if Pedersen were to make the flush, but those hearts give Pedersen a very slight statistical edge (52–48) on Can.

This seems to be cruising towards a split pot. But poker is rarely predictable, least of all when Phil Ivey is at the table. Now he steamrolls all-in, too, pushing 68,600 into the middle of the table, and swelling the pot to 118,300. Quite a welcome for Pedersen.

Ivey is holding pocket queens, Qc-Qh, which stack the odds heavily in his favour. There are only three cards in the deck that can beat his ladies, as another player has already folded one king, and we know that two aces and two kings are in play (although, naturally, he doesn't).

Pedersen folds his suited Big Slick, leaving Ivey and Can heads up, both all-in, but with the American the clear favourite. It's a good laydown from new arrival Pedersen, one that less experienced players might not have made. His raise brought two heavy-hitting reraises. His odds of winning the pot had – unbeknown to him – sunk to a mere 21%.

But the poker gods can be mischievous. How else to explain a flop of 5c-9h-Ac? That ace being one of those three magical cards that Can so desperately needed. A sporting shrug from

Can to Ivey. He knows he just got very lucky and is about to bust out one of the game's legends. Ivey offers a knowing smile. He has just a 9% hope of winning this one now, dependent on one of these next two cards being a queen . . .

. . . Which is exactly what the next card brings. Grins and whoops greet the appearance of Ivey's new fairy godmother, the queen of diamonds. Ever the sportsman, Can smiles along with the gallery. A handshake later, he melts into the casino crowd.

Aces cracked . . . a genuine bad beat

Thirty-five-year-old Bjorn Erik Glenne's previous EPT best had been a 19th-place finish in Copenhagen. A former chess champion, and the reigning poker champ of his native Norway, Glenne discovered Hold'em online and started playing live in 2005. Prone to nose twitches and big grins (when winning), Glenne hands out one of the tournament's most painful bad beats soon after the bubble.

With some thirty players left, Glenne raises – with the intention of stealing the 1500–3000 blinds and 300 antes, having not played a hand for some time – with 5h-6d. But Angel Blanco of Spain, a cautious, well-respected player, promptly reraises 45,000. Surprisingly, to say the least, Glenne decides to call. He doesn't seem to have enough chips to speculate this way on medium unsuited connectors, but chooses to go for it anyway. Blanco all but licks his lips. He is holding pocket aces.

The flop brings 6c-3s-7d. Glenne now has middle pair and an inside-straight draw. The Norwegian, his nose twitching, goes all-in. Blanco calls immediately. The pot is a healthy 463,500. This hand is still very much Blanco's to lose (he is, after the flop, a 67% favourite). Yet the veteran Spaniard shuts his eyes and shakes his head pessimistically on seeing his opponent's inferior hand. Blanco must have suffered too many bad beats over the years against hands that should not, by poker rights, still have been active or even prompted a call, let alone wound up winning.

His cock-eyed grimace deepens when the turn brings the 4c, giving Glenne an amazing straight. What would normally have proved a poor call and a fatal all-in mistake has freakishly paid off – as Glenne's beaming grin demonstrates. After the inconsequential river, Blanco shakes his head in bitter disbelief. He cannot look his lucky opponent in the eye as he shakes Glenne's hand and makes his exit from the table.

Never slow-play pocket rockets

Phil Ivey holds pocket sixes, and raises 24,000 – the blinds have now climbed to 6000–12,000 – before the flop.

But David Layani has pocket aces. The Frenchman feigns concern before calling Ivey's raise, bringing the pot to 86,000. Has Layani played it too weakly? Such contemplation can be dangerous, especially against a player of Ivey's calibre. Sometimes a player doth deliberate too much, and overdoing such tactics can backfire; instead of bogusly telegraphing the desired effect, that a player is not sure about his hand, it can just give away a hand's true strength.

The flop comes 2h-6s-Jc. That third six means Ivey's odds of winning the hand just leapt to 91%. He coaxes the Frenchman with a modest bet of 40,000. Layani ponders his next move. He lifts his shades in an ambitious attempt to read Ivey, notoriously poker-faced. Of course, the American's blank look gives away nothing.

Layani raises 60,000. It could have been more. Perhaps he thinks Ivey has a jack. No reraise from Ivey, who does not wish to scare his opponent off. A meaningless ten brings a bet of 120,000 from Layani. Ivey again chooses not to scare him off, and simply flat-calls. This is supremely confident play from Ivey. The river could bring many risky cards for him; conceivably, any face card could pose real problems for his set. Ivey's call raises the pot to 526,000.

Each player is bleeding money from his opponent, but only one can win. Alarm bells must surely be ringing for Layani, with little to draw to, watching a player of Ivey's calibre simply calling his bets.

The river brings a queen. Ivey checks, and Layani sets him in, to the tune of 162,400. Ivey doesn't hesitate to call. The pot has reached a whopping 1,027,000, as he reveals his winning set. Layani sits back down dejected, wondering if he has what it takes to compete in the Ivey league.

Should Layani have moved all-in on the river? The pot was raised before the flop; and with no obvious draw possible on the flop, he knew Ivey must hold at least a solid hand. If Ivey didn't hold a set on the flop, it must be top pair or an overpair. By the river, many of Ivey's possible hands (T-J, J-Q or Q-Q) had improved to beat him, not to mention the fact that Ivey could have had a set all along. Checking down the aces on the river may *seem* cowardly, but when there is such a high chance you are second best, it is the sensible play.

Ivey resists riding his luck against Layani

Ivey has not had time to stack all those chips from his set-to with Layani before the two are back at it again, *mano a mano*. The American raises before the flop with Ad-7d. Layani goes all-in, to the tune of 173,400, on As-Kd. With 36,000 chips already in the pot, Ivey has to figure that he is up against a medium/high pair, or a strong ace. He wisely lets Layani have the 36,000.

Unsurprisingly, perhaps, Ivey has the last laugh in this private duel. He goes on to knock out Layani, a suited 6-7 again meeting two friendly other sixes on the flop – and his trips again proving too strong for Layani. The Frenchman steps away from the table in eleventh place and €25,400 richer for his pains.

THE FINAL TABLE

As the players sit down at the final table, Phil Ivey lies in second place with 1,317,000. Glenne of Norway has 1,456,000. Jeffrey Lisandro of Italy lies third, not far behind the two leaders. Various short stacks soon ensure some quick exits. The blinds are up to 8000–16,000 when . . .

Ivey trips Lisandro

The first significant face-off between the three chip leaders comes between Lisandro and Ivey. The American raises 40,000 on the button, with pocket nines. Lisandro calls with Th-9h. The flop brings 5d-Tc-9d.

Lisandro's two pairs look very good from where he's sitting; little does he know that Ivey is holding a set of nines. It's a tough hand for the Italian to put down – but how will Ivey play it to maximise the chips he can extract from so key an opponent?

He bets 80,000 – a modest amount, in the circumstances, designed to draw his opponent into the pot, hoodwinking Lisandro into thinking that he has two high diamonds or the like . . . not the second nuts, for sure. With straight and flush draws distinct possibilities, Lisandro takes the bait and goes all-in with his two pair. Ivey, of course, calls the 942,200, boosting the pot to 2,026,000.

When the cards go on their backs, Lisandro cannot believe the set of nines he beholds. The turn and river bring two fours,

completing Ivey's full house, adding insult to Lisandro's injury.
He is less than generous to Ivey when he immediately, still in the
heat of the moment, comes before the television cameras. Of
his own hand, he says: 'No one else could play it any better.' Of
Ivey's, he moans: 'He's so lucky.'

Or, in Gary Player's famous dictum, as true of poker as of
golf: 'You know, the more I practise, the luckier I seem to get.'

Lisandro is out in sixth place, leaving the formidable Ivey almost
a million chips richer. And this EPT seems rapidly headed for a
duel between the maverick strategist Glenne and the 'Tiger
Woods of poker'. By the time the table is down to three players,
Ivey is chip leader with 2,142,000. But Glenne is not far behind
him on 1,733,000, with England's David Gregory in third place
on 925,000.

The blinds are up to 15,000–30,000, with 3000 antes. That's
54,000 in the pot before anyone makes a move.

Calling Ivey's bluff

All three players are in for the flop, which brings 6d-4h-Ah. Ivey
and Glenne both check. So does Gregory. But when fourth
street brings the 3h, Glenne bets 70,000, bringing the pot to
169,000. With Ac-3c in the hole he has made two pair, and
wants to put this hand to bed right here.

Gregory obligingly folds. But Ivey, now wearing diamond-
encrusted shades, quietly calls. Could one of the world's most
feared all-round players be holding a flush?

The river comes the 5s. Glenne checks. Ivey in fact has Th-9s.
He has no flush, no straight, no nothing. He is well beaten.
What can he be thinking? He has no pair, no draw, no overcards
to the board. How can the man often cited as the best player in
poker make such a bonehead move? His reasoning probably

went something like this: when the hand was checked around on the flop, Ivey began to suspect that nobody was holding an ace. When Glenne bet out on the 3h turn, there was a good chance he was trying to pick up an unwanted pot with no hand of his own, or possibly just a big heart, giving him a flush draw. Ivey had position, and believed that if he called, Glenne would be forced a good percentage of the time to check and fold on the river. Unfortunately for the Phenomenon, Glenne has played the hand perfectly – allowing Ivey to take a river card when he is drawing dead, and then snapping off his delayed bluff.

So can Ivey convince Glenne to fold? Hoodwink him into thinking he has, in fact, made the straight or flush? Ivey pushes 300,000 into the pot, with just that in mind. Is it enough to scare off the Scandinavian?

No: the Norwegian chess player calls Ivey's bluff right away, without the slightest twitch. His check on the river had been intended to test Ivey. By no means was it a statement of his true intent, or lack of it.

He nods to Ivey to reveal his hand, a right for which he had just paid 300,000. The American reluctantly flips over his cards. Bjorn Glenne rakes in a handsome pot of 1,119,000, and reassumes pole position.

A strong continuation bet

Ivey is dealt Th-6h and raises 50,000 before the flop. On the small blind, 15,000, Glenne looks down to see a pair of jacks. With three players left, he has to assume he's holding the best hand. Hence his reraise of 120,000.

Ivey has plenty of chips, and the button, so position is in his favour. Will he call? Glenne must be quietly thrilled as he sees Ivey do just that. Those varied earlier reraises have stood him in good stead. Ivey seems to be finding him hard to read.

The flop brings just what Glenne didn't want to see: Qs-Ks-8h. Those two face cards give him plenty to think about. After all, Ivey has raised and called his reraise. It's entirely possible he has just made an overpair, perhaps top pair.

Glenne tests his fearless opponent again, with a strong continuation bet of 300,000. Ivey decides discretion is the better part of valour – and folds. Glenne has seen off another of his typically bold challenges.

Pocket pairs

On the button with Ts-6s, David Gregory limps in, calling the big blind of 30,000 – cautious play that he can ill-afford as the low stack on this three-hander, unless he is to mix it up and throw his opponents off by limping in again later with pocket rockets or the like.

Ivey flat-calls with pocket fives. Glenne then raises them both 100,000. What can he be holding? The Englishman folds; Ivey, unhappy to relinquish his pocket pair, calls.

The flop brings 2s-3d-Kh. With only that one overcard, Ivey would expect to be ahead, always assuming there's no king in Glenne's hand. He checks. Glenne apparently takes the bait and pushes 150,000 into the pot. Ivey follows up on his check-raise strategy. He will now find out more about his opponent's strength by raising. The pot stands at 449,000. Ivey raises Glenne a further 200,000.

Glenne considers the proposition for a moment before dramatically going all-in. To the tune of 2,400,000. His nose twitches. The pot is now 3,199,000. Ivey leans back in his chair and crosses his arms. Does the Norwegian have a king? Glenne's nose continues to twitch.

Eventually, Ivey folds and Glenne scoops a huge pot. As Glenne tidies up his chips, they trade notes on what each figured the other was holding. Both get it wrong; Ivey thinks Glenne had either A-3 or the king, Glenne pegs his formidable opponent on A-5. David Gregory then pipes up and confuses his opponents by insisting that Glenne must have had trip threes, as he had seen a three when Glenne mucked his cards. Glenne denies it, but Gregory is adamant: 'I saw it! You had a three!'

Under pressure, Glenne reveals to them both his true hand: 'I had a pair of nines.'

'I don't know why he would lie,' says a po-faced Ivey, content in the knowledge that he had made the right decision in folding his weaker pair.

'I saw it! I saw your card!' continues a dogmatic Gregory – who will no doubt have grimaced upon watching the TV evidence that Glenne had indeed been holding those pocket nines.

Gregory goes all-in

After a few more hours of Bjorn Glenne running over the table, and the blinds now at 20,000–40,000, with antes of 4000, both Gregory and an unusually subdued Ivey are beginning to run low on chips. So when Glenne bets 85,000 before the flop, Gregory smiles, and cheekily says, 'Getting a big hand every hand, eh?', before defiantly raising all-in.

Glenne deliberates only briefly before making the 551,000 call. His huge stack means he can well afford it, but the call was worth thinking over. Glenne holds Ah-5h. It seems very possible that Gregory has a pair higher than fives, or an ace with a stronger kicker.

As the players turn the cards on their backs, Gregory reveals a weaker hand than expected: Ks-Th. The odds are marginally in Glenne's favour. The Brit stands up, knowing that he needs a king or a ten to survive. He's pretty much a 2-3 dog (58.7%). But the flop of 5d-Kd-7s suggests that the planets over Barcelona may just, after all, be aligned in Gregory's favour. He has his precious second king! Glenne has also made a pair, but his fives offer only a 20% chance of winning the hand. If Gregory's kings hold up, he will have more than a million in chips, more than enough to bring him back into contention.

But his hopes are dashed on the turn, when up smiles the five of clubs. Now, by the kind of miracle that wins you tournaments, Glenne has made trips. Gregory can only put his hands on his head and shake it in disbelief, like a footballer who has just missed a sudden-death penalty.

The river brings an irrelevant 4h. Gregory is a goner. He can console himself with €184,300 in prize money.

HEADS-UP

Ivey vs Glenne

For all his celebrated expertise, Phil Ivey would have to be some sort of miracle worker to win this tournament. Going into the head-to-head, with the blinds at 20,000–40,000, his 340,000 doesn't look like lasting too long against Glenne's near five million. The Norwegian has been playing shrewdly and aggressively. On their relative chip levels, Ivey effectively has a mere one-in-fourteen chance of winning. He's going to need to get very lucky in the next few hands if he's going to get back into this thing.

Dealt Qh-7d, Ivey rapidly goes all-in. Cursing his meagre 8d-5s, Glenne folds, wisely waiting for a better spot to administer the killer punch.

The back-and-forth continues awhile before two hands arrive that each deems worth playing. Glenne's Th-Td sees him declare all-in; Ivey calls with Ah-5h. The pot totals 800,000, with a first prize of €691,000 at stake.

Both players are strangely impassive as the flop of 5c-Jh-Ts brings Glenne a crucial third ten. The Norwegian smells victory at last, but manages to stem the trademark twitches in his nose. Only a pair of aces – or unlikely running hearts, or running fives – can save Ivey. Sure enough, the turn and river prove irrelevant. The rail erupts, the Norwegian fanbase in exultant voice. A huge grin spreads across the face of Norwegian poker champion Bjorn-Erik Glenne, in his understandable delight at seeing off the mighty Phil Ivey.

13

Dublin

Wolf in De Wolfe's clothing

Born in 1979, English poker pro Roland De Wolfe – variously nicknamed 'The Sheep', 'The Edge', 'Chopper', 'The Wolfman' and 'The Werewolf' – has been playing cards since the age of twelve. Prior to EPT Dublin 2006, he had one major title to his name, the World Poker Tour's 2005 Grand Prix de Paris, in which he bested the reigning champion, Finnish pro Juha Helpi. A sometime pool hustler, renowned for challenging all comers one-handed, De Wolfe began life as a journalist, finally becoming poker editor of the UK gaming magazine *Inside Edge*. The lessons he learnt covering tournaments eventually saw him turn professional in 2005.

After that WPT win in his first full-time season, De Wolfe cashed in the $1000 no limit Hold'em event at the World Series of Poker and the $15,000 main event at the WPT Five Diamond World Poker Classic. In early 2006, he finished third at the $25,000 WPT World Championship at the Bellagio, taking home more than $1 million. That June, Roland had two cashes at the WSOP, including a third-place finish in the $2000 no limit shootout. Then came Dublin, which saw him become the first player to win both WPT and EPT titles. So let's see how he did it.

Dublin's Regency Hotel saw 389 starters pay the €5000 entry fee to create a prize pool of €1,847,750, with a first prize of €554,300. Past EPT winners and top poker stars such as Ram Vaswani, Noah Boeken, Chris Moneymaker, Greg Raymer, Dave 'Devilfish' Ulliot and Johnny Lodden – not to mention PokerStars-sponsored Anthony Holden – have all been eliminated as we join the action.

Wisely erring on the side of caution

In late position, Roland De Wolfe raises 33,000 with just 4s-2h. With the blinds at 6000–12,000, the chip leader, Sweden's William Thorson, calls with Ad-Jd. The flop comes 3d-5d-Qs, and both check.

When fourth street brings the Kd, Thorson bets 60,000. De Wolfe flat-calls, still hoping for a straight, apparently not suspecting that his opponent holds the nut flush. This is not, to put it politely, a great call; as Roland is up against a flush, he is drawing dead. If he hits his straight as the river brings a fourth diamond, he will be far from comfortable with the strength of his hand. Perhaps he is calling partly for the chance to make a straight, and partly to use any fourth diamond as a phantom out to push Thorson off his hand. Little does he know that Thorson will have the nuts regardless.

The river brings the 10c. First to speak, Thorson bets 170,000. De Wolfe wisely retires his hand. As he stacks the 395,000 pot, Thorson manfully shows his opponent the gleaming diamonds in his hand – not something I normally recommend. But maybe he was trying to show De Wolfe something about the strength of the hands he plays. This was to prove just one early clash between two aggressive players who would fight to the end in this tournament.

Making your own luck

With the blinds still at 6000–12,000, De Wolfe raises 26,500 before the flop with Jd-Qh. Thorson calls with Ad-Ks. The flop comes As-3d-Kc.

De Wolfe checks. Thorson thinks a moment before checking, too. The free turn card is the 4d.

De Wolfe considers his move for a while before betting 65,000. Thorson's check on the flop has yielded a return. With the pot at 192,000, the Swede calls.

But, cruelly for Thorson, the river brings De Wolfe the very card he needs: 10h, to make him top straight, Broadway. The odds against his receiving a ten were a hefty 10-1. Thorson was, after all, mistaken in slow-playing the hand and not killing it off earlier. For a slow-play to be correct, the chances of your opponent improving to beat you must be slim; but, crucially, there must be hands he may improve to that entice him to pay you off. This second condition was not really met here, so there was no value to Thorson's slow play. The only card that would make De Wolfe happy to commit more chips is a ten, and that loses Thorson the pot.

Now De Wolfe bets 150,000. Thorson, who has an impressive stack in front of him, goes into the tank for a moment. De Wolfe's previous bet on the turn has bamboozled the Scandinavian. Eventually he calls, bringing the pot to 557,000. He peers over the table to see the Englishman's hand: 'What's that?' Back comes the monosyllabic answer: 'Nuts.'

THE FINAL TABLE

As the last nine players sit down at the final table, Sweden's William Thorson, now 23 but a pro since the age of 18, has 773,500. But the man to beat is in Seat 7: England's Roland De Wolfe, with a mammoth stack of 1,352,000.

Wait your turn!

The blinds are still 6000–12,000 as Thorson raises 12,000 pre-flop, with As-2s, and De Wolfe calls with 9s-Ts. France's David Tavernier also calls, with Ad-7d. The flop brings 5c-3d-9d.

So De Wolfe has top pair, Tavernier is four-flushing, and Thorson has a gutshot straight draw. First to speak, Thorson tries to represent an overpair with a bet of 100,000. Tavernier immediately reaches for his chips, to go all-in with 273,000. De Wolfe tells him to wait – it's not his turn! – before folding.

Tavernier's over-hasty manoeuvre has led De Wolfe into laying down the leading hand. But, sure enough, Tavernier still goes all-in. His bluff called, and then some, Thorson also folds.

Had Tavernier not jumped the gun, De Wolfe would probably have called his chasing hand with his made top pair. Tavernier might have then lost out on another 100,000 in the pot. Or – another way of looking at it – he could inadvertently have seen off his biggest challenger for the hand . . .

Either way, the pot is his. Next case.

The big breakfast

De Wolfe raises 18,000 pre-flop. He's holding Qs-5s. 'Have you got a big hand, Roland?' asks his compatriot and friend, Robert Yong, before raising 60,000 with pocket tens.

'We had breakfast together!' Yong tells the gallery. 'Just set me in!' he dares De Wolfe, after his friend asks him for a chip count. This proves enough to see off his opponent, who told Yong that the sight of that reraise was bringing his bacon and eggs back up . . .

Slow-playing the nuts

With the blinds still 6000–12,000, De Wolfe raises 38,000 pre-flop, making it 50,000 to play. This time *he* is the player with pocket tens. Tavernier calls with a decent enough hand, As-Js, which gets a whole lot better when the flop brings Ah-Jd-Ac.

Holding the nuts, but not wishing to scare his opponent off, Tavernier checks. To his disappointment, De Wolfe follows suit. The turn comes the 7c. Again, Tavernier checks, in the hope that his opponent will bet at him. But again De Wolfe checks back.

On the (irrelevant) river, Tavernier bets a modest 40,000. With his pocket tens, De Wolfe calls – and then laughs in disbelief at the sight of Tavernier's boss hand. But Tavernier could not have played it any other way. It is nearly impossible to capture an opponent's chips when out of position with a hand so powerful that there is barely a good card left for him. Checking twice and betting modestly was about all Tavernier could do. Furthermore, if De Wolfe *had* hit his ten, Tavernier's bigger full house would still have held up, so there was no risk of losing the pot by slow-playing the flop and turn.

A pricey pair of ladies

Soon enough the breakfast companions are *mano a mano* again, with the cards on their backs. Dealt pocket queens, De Wolfe raises the pot to 24,000. Yong, with Ah-Ks, reraises all-in, to a total of 217,000.

De Wolfe calls immediately, building a pot of 544,000. If De Wolfe were to win this hand, he would have a stranglehold on the game.

The flop brings 5d-9h-Jc. No change. It is still De Wolfe's hand, with his chance of winning the pot now at 76.5% to Yong's 23.5%. Yong needs a king or an ace, with a runner-runner straight as a real long shot. Yet the turn brings him his king, to roars from the crowd.

Now the tables have been turned. With his chance of winning the pot down to a meagre 13.6%, and Yong's up to 86.4%, De Wolfe needs a miracle card: a queen for trips or a ten to make the straight. But the river brings only the six of spades.

A rash all-in

Yong calls the big blind of 12,000 with pocket fours. William Thorson also calls, with Qd-Jc. The UK's Gavin Simms limps in with Ad-Qs. Nick Slade, the small blind, also limps with Jh-9s.

But the big blind is chip leader Roland De Wolfe – who now, in an effort to sort the players from the limpers, makes it 100,000 to go. He is also seeking to protect his hand, Ah-Qc, by thinning the field.

And he succeeds: after some deliberation, Yong folds his fours. Then Thorson folds his Qd-Jc. Holding A-Q, like De

Wolfe, Simms makes a tight fold. It is left to Slade to take on De Wolfe. He doesn't know it, but he's a 2-3 dog.

Slade sets himself in, a total of 300,000. It is ironic that the player with the weakest hand pre-flop should have turned out to be the only one who feels compelled to take on the raiser. His push here is hyper-aggressive and foolhardy. When he saw the rest of the table fold, he decided to make a play for the chips in the middle, hoping that De Wolfe would fold. Two factors make this unlikely, and point to Slade ending up all-in with a far inferior hand. De Wolfe may be chip leader and the table bully, but this time he has raised from the blind into a large field of players – an indication of real strength. Not only that, but Slade's reraise to 300,000 total leaves De Wolfe facing a call of 200,000 into a pot of roughly 450,000. De Wolfe can't give Slade credit for a high pair; nobody just limps on the small blind in a five-handed pot with a monster. His Ah-Qc is unlikely to be enough of an underdog against Slade's hand for him even to consider folding. Slade's best-case hope here is to end up all-in with live cards – and get lucky. Not a spot you want to find yourself in during a tournament – any tournament, let alone one this big.

Then Slade pairs his nine on the flop! Unfortunately for him, however, De Wolfe also pairs his queen and his ace. This is a highly unlikely development, as Thorson folded one queen and Simms another, with an ace kicker. The flop of Qh-9d-As has been very kind to Roland De Wolfe.

When the turn comes the 4s, only a third nine can save Slade. But the river brings the 2h, and with it the end of Slade's tournament. He leaves in seventh place, with just over €70,000 for his troubles. The 718,000 pot belongs to De Wolfe. Slade walks away, saying: 'I thought he had nothing, I really thought he had nothing . . .' testament to the fact that De Wolfe may be on a roll, but he's playing it to perfection.

Mixing it up pays off

Now the blinds are up to 8000–16,000, with 2000 antes. With the pot starting at 36,000, Thorson calls the big blind with As-Ts. De Wolfe also calls, with pocket deuces. In the big blind, Robert Yong checks his Qs-9c.

The flop is a beauty for De Wolfe: 2s-Ah-3c.

Yong checks. So does Thorson. De Wolfe bets an enticing 70,000. Yong folds. Thorson, with aces, calls. The river brings the Qc. De Wolfe doubles his previous bet, boosting the pot by 140,000.

Now Thorson thinks long and hard. De Wolfe has been mixing up his play, so the Swede would find it difficult to peg him to any one hand. This and the myriad possibilities available on the board, allied to Thorson's shining top pair, eventually prompt him to call. Little does the Swede know that only another ace can save him.

The river brings the 8s. Thorson checks. De Wolfe sighs and asks him how much he has – always a good ploy, if only to gauge your opponent's mood when he responds. The answer is 670,000.

De Wolfe bets half that, 350,000. His bets had gradually escalated, in a smooth and rather swaggering manner, throughout the course of the hand. But this proves a bet too far for the Swede. Thorson wisely folds.

Aggression nearly pays off

De Wolfe's aggressive play continues when, before the flop, the Brit Gavin Simms makes it a huge 50,000 to go, with the blinds still at 8000-16,000. De Wolfe glances at Simms's short stack, and reraises him by 96,000. The other players all fold. Simms set himself all-in, with 185,000.

De Wolfe calls. His Jc-Th is up against Ad-Qc. The flop brings a tantalising 2h-Kd-7h. Could De Wolfe's heart make all the difference? Surely not.

Fourth street produces the Jd. Simms tries to maintain an Englishman's sporting smile, but his face betrays him. De Wolfe is winning this 506,000 pot, against the odds. Simms needs an ace or a queen, or a ten to make his straight.

The river takes pity on the underdog and brings him his Qs. Simms's defiant play has paid off – and he sits back down and smiles, albeit a little sweatier, but only too happy to live another day. De Wolfe now has 1,146,000. His nearest challenger, the Frenchman David Tavernier, is on 880,000.

Unpredictable play

The blinds are still 8000–16,000, with 2000 antes. Thorson raises with pocket nines, to 60,000. De Wolfe, with Ks-3d, and still incessantly bullying the table, is the only caller.

The flop brings Js-Jd-3s. Both players check. The turn brings the 6h. William Thorson bets 45,000. His percentage chances of winning the hand are 89%. De Wolfe boldly raises 120,000. Thorson contentedly calls.

And the river brings De Wolfe a third three!

Thorson checks. Coolly, De Wolfe checks back.

Once the trips are revealed, Thorson openly vents his frustration at the unpredictable nature of De Wolfe's play.

Another bad beat

De Wolfe's breakfast buddy, Rob Yong, decides to take him on again. And so they both wind up all-in, with Roland's As-Js looking like losing to Rob's Ad-Kd . The pot is a handsome 1,532,000.

The flop brings Ah-2h-6s. The turn is the 7s.

But sometimes when you're on a roll, and the poker gods are on your side, all those gambles finally pay off. You make, as I've said before, your own luck. And so it is that the river brings De Wolfe one of only 12 of the remaining 44 cards that can win him the hand, the Jd. Yong can scarcely believe his bad luck as it hits the board. He has been beaten, in the end, by De Wolfe's incorrigibly cavalier play.

The odds hold

With the blinds now up to 20,000–40,000, and antes at 4000, David Tavernier reraises De Wolfe's initial pre-flop raise of 80,000, going all-in with a total of 364,000.

With 2,213,000 in chips, way more than double his nearest opponent, and having knocked out three (out of four) challengers already at the final table, De Wolfe cannot resist calling.

On their backs: Tavernier has Ac-7c, De Wolfe Kc-6h. This one really is a long shot for the chip leader.

The flop brings 2d-Qh-5d, the turn the 4h.

Can De Wolfe *again* beat the odds on the river? He needs a king, a three, or a six, meaning that he has ten outs, i.e. almost 4-1 against. Surely lightning won't strike twice?

No, it doesn't. The river brings a ten – and Tavernier, the 50-year-old Parisian veteran, scoops 804,000.

So De Wolfe is not invincible, after all.

Flopping a set

Now the blinds have risen to 30,000–60,000, and the antes to 5000. Gavin Simms raises pre-flop by 80,000 with 7d-Jd. And the antsy, impatient Roland De Wolfe, sitting to Simms's right, reraises him 280,000 with pocket sixes. Simms calls all-in – a total of 423,000.

The flop brings Th-6d-Ac, giving De Wolfe a set of sixes.

The turn taunts Simms with a seven for a pair. So his EV moves from a pathetic 0.059 to a round 0.000. Another seven would simply give his opponent a full house. Simms is drawing dead. The river brings a nine.

De Wolfe has knocked out yet another final-table challenger. Gavin Simms can console himself with €138,580 in prize money.

A pricey bad beat

De Wolfe calls the big blind of 60,000 with Ah-4s. Tavernier, on the small blind, calls with Qc-8h. Big blind Thorson checks his Jd-9c.

The flop of 8s-Tc-Qd brings Thorson a straight and Tavernier two pair. With just three players left, these cards promise a lively hand.

First to speak, Tavernier bets 100,000. Thorson calls. Wisely, De Wolfe decides to watch, and folds.

When the turn brings the 7h, Tavernier goes all-in with 605,000.

Thorson calls. Tavernier obviously knew that the straight was on, but nevertheless felt that he had to go for it. Now, in need of an eight or a queen, the odds are 9-1 against him. He stands up, ready to walk away and leave the 1,665,000 pot to Thorson.

But instead he claps his hands and sits right back down . . . as the river brings the 8d.

Thorson can only shake his head. He has lost so many of his chips to Tavernier that De Wolfe thinks there has been a mistake when he sees how much Thorson has left. 'That's all you have? Wow!'

And then there were two

Tavernier holds Kh-9s, Thorson As-Ts. With pocket sevens, and the blinds still at 30,000–60,000, De Wolfe makes it 350,000 to go – a raise of 290,000.

He knows how little Thorson has left, and wants him to hand over those chips, too. The Swede calls, all-in with just 90,000. Tavernier folds, happy to sit and watch.

De Wolfe and Thorson shake hands with old-fashioned poker chivalry before the flop – which brings Jd-2h-9h. Thorson's flush hopes have evaporated; now he needs to see an ace or a ten. He has six outs.

The turn brings a queen. Could Thorson's bad luck be about to change? He now has eight more outs, as a king or an eight would also save him. But the river brings a meaningless 6c.

Thorson has played a strong tournament, but he'll spend a while ruing that bad beat against Tavernier, which pushes him back into third place, walking away with €184,780.

HEADS-UP

De Wolfe vs Tavernier

Roland De Wolfe has more than 2.5 million in chips, David Tavernier half that. The Frenchman needs to double-up soon. But De Wolfe continues to hit cards in the first major hand between England and France.

The importance of the continuation bet

On the small blind, still 30,000, Tavernier calls with Ks-3d. There is no raise from De Wolfe, who has 5s-6c.

The flop brings Qd-4h-7s.

Now De Wolfe has an open-ended straight draw, and Tavernier nothing much beyond his king. De Wolfe checks; Tavernier bets straight at him with 60,000. De Wolfe calls his bluff.

The turn brings the Jd. Tavernier needs to make a continuation bet after De Wolfe checks again. But he chooses not to, foolishly giving his opponent a free card.

And his weak play brings big trouble on the river, which comes the 3s, giving him bottom pair, but also De Wolfe his straight, which also happens to be the nuts. He bets 230,000, leaving Tavernier with a problem.

Tavernier pretends to think long and hard. He has to represent that he had something the whole time – enough, anyway, to justify that rogue post-flop bet – and that folding is now a tough move. As he does so it is in truth, of course, a no-brainer.

Out-representation

With the blinds and antes still adding up to 100,000 before a card is dealt, De Wolfe raises 40,000 pre-flop with 9h-5d. Tavernier calls with 6s-4s.

When the flop brings 3h-Kd-Js, both players check. When the turn brings the Ac, Tavernier checks. De Wolfe, having raised pre-flop, chooses to represent the ace and bluffs all of 140,000. But Tavernier gets one over him by swooping back with a check-reraise, to the tune of 460,000.

De Wolfe folds straight away. This was a great move by the Frenchman. He convinced his opponent that he had been holding the ace all the time, when in fact he had an even worse hand than De Wolfe.

Surprisingly, Tavernier now chooses to reveal his cards to De Wolfe, who smiles, knowing that he has been outplayed. Perhaps the Frenchman wants to show De Wolfe that he can mix up his play when necessary – and to send out mixed signals, to throw the Englishman off balance.

But I still maintain that – when playing a solid, aggressive game, as Tavernier had been – it would have been wiser *not* to have shown his bluff to De Wolfe. If in doubt, do not reveal a winning hand to your opponent.

A bluff too far

The blinds have gone up to 40,000–80,000, and the antes to 5000. Neither player raises before the flop comes 3h-5d-As. De Wolfe checks his 4c-5s, and Tavernier his Qs-Jh. This is tentative stuff.

But the turn brings the 5h, giving De Wolfe a set. He bets 70,000. Having seen his efforts to represent an ace pay off handsomely earlier, Tavernier deliberates a moment before raising 220,000.

De Wolfe must have wanted to lick his lips, but pretends to think a minute before just calling. A reraise would likely scare his opponent out of the pot. He smells blood in this hand: a set is a big hand heads-up, and De Wolfe is determined that this one will pay off.

The river comes the 9c. Unbeknown to both players, it's an irrelevant card. Tavernier was drawing dead.

First to speak, De Wolfe makes a moderate bet of 220,000, hoping to coax Tavernier into another large play, perhaps even an all-in, with only queen-high to fall back on. And the Frenchman duly obliges, going all-in over the top with 995,000.

In this moment, as he calls, Roland De Wolfe becomes the first player to have won titles in both the World Poker Tour and the European Poker Tour. After the tournament, the French doctor acknowledged: 'Quite a few bluffs worked really well. Until the end . . .'

Roland De Wolfe had a great run of cards throughout the tournament, and proved a very modest winner, at least to the cameras: 'I've been blessed the whole week – I won key coinflips. I've had a really lucky run. Every time I've been behind, I've come out on top. You need to get lucky in a tournament; the lucky ones will always win.'

Later, he gives his winner's bottle of champagne to the press corps, saying: 'Before I was a half-decent poker player, I was a really bad journalist.'

In 2008 De Wolfe reached the final table of TV's *Late Night Poker*, finishing in second place. By the spring of 2008, his tournament winnings exceeded $3,900,000.

14

Monte Carlo

The Pink Panther

Only as recently as September 2004 did the principality of Monaco finally see fit to move with the poker times and allow a major cash tournament to take place within its tiny boundaries. For such an iconic destination, famed for its luxury casino culture, this comes as something of a surprise. All too soon, however, Monaco was welcoming poker with open arms.

By the time of the showpiece event of the third European Poker Tour – the €10,000 buy-in Grand Final – Monaco was hosting the biggest poker tournament ever held outside Las Vegas. With 706 players competing for a prize pool of €6.6m at the Monte Carlo Bay Hotel and Resort, this was not just the richest but also the largest tournament ever to take place in Europe.

To the players, too, this was the Big One. True to form, the top names in poker descended on the principality, some of them to head back home all too soon. Early casualties included Phil Ivey and former world champions Phil Hellmuth, Greg Raymer and Joe Hachem. PokerStars' Anthony Holden, for once, actually made it through to day two – only for A-Q to see him eliminated, despite a flop of A-Q-x, on its very first hand.

Open-ended muscle

With the blinds at 2000–4000, Norway's Gunnar Ostebrod raises 8000 before the flop with Kh-Jh. The USA's William Hill – a betting man, as befits his name – calls with a pair of threes. Speculating in the hope of accumulating, Britain's Ram Vaswani, the 37-year-old EPT top earner, also calls – with the less promising Ts-7c. The flop helps Vaswani, bringing him an open-ended straight draw, with 2d-9c-8s.

Ostebrod checks. The young American, Hill, bets 30,000, taking the pot to a healthy 71,200. Vaswani bullishly moves all-in, to the tune of 195,000. Not for nothing is he called 'Crazy Horse'. Hill has no choice but to fold. Vaswani merely muscled him out of the pot. It's the only way to play a chasing hand like that.

A good call

It's just before the bubble, and Norway's Halldor Sverrisson is holding 8d-8h. He calls the 4000 blind. Maybe a raise would have got rid of the two opponents who also go on to call. Will Sverrisson's pocket pair stand up to Ram Vaswani's Jh-Ts and German Jan Veit's Jc-8s?

The flop brings 9s-6d-Th. Vaswani has made a pair and is now a 62% favourite, while Veit has an open-ended straight draw. Vaswani bets 5000, Veit calls, and Sverrisson lays down his eights, neither fancying the inside-straight draw nor liking the look of those overcards. A shrewd fold. He was beaten as soon as he neglected to raise pre-flop.

Fourth street brings the Ac. The remaining two players check. Then the river brings the Ks.

It's Vaswani's hand. But with the bubble approaching, and those overcards on the board, he cautiously checks. So Veit bets at him, pushing 20,000 into the pot. Vaswani has to think hard. There are plenty of worrying permutations available and 45,200 in the pot.

He calls. Veit mucks. And Crazy Horse smiles.

A classic check-raise

Ireland's Andy Black sits down for day two as tournament leader, with 709,000 in chips. With pocket fives (5d-5s), and the blinds up to 4000–8000, he raises pre-flop to 15,000. Canadian Marc Karam, who came fourth in this event last year, calls. He has a not insignificant 260,500 in chips. With the chip average for the remaining 32 players now at 330,937, however, Karam needs to win a pot or two to stay in the running.

The flop brings 3s-2d-Kh. Karam's Ks-Qd is first to speak. He checks, no doubt suspecting that the cavalier Black is bound to bet at him. Which the Monk duly does, to the tune of 35,000, trying to persuade Karam that he's holding a king. But it's actually Karam, of course, who has the king! All-in he now goes, to the tune of 185,000. Black folds, his stack severely dented by a classic check-raise from Karam.

A bold call pays off

Just 20 players are now left in the tournament, and the blinds have reached 6000–12,000. At the TV table, three players have called the 21,000 raise made by the USA's Gavin Griffin, leaving four contenders for a pot totalling 139,000. They are

England's Dean Sanders, with the Hammer, 7c-2s; Holland's Eric Van Der Berg, with 5s-4s; Norway's Kristian Kjondal with Ks-Js; and Griffin, holding 9s-9c.

The flop brings 3h-Th-Ts, and the table checks to Griffin – who chooses to play it cautious and checks along. In truth it's a weak check. With no pre-flop reraise, it is unlikely that Griffin is up against a higher pair than his nines. There are only two tens left in the deck for one of his opponents to hold. Griffin can be confident his nines are good, even up against three opponents. Any J, Q, K or A on the turn will effectively kill his hand. A bet here was certainly called for.

The free turn is the 3s, making two pairs and flush possibilities for Van Der Berg and Kjondal. Van Der Berg sets the pace with a 20,000 bet. Kjondal and Sanders fold. Griffin, with a large stack in front of him, just calls.

The river brings the Kh. No flush for Van Der Berg. As Griffin beholds another dreaded overcard, the pressure is on Van Der Berg. Will he fire the second barrel, to try to squeeze out the American, as if he were holding a heart flush or a rivered pair of kings? Even tens full of threes?

Van Der Berg bets 75,000, taking the pot to 254,000. A sizeable sum – but will it be enough to force Griffin out?

No. The American calls and takes the hand down.

This was a strong call from Griffin. So strong that spectators wondered whether he had seen some tell in the Dutchman's play. In fact, sitting back and playing a solid hand passively can induce an aggressive opponent to fire bluffs; but the conditions to make such a play correct don't seem to be met here. Griffin's hand was vulnerable to plenty of turn cards. He was up against multiple opponents and in the middle stages of a tournament, players aren't often inclined towards super-aggressive play. The play worked, but it had risked losing Griffin a sizeable pot at a crucial stage of the tournament.

Another genuine bad beat

Four players are in before the flop, three of them calling a raise of 24,000 from the USA's David Peters on top of the 12,000 big blind. Just 19 years old, Peters cannot yet play legally in his home country, yet here in Monte Carlo he can compete with the world's best for millions of dollars.

Peters is holding Ah-Jc. Eric Van Der Berg calls with As-5s, Dean Sanders with 8h-7c, and Marc Karam with Tc-9s. The flop brings 9c-Ts-6h. So Karam now has two pairs, but Sanders has filled his straight, making him a 72% favourite.

Sanders, first to speak, checks. To his disappointment, so does Karam. How they must both be purring now that Eric Van Der Berg decides to take a punt at the pot, his acute positional play spoilt by the unwise assumption that his ace gives him some sort of edge. He bets 60,000, not knowing that he's a 25-1 longshot to win this hand.

Sanders is first up to respond. Holding the nuts, he just calls, hoping to build the pot and suck in more players. Karam, next to speak, chooses the wrong moment to lob in a big raise – no less than 200,000.

Sanders, of course, now goes all-in with 294,000. Karam calls immediately. With 919,000 up for grabs, and no one else left in the hand, the winner of this pot will be very strongly fancied to reach the final table, which is fast approaching.

Karam's annoyance is all too visible when he sees that his two pairs are losing to Sanders's straight. Both players stand up to watch the turn, which comes the 6s. Now only a house can save Karam; he needs a third ten, or a nine, or another six. The odds are 7-1 against him.

But the Monegasque poker gods are in fickle mood. The river brings a miraculous 6d, giving a delighted Karam a back-door house. As he claps his hands and reaches for the chips, Sanders strides sharply away.

Both men have played the hand absolutely correctly. Whoever lost would have felt hard done by. But there was no doubting that Sanders had just experienced one heck of a bad beat. 6-6-6 – the Sign of the Devil – had proven fatal for his straight.

Mixing it up

With just fifteen players left, Andy Black has been raising at Eric Van Der Berg, in the seat immediately behind him, throughout the penultimate day's play. Eric seems aware that, in his crafty way, Andy is playing a kind of inverse position – and that the Monk likes to bet big.

So when Andy raises the 12,000 big blind yet again, this time by 20,000, and Eric looks down at pocket eights, the Dutchman feels that the moment has at last come to reraise the Irishman – which he does, to the tune of 68,000.

Black thinks for a moment – and then sets himself all-in. The two players have been fighting over pots all afternoon, but this long-running stand-off has now reached a new level of aggression. It seems as if Black has lost patience with Van Der Berg. The Monk has clearly grown fed up with his neighbour's manipulating his position at the Irishman's expense; now he definitely wants to take some chips off his opponent.

It's on Van Der Berg. He takes a deep breath, wriggles in his seat, rubs his eyes. Perhaps Black is holding A-K or A-Q; but equally, the way he's been betting, he could just as well have rags.

'It's only chips, thank God,' says a smiling Black, his entire stack now in the middle of the table. Doth the Monk protest too much? Is he hoping not to be called? They may only be chips in the middle, but there's big money at stake at the end of all this.

'Yeah, you're right about that,' says Van Der Berg, calling Black's 417,000, and swelling the pot to a hefty 906,000.

Black hurls pocket rockets on their backs and stands up.

The flop is irrelevant to either player. Then the turn brings Black a third ace. His bold, constant raising had stood him in very good stead to make such a run at his opponent. He has won this hand through maverick betting.

Van Der Berg, on the other hand, knows that his chances of scooping the supreme prize have just taken a huge dent.

Play the man, not the cards

Gavin Griffin has been chip leader for some time. In early position, with pocket fours, and the blinds up to 8000–16,000, he makes a 29,000 raise. Eric Van Der Berg, now playing a lot of pots, calls with suited connectors, Qd-Jd. The flop comes 5d-9s-Kd.

Seeking to gauge his opponent's interest in the hand, Griffin bets 65,000. For all the Dutchman knows, Griffin could have A-K. Van Der Berg, who is flushing on top of his gutshot straight draw, calls. Fourth street brings the 6s.

Eric checks. In previous hands, he has been betting winners. So Griffin now preys upon his opponent's new passivity, and plays him on his betting record; he pushes 95,000 into the pot. With 20 outs, 14 of which are to a seriously strong hand, Van Der Berg calls.

The river brings the Jh. He may not have made his flush, but Van Der Berg surely now has to throw caution to the wind and bet his pair of jacks. Or does he have Griffin pegged for a pair of kings?

Van Der Berg checks. Griffin smoothly comes up with

another bet of 225,000. This continuation tactic again suggests that he's holding the king – that he has had the winning hand all along – even if, in reality, he no longer holds it at all . . .

Van Der Berg thinks long and hard before folding.

It seems likely that Van Der Berg has been drawing to something. But if he has missed his hand completely, Griffin could check behind and win in a showdown with his pair of fours. Van Der Berg may have been making good calls with middle pair, or perhaps Griffin fears that Van Der Berg has indeed been drawing, but has hit a six or jack, giving him a higher one-pair hand? In this case, a third barrel is needed to represent the king a third time, and take the Dutchman off his hand. This is indeed exactly the case. This was confident, stylish play from the young chip leader – and a fine example of that sage old dictum: play the man, not the cards.

Maximising pocket rockets

Dealt pocket rockets, Gavin Griffin raises the 16,000 blind by another 29,000 pre-flop. The Hendon Mob's Ram Vaswani likes the look of his Jh-Qd enough to call. And the flop, by the look of it, is a good one for Crazy Horse, giving him top pair with Ts-Qh-4s. In reality, of course, it's the cruellest of flops. He's not to know it, but he has only a 4-1 chance of victory. Ram trap-checks; so does the crafty Griffin.

The turn brings the 4h. It's another cruel communal card for Vaswani, though again he cannot know it, for his jack is now irrelevant, given Griffin's two pairs. Understandably, however, Vaswani bets: 60,000. No doubt praying that Vaswani holds a queen, Griffin raises 200,000. The Brit – maybe worried about a queen with a higher kicker – just calls.

The river brings the Kh. Will the overcard – though, in truth, irrelevant – scare off Vaswani? He checks. Griffin boldly bets

225,000. Clearly, he wants as many chips as he can get out of this hand. Will that king, married to this strong play from the young American, push out the canny Vaswani?

From his point of view, however, would Griffin have kept betting throughout the hand in the hope of pulling a king on the river? Surely not ... maybe he's using his stack to steal? So Vaswani calls. Griffin's cue to turn over the aces, safe in the knowledge that he has maximised the profitability of this most handsome of starting hands.

THE FINAL TABLE

Heading into the denouement, 26-year-old Canadian Marc Karam is in second place, with 1,472,000. But still leading the pack is Gavin Griffin with 2,597,000. Twenty-five years old, from Orange County, California, Griffin became the youngest ever World Series bracelet winner in 2004, at just 22, when he walked off with the $3000 pot limit Hold'em event.

With some aggressive and inventive play, Griffin has maintained a very healthy lead for some time in the Grand Final, and is now hoping to take that lead all the way to the bank. Six different nationalities have sat down to finish the job. Half of the table has qualified online, including Griffin, who won his entry via a €240 tournament.

Don't think *too* hard

With the blinds up to 12,000–24,000, and rolling antes of 3000, Marc Karam is dealt pocket nines. He raises 41,000 pre-flop.

The 32-year-old American Josh Prager, who has also qualified online, calls with pocket jacks (also known as 'Fish Hooks' – see table, page 23). Steve Jelinek, a Brit who has recently been made redundant from his day job, also calls with low suited gappers, 5c-3c. The flop comes 6h-Kd-7h.

Fancying his nines, but also hoping to represent a king, Karam tests the waters with a bet of 110,000. But the overcard seems to have spooked Prager, who must now either fold or raise without stopping to think too much. After a moment of thought he goes for the latter, to the tune of another 130,000.

That moment of thought, however, may have been just a second or so too pregnant. Noting his opponent's apparently genuine hesitation, Karam discounts the idea of Prager holding the king – and reraises 300,000.

Now Prager has to make up his mind whether Karam has the king. Erroneously, he decides he has walked into a trap, and folds the winning hand. The Canadian has comprehensively outplayed the American.

Seeing off a bare ace

With 8s-4s and good position, Denmark's Soren Kongsgaard, 19 years old – who, like Griffin, won his entry online – chooses to raise the 30,000 blind by 55,000 pre flop, in an apparent attempt to steal the blinds. Sat to his left, however, is Griffin, who has just been knocked off his perch as chip leader by Karam. Griffin sees through the attempted steal and reraises 65,000.

Kongsgaard seems to be feeling irked by having the big stack on his left, and decides not to play to the American's tune. He pays no heed to the raise and goes all-in, with a re-reraise totalling 1,428,000.

It's a very strong play, which flummoxes Griffin. He errs on the side of caution, and mucks his weak ace, unwilling to throw away the fruits of his hard labour with so little information.

Fight your corner when the chips are in your favour

Chastened by his recent defeat to Canadian Marc Karam, Josh Prager triples the 30,000 blind pre-flop with Ah-3d. Like Kongsgaard, he is hoping to steal some blinds. But Griffin, the small blind, is also apparently still smarting from being outbet by Kongsgaard. With Tc-8c, he calls his fellow American.

And the flop of 9h-7d-5c brings him an open-ended straight draw, while giving Prager no help at all. Griffin is first to act. No doubt pegging his opponent for high cards, after that pre-flop raise, he bets 135,000. The odds are still fairly even. Game on.

Despite getting caught out by Karam in similar circumstances, Prager boldly comes over the top again, raising Griffin 365,000.

This time there is less deliberation from Prager. His hand promises more possibilities, as there is no worrying high card (like that troublesome king during his skirmish with Karam). If he can hold his nerve and look stoic, maybe Prager can take some chips off Griffin here, just like Soren Kongsgaard?

But Griffin, who is used to being chip leader, seems to have grown fed up with being pushed around. He is also feeling unwell after a week of hardcore Hold'em. It looks like he has had enough, and is ready to throw his weight around. He goes all-in, with a total bet of 1,793,000.

Prager has nowhere to go. Again, he lays down his cards, bullied out by the bigger stack.

Thirty-three-year-old Prager soon leaves the final table, after himself going all-in with pocket sevens. Again, he runs into a player with more chips who is not taking any prisoners. Kongsgaard, with pocket tens, knocks out the bold American, who walks away with €391,500 for his trouble. If he had taken a stronger stand against the heavyweight Griffin, or maybe played those fish hooks better against Karam, he could have left Monte Carlo with even more.

Burn, baby, burn

Even at the final table of the biggest tournament ever held in Europe, cards are misdealt, exposed and must be burnt on their backs. And so it is that Gavin Griffin is dealt a three, but one that lands face-up. So it becomes the first 'burn' card, before the flop, as is the rule when this happens, and a fresh card is dealt to the American.

And that new card just happens to pair his hole card, a queen. Those two ladies now seduce him into raising 50,000 under the gun. Soren Kongsgaard, holding pocket jacks behind him in the big blind, reraises 220,000. Griffin goes all-in with his ladies, to the tune of 1,820,000 – and Kongsgaard has no choice but to call.

The board proves unhelpful to the Dane: A-A-5-K-3. So Griffin's freak queens stand up. Kongsgaard has played the hand right within the tighter confines of a four-hander. But Griffin is back in charge.

The 'trap-bet' pays off

With three players left, Griffin and Kongsgaard continue to rub up against each other, Griffin emerging the victor each time.

The blinds are up to 20,000–40,000, when Kongsgaard is dealt tempting suited connectors, 9s-Ts. He calls from the small blind. But he has run into Griffin's As-Jh; a 60% favourite to win the hand, he raises Kongsgaard 100,000.

Kongsgaard calls, and both players check the flop of 5h-4h-6c.

The turn brings the ace of hearts. Again Kongsgaard checks. Now Griffin swiftly bets out 200,000 – a clever, instinctive move.

The speed with which he reached for his chips, and the size of the bet itself, are both designed to make his opponent think he is trying to steal the hand, that he is bluffing an ace in the hole. A sophisticated trap-bet strategy, in keeping with Griffin's play throughout the session, it works a treat. Kongsgaard immediately goes all-in with just ten-high, his last 890,000, taking the pot to a total of 2,072,000.

The Dane is drawing dead. Griffin happily calls and busts out his opponent, the last European standing, who leaves with €610,500.

HEADS-UP

Griffin vs Karam

As we reach the heads-up, there is everything to play for: Gavin Griffin, a World Series bracelet holder, and Marc Karam, EPT and Aussie Millions finalist, are pretty much level on chips. Both have been playing with great coolness and style. As so often, however, it will take just one freakish hand to tip the balance.

A good laydown

Dealt Kc-7d, Griffin raises the 50,000 big blind pre-flop by 75,000. A king with medium kicker is a decent hand, heads-up; but Karam's Ks-Qd, is a whole lot better. He reraises 275,000.

Griffin could easily lay down that hand on the back of this reraise, but he chooses to play on. If the board were to bring a king, he would be in big trouble; as it is, the odds against his winning the hand are less than 3-1. But when the flop proves as much, by bringing the American another seven, 5h-7s-5d, he has the perfect cards to sucker-punch Karam – whose only hope of winning the hand, unbeknown to him, is now one of the three queens left in the deck.

But Karam understandably bets 500,000. Correctly assuming his opponent does not have a pair, Griffin calls comfortably enough before the turn brings the 3c. Karam checks. Griffin also checks, slow-playing his pair, hoping to entice the Canadian into calling after the river – which turns out to be another three.

This time Griffin bets – a total of 700,000. Karam thinks long and hard. If he had the ace kicker, perhaps he would have raised at some point, even before the flop? But he lays down his hand. A tough but smart fold.

Take me to the river

They have been playing heads-up for quite some time. Griffin has built up around a two-to-one chip lead, with 5.6m to Karam's 2.47m. Just one big all-in hand could change that round. Or finish things off.

With Kd-5c, and the blinds still at 25,000–50,000, Griffin raises pre-flop by a mere 75,000. Holding 7h-4s, Karam attempts to steal with a reraise of 275,000. Griffin calls.

The flop of 3c-2s-4d brings a dangerous host of possibilities, giving Karam a surprising top pair, and Griffin an inside straight draw. That big all-in hand has arrived.

Karam bets 500,000 on his pair of fours. Griffin, still feeling ill, thinks his straight draw worth pushing it up to 1,500,000. This prompts Karam to go all-in, to the tune of 4,155,000. A bold move, especially when he cannot know that he is in fact ahead.

'You have the best hand,' muses Griffin, with some accuracy, to his opponent. But the situation is not too bleak for him. With two overcards to Karam's pair of fours, and an open-ended straight draw, he is only a 48-52 underdog to win the hand.

Karam replies simply: 'You're calling?'

With the fateful words, 'Yeah, I call,' Griffin does just that. He is clearly hoping to put the tournament – and himself – to bed right here. When the cards go on their backs, however, it is clear that this one might yet run and run.

Karam puts his hands on his head, knowing that he is a 52% favourite. Here is his chance to take pole position. The pot totals 10,110,000. The turn brings the 3h – and, in turn, a jubilant clap from a tense Karam. With one card to go, he is still winning the hand.

Griffin is steeling himself for plenty more heads-up play. He looks resigned and relaxed – perhaps thinking that he is the underdog, even though he in fact has 14 outs. Karam's lead is deceptive and marginal, actually.

The announcer tells the gallery that Griffin needs an ace or a six. The kid from Orange County smiles and adds: 'How about a king or a five? I'd just take a five!'

But the river does not give him his five. It brings the king! Now it is young Gavin Griffin's turn to clap. He has won the EPT main event.

Griffin has also just given a masterclass in long-legged tournament play. And he has turned that €240 online entry fee into the €2.4 million first prize. All this on his first ever visit to Europe.

As Griffin told the post-tournament interviewer: 'I've been sick all day, and I'm really tired, but I've had the support of my girlfriend here, who has been fantastic. Marc played great. It was a hell of a move on that last hand, but by the time he moved all-in I had to call.' Griffin played the entire tournament with his hair dyed pink, to signify his support for breast cancer charities, after his girlfriend was diagnosed with the disease at the age of only twenty. Some of his followers in the bar, as a result, have nicknamed him 'the Pink Panther'.

The following January, 26-year-old Griffin capped Roland De Wolfe's record by winning a WPT event, the Borgata Winter Open, to follow up on his WSOP and EPT wins. This made him the first – and, at the time of writing, still the only – player to win titles in all three competitions.

Now that you've learnt from the masters, why not try entering the low-price online satellites for EPT events? The vast majority of entrants are online qualifiers, whose airfares and hotel bills are also taken care of. Whether or not you wind up in the money, it's a great way to see Europe – in congenial (on the whole), like-minded company!

But now we move on to the Big Daddy of all poker tournaments: the $10,000 entry main event of the annual World Series of Poker in Las Vegas, which sees one player from several thousand wind up a multi-millionaire and poker's official world champion for a year, earning himself – or before long, for sure, herself – an immortal niche in poker history.

15

WSOP Diary

Everything you've learnt in this book can, of course, go seriously wrong at the tables; or it can go seriously right. The only way to find out is to play. And play, and play. When it does go wrong, it can hurt, really hurt; when it goes right, it's a thrill encapsulated in one of the favourite one-liners of my old pal Al Alvarez: 'Sex is good, but poker lasts longer.'

Well, you hope it does. The worst time for things to go wrong – or the best for them to go right – is in the main event of the World Series of Poker, the $10,000 event held in Las Vegas each summer. I've played in it many times, but have never managed to realise the dream shared by all poker players of winning that world crown.

With so many starters, many thousands since online poker so boosted the number of qualifiers, freakish things happen by the minute all over the giant cardroom in the garish Rio hotel-casino on the Las Vegas strip. As the blinds rise on day one, for instance, aces get cracked on all sides. The most diligent of bloggers could never capture everything; but in 2007 I kept a diary of the event, including my own (all too brief) participation, which I hope captures some of the excitement unique to those heady summer Vegas days.

Now that you've mastered the rudiments of the game, come on out to Vegas and take your own crack at poker immortality!

7 July

On Thursday, the day before the world-title event of the 2007 WSOP, poker pro Annie Duke and Hollywood star Don Cheadle hosted an event named 'Ante Up for Africa'. George Clooney didn't show up, as advertised, but those who did included Matt Damon, Ben Affleck and Martin Sheen – whom I saw walking through the lobby of the Rio in darkest Hollywood shades, acknowledging the applause of the crowds with a practised Queen Mother wave – as if he actually *were* the President of the United States.

The $5000 buy-in event, in which cashers were encouraged to give half their winnings to the victims of Darfur, ended when the last two men standing out of 167 starters agreed to give *all* their prize money – $386,738 between them – to the relevant charities, the Enough Project and the International Rescue Committee. And so it came to pass that big-hearted Daniel Shak and Brandon Moran were formally declared joint winners. At the star-studded post-event party, a glowing Annie Duke predicted the event would wind up raising a sum close to a million bucks.

By noon yesterday, Friday, all this had become one of the finer moments in World Series history when Day 1-A of the main event saw 1287 players settle down to the ten-day task of pursuing this year's multi-million-dollar first prize as 2007 world champion of poker. By the day's end, 16 hours later at 4 a.m., such illustrious poker names as former world champs Doyle Brunson, Johnny Chan and Amarillo 'Slim' Preston had all been eliminated, as had top Europeans Andy Black, Dave 'Devilfish' Ulliott, Dave Colclough, Roy 'The Boy' Brindley and Ram Vaswani (who snagged his first WSOP bracelet 48 hours earlier, as the $217,438 winner of the 720-entrant, $1500 buy-in limit Hold'em shoot-out. While I'm updating the back story, the next day saw the genial Erik Seidel win his eighth WSOP bracelet with the $538,835 first prize in Event 54, $5000 no limit 2-7 draw lowball with rebuys).

The early departure of Brunson and Chan from the main event ensured that happy new Hall-of-Famer Phil Hellmuth's record haul of 11 WSOP bracelets would now remain intact until at least next year.

The dubious honour of being the first person out of the 2007 world title event went to one Matt Jansen – who began his bad-beat story, like so many others, with those familiar words, 'Well, I had pocket rockets . . .' Jansen held Ah-Ad to George Dolorfan's Kh-Qh. All the money went in after a flop of Jh-Th-5h. When no fourth heart came on the turn or the river, Jansen became the first player to be 'sent to the rail'.

It's still early days, of course – and WSOP history shows that no day one chip leader has ever gone on to win the world title – but, for the record, the field at the end of day one was led by a Frenchman called Tinten Olivier with 270,500 chips. Also among the 450 weary survivors were Britain's Julian Gardner in seventh place with 243,000, 'Gentleman' Joe Beevers with just under 100,000, and . . . yes, poker writer and pal Des Wilson with, er, just 12,500 of the 20,000 he started with.

Given that the brutally revised structure scoops some 40,000 in blinds and antes over those hours, however, this was no mean feat from Des. The cheers could be heard all the way from Cornwall as the New Zealander-turned-West Country boy achieved his prime objective of surviving day one. In the process he won his $100 last-longer bet with snooker champ Steve Davis – a very canny player, who got into the money last year –

and, even better, also outplayed Dave Ulliott, prime subject of the poker book Des published last year.

Des will also have gathered enough good material to write himself into poker history in the final chapter of his imminent history of poker, *Ghosts at the Table*. Halfway through the day, he found himself short-stacked enough to go all-in with A-10 of hearts. 'To my horror,' Des reports, 'the guy on my right said "call" and tabled A-K. As if that was not bad enough, he got two more kings on the flop. So it was all over? Well, actually, no, because two of the cards on the flop were hearts – and guess who got a lucky break on the river!' Clearly, Des's name is on the trophy.

I will certainly be pleased if I manage to do as well on Monday, Day 1-D, when Mike (*Suicide King*) Craig and I will be among the weirdos and mavericks who signed on for that day for no other reason than pure eccentricity. This was before Harrah's suspended entries for Saturday and Sunday, ensuring that all the last-gasp satellite winners and last-minute celebrity alternates will also be arriving in droves to make this last day one pretty chaotic.

We won't know the final tally of starters until halfway through Monday, so that figure will have to wait until I chronicle my own progress (or, more likely, lack of it) early next week. In the meantime, Day 1-B is well under way as I write, characterised by a clutch of top pros playing because it's the best day for phasing your progress through days two and three, and countless superstitious morons who believe that 7/7/07 is 'the luckiest day of the century' (what, I ask, about 7/7/77, when I will be signing on at the tender age of 130?). The Strip is teeming with bridal couples today, all of them figuring that it is the luckiest day of the century to tie the knot. Vegas being Vegas, the wedding chapels have all doubled their rates.

So I will now go score a free meal off someone – Des Wilson, I hope, in my new role as the eternally freeloading Anthony

Holden he portrayed in a vivid, warts-and-all profile in *Poker Pro Europe* – while waiting to bring you the highlights of Day 1-B. Among those playing is my dinner companion of last night, EPT London winner Victoria Coren, who has already cashed once this year and is currently playing as well as any Brit, nay European.

Could this be the year of the poker writer? How dumb of Des Wilson not to insist on a last-longer bet with his pals Anthony Holden and Michael Craig (who has already reached two WSOP final tables this year) over the several meals I got him to pay for in return for copious advice on how to survive day one. I would, of course, have taken it then. Not now I won't . . .

8 July

'Luck is nothing but probability taken personally,' declared Penn Jillette, of the Rio's resident double-act Penn and Teller, before intoning 'Shuffle up and deal' to get Day 1-B under way. Many seem to believe this mildly amusing thought is Penn's own, but he is the first to acknowledge that it was coined by an eminent American statistician with the spot-on name of Chip Denman.

Sixteen hours later, the second day one's dust-biters included such big American poker names as Howard Lederer, his sister Annie Duke, Erik Seidel, Sam Farha, John Juanda, Scott Fischman, Jeff Shulman, Kathy Liebert and Jennifer Harman, plus European pros Isabelle Mercier, Simon 'Aces' Trumper and the Hendon Mob's Barny Boatman – whose brother Ross survived (in good shape with 68,000). Among others to have made it through 1-B are former world champions Joe Hachem, Dan Harrington, Scotty Nguyen, Tom McEvoy and Berry Johnston.

For the second day running, the field is led by a European, Norway's Dag Martin Mikkelsen with 253,000. High among the other survivors are Brits John Duthie on a handy 135,000,

Neil 'Bad Beat' Channing with 65,000 and Roland De Wolfe (31,000). Vicky Coren made it through with 33,000, while Donnacha O'Dea and his son Eoghan both kept Ireland's flag proudly flying. Reigning champ Jamie Gold has yet to play, but his mother Jane is still in there with 40,000. Yesterday's literary survivors, all American, include Lou Krieger, Charlie Shoten and Avery Cardoza.

I am writing this halfway through Day 1-C, whose casualties already include former champ Greg Raymer, Phil Ivey, Andy Bloch, Phil 'The Unabomber' Laak and his girlfriend Jennifer Tilly, Men 'The Master' Nguyen and Britain's 'Gentleman' John Gale. And that's all for now about the day ones until I've played in my own, 1-D, tomorrow. With fields growing by the day – 1287 for Day 1-A, 1545 on 1-B, and 1743 on 1-C, chancers like me who chose to play on 1-D are expected to find themselves battling against the largest field. The total number of starters will still have trouble getting much beyond 6000 even if 1-D turns out to be as last-gasp chaotic as feared. One of the promises from the organisers was nine-handed tables. But they're already cramming in ten, and overflowing into the tent outside, where the great T. J. Cloutier has been among those shivering in the air-con or burning up in the heat, depending where they're sitting.

Otherwise, Harrah's is generally thought to be looking after the players better in this, the third year at the Rio. Thanks to the Players' Advisory Committee recruited by the commissioner of poker, Jeffrey Pollack, even the 'f-word' has been redeemed. In 2006 its use warranted an automatic ten minutes in the sin-bin. Now you can utter it with impunity as long as you're swearing at yourself rather than anyone else, be it an opponent, a dealer or Lady Luck. Which should have Tony G (who survived yesterday) and Mike 'The Mouth' Matusow (playing today – or, whoops, he was till he just went out) in more schizophrenic mode than ever.

For the most part, there's a more restrained atmosphere than usual in the Amazon Room, which some are crediting to the drop in the number of internet qualifiers – many of whom have clearly found another, supposedly better use for their 10k. Me, I'm thrilled to be sitting down yet again for my eighth shot at the world crown in some 20 years. This time, what's more, I don't plan to chronicle my progress in the closing chapter of a book. I can just play my normal game – or maybe mix it up a bit more than is my wont, and hope the poker gods smile on me. That way, as one friend has predicted by email, I'll probably wind up doing either 'extremely well or extremely badly'. There is no room for any in-between. Nor should there be.

This year, in other words, I'm not going to play merely for survival to day two. I'm playing, from the off, to win this damned thing. So let's hope luck – or probability – stays on my side.

PS: The above should also contain an honourable mention of Britain's David Flusfeder, the *Sunday Telegraph* poker columnist and *Telegraph* website poker blogger, who survived Day 1-B with all but 40,000 in chips. Day 1-C fallers include David Sklansky and Clonie Gowen (who left her chewing gum at the table, which will apparently be on offer on eBay).

10 July

'It's the worst moment of the year,' says two-time world champ Doyle Brunson, dean of living poker players, of the day you're knocked out of the 60-million-dollar main event of the World Series. From personal experience over the last 20 years – in which I've made it through to day two four times out of eight – most recently in 2005, at the beginning of *Bigger Deal* – I can tell you that the dread, odds-against card that seals your fate socks you in the stomach like a sucker-punch to the solar plexus.

Whether already up on your feet or not, you reel away from the table winded, and stagger out of the room like a vaudeville drunk – dazed and alone, blind with rage against the world and all its works, maybe even (if you're a *real* wimp) disappearing to a lonely, self-pitying corner to shed an over-the-top tear or two.

But hey, brother, come on, so what? Two-thirds of the field (i.e., this year, more than 4000 people) goes out on day one. Pull yourself together and go play in a cash game. That way, you can begin to feel better by thinking of all the time you're not wasting joining the day two, three, even four suckers who grind on red-eyed and wasted through those exhausting, interminable, 16-hour days – still without making it into the top 10%, and so the money.

The worst place to go out of this thing, we all know, is the bubble – one off the money. You've played all that time, beaten all those world-class players, and what have you to show for your $10,000 entry fee (however you may have come by it)? Precisely nothing. Neither for professional or amateur players is that a good rate of pay for four long days' extremely hard work. Better, by far, to go out in a blaze of doomed glory on the first hand of the first day.

Day 1-D – the first day of *my* main event – begins unusually promptly at 12.10 p.m., after a rabble-rousing speech from ex-Senator Alfonse D'Amato, representative of all our interests in Washington DC, as the leading lobbyist working to get poker exempted from the absurd new American legislation against online gaming. God alone knows how much Al D is paid by whom, but I've never heard anyone cry 'Shuffle up and deal!' with quite such passion, such intensity, to quite so much foot-stamping applause.

Among today's players, apart from little old me, are reigning world champion Jamie Gold, former champs Phil Hellmuth and Carlos 'The Matador' Mortensen, Gus Hansen, Chip Reese, Ted Forrest, Antonio Esfandari, Robert Williamson III, Chip Jett, Mimi Tran, H.O.R.S.E. champion Freddy Deeb and new Hall-of-Famer Barbara Enright. Plus Michael Craig, intent on his third final table this year. As opponents go, yup, this is a not un-intimidating group.

My own table (37) gradually reveals itself to be quiet, genial, intense, and full of solid if occasionally brash players – including, in my view, myself. I get off to a terrible start, losing a quarter of my $20,000 stack within 20 minutes, but it isn't (of course) my fault. What are you to do if you raise pre-flop with A-Q red-suited, get called by what turns out to be 5c-6c, see a flop of A-Q-x containing one club, bet out big again, get (believe it or not) called – and watch your opponent pull a runner-runner flush? Decide it's not going to be your day, that's what you do. Then you pick yourself up, dust yourself down, and start all over again.

In, for a while, vain. By the end of the first two-hour session, I am still down at 15k. There follows a soul-searching, ten-minute cigarette break with friends old and new in the 120-degree heat. By the end of the second level, however, after some manful bluffing, I am back up to all of 25k. During the third, I bumble my way back down to my original 20.

Now, after six hours' play and the welcome 90-minute dinner break, the $50 antes are about to kick in. In Antonio's, my eponymous Italian restaurant in the Rio, there is much futile discussion of tactics with Des Wilson and ESPN super-blogger Gary Wise before Mike Craig and I head back to the combat zone.

Some ten hours into day one (or seven hours' play, plus breaks) – around 10 p.m., with a mere six hours to go to day two – I am dealt Ad-Jd in the cut-off seat (the one before the button, often even better for running a bluff if you smell weakness around the table). I raise 5000 and the whole gang folds apart from a dour, bearded Yank with twice as many chips as me, who thinks long and hard before calling.

The flop brings Jc-Td-8d. I've got top pair with top kicker, and four to the nut flush. With 12,000 left in front of me, and much the same in the pot, I pretend to think for a while, then push all-in. Beardy thinks rather longer – then calls. We roll them over. He has 9-8 off-suit, both black. The turn brings the Js, giving me trip jacks with top kicker. This pot must now be mine, doubling me up to a very respectable, workable-with 35,000. The bearded one has only six outs – for Qd or 7d, which would give him a straight, would fill my flush. With eight cards seen, and so 44 unknown, I make that 38-6, i.e. better than 6-1, in my favour.

The dealer bangs the table, burns a card, and shows . . . a black seven, giving Beardy a beyond-fluky straight. He rakes in my chips as if they were his natural due – without even looking at devastated me, let alone offering any gallant apology or embarrassed sympathy – as I suavely rise above the Matusow routine of telling him in many colours what a lousy call he made on the turn, if not the flop, and before it.

'Wow,' says the guy on my left, 'that was a *really* bad beat.'

'Can I have that in writing?' I ask him with a smile, and true-Brit insouciance, as I gather what's left of my worldly goods, nod knowingly to the rest of the table, and make a relatively dignified exit.

But who, apart from me, cares? It's just another day one exit, in impressive company today: reigning champ Gold, along with Hellmuth, Reese, Williamson, Steve Zolotow, Cyndy Violette, David Benyamine, Paul Darden and (alas) Mike Craig – along with myself, just some of four thousand departees not to have made it through this last first day, leaving a third of this year's starters to struggle on tomorrow. I've outlasted maybe half the field, but that of course means nothing. I must square up to the fact that I'm not going to win this year's $8.25-million first prize, nor even the $20,320 which goes to 621st place out of the 6358 starters.

No, I've just got another ten days here to watch the others battle it out, and keep this diary going, while attempting to restore my shattered pride in the cash games.

Doyle is so right. Soon after 10 p.m., until which point I'd really enjoyed myself, this has turned out to be the worst day of my year. But I'm fortunate enough to know that the consolations will swiftly kick in. Unlike most poker pros, I will soon be able to wrench my mind back to the real world so blithely absent from Las Vegas, enjoy the rest of what passes for my summer vacation, savour the company (even here) of family and friends – and remember that, in the immortal words of the Sage of Stratford, there's a (wonderful, most of the time) world elsewhere.

PS: Late Day 1-D victims also included H.O.R.S.E. champ Freddy Deeb and Erick Lindgren. But not the oldest competitor in the field, 94-year-old Jack 'Jeffrey' Ury, who survived the 16-hour stint that ended just before 4 a.m. At one point Jack doubled up in middle position, calling after two players before him had limped. After the flop, the big blind raised it up to 3000 and the third player folded, but Jack made the call. After both checked the turn, the river paired the board, and the big blind fired out a 10,000 bet – enough to put Jack all-in. He then said he couldn't see the board properly, so the dealer moved it over right in front of him. Jack looked back and forth between the board and his hole cards several times before announcing: 'I got a straight, I call!' He rolled over pocket sixes – no straight, just two pair, but enough to win him the pot. Jack's opponent mucked, and the gallery let out the loudest cheer of the day. Jack's now got 24 hours to recover before embarking on Day 2-B.

Email from 'the Moll' of Big Deal, *Cindy Blake:*

Whoa. Forget odds. This sucks. Poker is a terrible, terrible, merciless game. That guy will get his comeuppance and it will hurt him even more when he does because he'll be having delusionary dreams of glory, if there is such a word as delusionary . . .

Email from 'The Crony' of Big Deal, Al Alvarez:

The Book of Bad Beats is longer and more bitter than the Bible – or, for all I know, than the Koran, but yours has to be up there with the worst of them. Maybe that in itself is immortality of a kind, but who needs it? Console yourself with the thought that reason was on your side, even though God had other ideas. As for Lady Luck: she's a bitch with the morals of an alley cat. Always was, always will be.

12 July

You can rely on the World Series of Poker for enlightening new takes on the game. Among the new rules introduced this year by the Players' Advisory Committee is an intriguing clause making it illegal to 'induce' a call. Sometimes, amid all the Machiavellian chat at the table made so fashionable by television, this can clash with the established rule about not revealing your hand during play.

This was the one that got 2006's champ, Jamie Gold, into such trouble. After conceding, some months after the event, that he had broken it more than once (as seen on TV), Gold was given an official pardon – which did not stop an ill-tempered front-page editorial in the US version of *Poker Player* magazine demanding that the reigning champ be barred from entering the tournament this year.

All of which may explain a pretty harsh ruling made yesterday, midway through Day 2-B, when an opponent contemplating a call asked a player named Tommy Giampaolo, 'Do you have the king?'

'Yeah,' replied Giampaolo, 'I got the king.' The opponent

chose to believe him and mucked, then summoned a floor-man for a ruling. His decision was to give Tommy G a nine-hand penalty for disclosing his hand. 'Had you lied about the hand,' the official told him, 'that would have been OK.'

Does this buttress my long-held conviction that poker is a metaphor for life? I am still pondering the matter. But it certainly reaffirms my belief that TV has a lot to answer for when it comes to poker etiquette.

Today is the big day, when we – that's to say, they – finally reach the money. Of some 2300 day two starters, from the initial field of 6358, only 808 have survived to day three. The cash kicks in at 621st place, which we should reach early this evening after all the TV delays associated with the dread bubble.

'All-in and call' will echo around the Rio's Amazon Room as the television cameras rush to catch numerous potentially dramatic moments before finding the actual 'heartbreak' one; and the entire room will grind almost to a halt for a while as the tables are kept in synch. Whoever finishes 622nd will get nothing for three long days' work, in which he or she will have vanquished 5737 of the world's top players. Unless, of course, like in 2006, Harrah's takes pity and awards a free entry for the following year – in which case the worst place to finish (and the *real* bubble) will be 623rd. Either way, the player who finishes in 621st place will double the entry fee with $20,320 – and so on upwards (over another five days) to the $8.25-million first prize.

The 2007 main event may be smaller than 2006's – a record 8773 starters, with a $12-million first prize – but that's the only visible impact of the US anti-gaming legislation on the year's World Series of Poker. Many of the lesser events have proved record-breakers – as is this year's number of registered players for all 55 events, which totals no fewer than 54,288.

Now, at last, the Rio can fit all surviving main event players into one room. Among those who won't be there, having fallen yesterday, are former world champs Joe Hachem, Dan Harrington, Tom McEvoy, Chris Moneymaker and Brad Daugherty, plus such other poker names as Daniel Negreanu, Barry Greenstein, Phil Gordon, Allen Cunningham, Hoyt Corkins and Tony G. Also gone are Britain's Vicky Coren and Ross Boatman and Ireland's Padraig Parkinson. The tournament's oldest player, 94-year-old Jack Ury, was also an early departee.

Of the survivors, John Duthie leads the British charge with 381,500, closely followed by Jac Arama with 302,000, Willie Tann (282,000), Julian Gardner (130,000) and Neil Channing (125,000). Former champs still in with the chance of a repeat are Huck Seed on 280,000, Carlos Mortensen (260,000), Berry Johnston (191,000), and Chris 'Jesus' Ferguson (150,000); Bobby Baldwin is hanging in there with just 16,800. Chip Jett (260,000) and Ted Forrest (250,000) are also well placed, while Hollywood last-longer bets have been won by Tobey 'Spiderman' Maguire, still there on 150k. In the family department, Doyle Brunson's daughter Jennifer (125k) and son Todd (95k) have both outlasted their old man. Leading the field with 622,300 is none other than Gus ('the Great Dane') Hansen, to the surprise of many fellow pros who regard him as a poker eccentric. But there's still a long, long way to go.

Having started Day 2-A with 40,000, the *Telegraph*'s David Flusfeder is also right up there with 265,000. At lunchtime yesterday I bumped into the novelist-cum-cardsharp outside the poker room in our hotel, and he told me that there finally came a point when he developed the feeling all we amateurs yearn for: that he was still there as of right, not by dint of luck more than judgement. Go, Dave!

Whatever happens now – and he has a great chance of getting into the money, maybe going deep – Flusfeder will surely achieve the all-time best finish (I blush to say) of any British player-writer. Play begins in half an hour. So off I go to monitor developments. Or maybe I'll go play in the noon tourney at the Wynn . . .

14 July

'How do you spell "devastated"?'

John Duthie was in mid-text to his loved ones back in Blighty, all asleep as Gus Hansen's bare pre-flop ace sealed Q-Q Duthie's doom, when he asked me this poignant question. Walking back from dinner towards the tournament room late on Thursday, day three, I bumped into John coming the wrong way up the Rio's corridor of fate. He had played well enough to get into the money – $25,101 for coming around 500th – but he was far from happy about it. After sorting out his spelling, I made a futile attempt to cheer him up.

'At least you've got the 25k, John,' I ventured. Infected by the local lingo, I even added: 'You played great!'

'I don't want the frigging 25k,' he snapped back. 'I'd give it up right now to be back in that tournament.' Then he stalked off.

Yup, Duthie was devastated. D-e-v-a-s-t-a-t-e-d.

I was put in mind of Dr Freud's theory that no gambler is truly fulfilled, if not happy, until he goes broke. Here, in the shape of John Duthie, was flesh-and-bones proof to the contrary. Or: a new twist on an old theory. Those who have won some money are distraught that they haven't won more.

This was confirmed the following night, Friday, when I dined at the Wynn with David Flusfeder, who'd made his exit early on day four in 321st place, winning $39,445. Not a bad return, you might think, on the $10,000 entry fee – especially as it was in fact a freeroll sponsored by those shrewd folk at PokerStars.

What an achievement – the best ever, to my knowledge – by

a British poker-writer! Flusfeder confessed to being quietly satisfied, but hungry for more. Hungry not just for more tournament play, now that he's built up such self-confidence, but for more money. His all-in move early on day four was designed to make him a contender.

With 275,000, and A-K in late position, David sensed his chance when the short-stack pushed in for 40k, only to be called from mid-position by a guy with slightly more than David himself. 'I'd already decided, before the start of play, that I was going to be prepared to gamble. I wasn't going to just sit around hoping to limp up a prize level or two. This had to be my spot. I was sure I was way ahead of the short-stack and at worst I was in a coinflip against the medium-stack. If he'd had aces or kings, I felt sure he'd have reraised, so I was confident that, at worst, I had two overcards.'

David pushed all-in, and medium-stack eventually called. The cameras arrived to record the moment for posterity. Short-stack had 9-10, medium J-J. David needed an ace or a king to leap to 600,000, not far off the chip average at the time. As fate (or Anna Kournikova) would have it, he finished third in the hand, when the board gave short-stack two pair and medium a set of jacks. Flusfeder's tournament was over.

As he waited in line to pick up his prize money, David told me, he got annoyed by people saying 'Congratulations!' Commiserations were what he wanted at that particular moment. So he got both from me, in the right order – and duly paid for dinner.

Then my son Ben arrived with his wife Salome, in town from LA for the weekend, and we had a nightcap at the Sports Bar before checking out the stunning view from their plush top-floor room at the Wynn. En route to the elevators we bumped into Neil Channing, clutching a white plastic bag. It was around 1 a.m. Had day four just finished? Or had Neil been knocked out?

The latter, it transpired, with an authentic 'bad beat' grimace.

After a terrific four-day performance, Neil had just finished in the low hundreds, with $58,570 to show for it. 'It's here,' he said gloomily, 'here in this bag.' Ben and I squeezed it longingly.

But Neil was, to say the least, glum. Had he been right to push all-in with queens? Should he have read the other guy for aces? As I stammered to reassure him, Barny Boatman appeared out of nowhere to back me up, with rather more authority. Neil had done the right thing. How can you read someone for pocket aces? Victory would have made him a contender.

Duthie, Flusfeder, Channing – they could all have been contenders.

Compared with me, they *were* all contenders. Between them they'd won more than $100,000. But none of them was happy. They'd all been close enough to the *real* money to smell it, almost touch it, to start dreaming about six figures, maybe even seven.

Not for nothing was it Friday the 13th.

16 July – The final table

After ten long days of play, not to mention 54 previous events over six weeks, we're at last down to the final table of the WSOP main event. The elimination of Washington State's Steve Garfinkle soon after 4 a.m. this morning left just nine players still standing out of the 6358 starters aspiring to the title of 2007 world champion.

And the chip leader is a Brit! Well, kinda. Leading the field, with more than 22 million, is Philip Hilm, billed as a Dane now living in Cambridge, England. So, OK, it's a stretch. But what I want to know is this: how come Hilm played for the Polish team that won the 2006 World Cup of Poker in Barcelona, in which I was playing for England (see Chapter 10 of *Bigger Deal*)?

I, too, aspire to be a Citizen of the World. But this is ridiculous.

A look back at one of the blogs from Barcelona reveals that Hilm was Team Poland's 'celebrity' player (my own dubious billing for England), then described as 'based in Denmark, although his family background is Polish'. Hmm.

Nationality is irrelevant, of course, at the WSOP final table – apart from noting the very 'new poker' fact that only four of the nine remaining players are American. Three are Europeans – two, if you count Hilm, Brits. You may wish to root for a dashing Polish Dane living in Cambridge, or you may prefer to support the only true Brit at the table: the less dashing but extremely proficient online favourite John Kalmar from Chorley, Lancashire, better known as 'Skalie', who lies in third place with 20,320,000.

The only problem is that Skalie's support team have been behaving like classic English football fans abroad, drunkenly spraying f-words around the bleachers every time he's involved in the action. More than once yesterday, after his wife told him they were making him 'look bad', and the tournament director gave them an official warning – one more f-word, and they'd be ejected from the room – their hero felt obliged to go over and have a word with these uncouth specimens, asking them to 'chill out'. Let's hope they don't besmirch our national pride during the long hours of play at the final table.

Between Hilm and Kalmar in second place, with 21,315,000, is a 40-year-old Vietnamese Canadian, a former dealer from Ontario named Tuan Lam – whose supporters, by contrast, quietly play hand-held video games during the action. Except when Lam is in a pot. Once they hear the announcer mention his name, they all look up, shut down their Gameboys and yell, 'Go, Tuan.' Well, poker – even the final table of the World Series – can be very boring to watch.

One of four online qualifiers at the final table, Lam's screen-name is 'BabyIIam'. Behind him in fourth place, with 16,320,000, lies another – and my personal favourite, if only because of his age: 62-year-old Raymond Rahme from South Africa, a 'semi-retired entrepreneur' who took up Hold'em only two years ago, after decades as a stud player. Genial, white-haired Rahme has had a South African film crew following his every move since he got here – and indeed before. Have they stumbled upon the greatest fly-on-the-wall documentary subject ever?

Fifth with 13,240,000 is Lee Childs, a 33-year-old Virginian former wrestler, as you can tell by looking at his formidable frame, complete with menacingly shaved head. Add the shades, and Childs is a tough opponent, even if he turned pro only last month, and this is his first WSOP event. Tangle with Lee at your peril.

Half a double-up behind him in sixth place, with 9,925,000, is the most experienced player at the table, 40-year-old respected professional Lee Watkinson, an economics graduate from Washington State with one World Series bracelet already to his name (for the 2006 $10,000 pot limit Omaha event). Ironically, Watkinson lists 'wrestling' as one of his recreations, so it will be interesting to watch him butting heads with Childs. With career winnings in excess of $2.6 million, Watkinson qualified for the main event on FullTilt, who are committed to throwing in a bonus of $10 million if he wins the top prize.

To help him more than double his prize money, Watkinson has FullTilt's top 'sweater' among his classy supporters on the rails: FullTilt pro and WSOP bracelet winner Perry Friedman, who claims to be one of the most successful sweaters in the business. He sweated his friend Chris Ferguson to four of his five WSOP bracelets, including the 2000 world crown. Friedman's job, in his own words, is 'to ensure that a powerful winning force surrounds the player in the field'. Yesterday he was joined in the bleachers by Jesus himself, making Watkinson's progress to the final table all but inevitable. The same forcefield will no doubt be there for him. In, as it were, force.

Next, with 9,205,000, comes an excitable young PokerStars qualifier from Poughkeepsie named Hevad 'Rain' Khan (online name 'RaiNKhaN'), who gives the TV cameras value for money every time he wins a hand, leaping around and yelling to a degree unseen before the advent of televised poker.

Eighth with 8,450,000 is Californian Jerry Yang, an LA hospital worker with five children whose Laotian parents have made their first visit to Vegas, forgetting briefly about all 32 of their grandchildren, to root for him from the rails. 'Hallelujah!' cried his mother yesterday, when Jerry's all-in 8-8 beat two overcards to put him briefly in the chip lead. 'Son – very good boy!' she tells all enquirers in her barely existent English.

Bringing up the rear with a mere 6,570,000 is Alex Kravchenko from Moscow – the first Russian ever to reach the final table of the WSOP main event. Winner of several European events – the Austrian Masters, the St Petersburg Winter Tournament, the Helsinki Freezeout and the UK's Pacific Poker Open – this self-styled 'businessman' has enjoyed a stellar World Series, winning the first-place bracelet in the $1500 hi-lo limit Omaha event, and cashing in no fewer than four more (including the $50,000 H.O.R.S.E.). Also the first Russian to win a World Series bracelet, Kravchenko has won a total of some $267,000 so far – and now stands to add a minimum of $525,934 more when play begins tomorrow.

That is the prize money for ninth place. Eighth wins $585,699, seventh $705,229, sixth $956,243 – and the top five all become dollar-millionaires (if they aren't already), winning $1.255m for fifth, $1.853m for fourth, $3.048m for third, $4.841m for second and $8.25m (not to mention the custom-built gold bracelet) for the title.

I'll be watching from the comfort of the ESPN truck, where my friend Eric Drache has reserved me a behind-the-scenes seat to watch – and maybe join the commentary team. Apparently this is no ordinary truck; there are comfy seats, food and drink, interesting companions. Who will, one assumes, behave decorously – making it the perfect seat from which to disown the foul-mouthed yobs supporting 'Skalie'. Apart, of course, from the impeccably mannered snooker champ Steve Davis, into whom I bumped on the bleachers yesterday, rooting for his Ladbrokes pal. If Steve gives Skalie some tips on the pressure out there under the lights – his immunity to which, says Steve, helped him make the money himself here last year – Britain could yet have its first world poker champion since Iranian-born, Cardiff-based restaurateur Mansour Matloubi in 1990 – the year *Big Deal* was published.

Yes, *that* long ago.

17 July: Interlude – ye olde merrie Englande

'You don't want to be photographed with me?' asked the Queen indignantly.

'No way,' I replied brusquely, sweeping past Her Maj and her baffled Beefeater bodyguard without even saying hello, let alone genuflecting. This was – as veteran royal-watchers would (if asked) confirm – my first royal red carpet in, well, yes, a few years.

On past the paparazzi, there was another one to snub – another Queen, that is – before finally reaching the free drinks beyond. Well, neither of them looked much like Helen Mirren – more, in truth, like the Real Thing, specs and all – and neither was offering my overdue knighthood for services to sport, after representing Britain no fewer than eight times over 20 years in the world championships of poker. So I savoured giving both the right royal brush-off they deserved.

Once inside, the Queen herself – the real one this time, if

only on CGI-enhanced celluloid – was waggling her head in
time to some jaunty music as a *Monty Python*-style graphic
sequence on giant screens throughout the room asked: 'Who
will be the next King of Europe?' Julius Caesar, Napoleon,
Henry VIII, David Beckham and others, maybe Genghis
Khan – they were all there, the over-the-years contenders, jock-
eying for position as America offers to send over the new
monarch they think we Brits deserve, probably need.

Yes, the World Series of Poker is coming to Europe. For which,
read London. This is why one of those grey-haired Queens is
even now wandering by, flanked by men in anorexic Busbies,
waving affably. This is a party in Caesar's Palace – at its hot-
spot night club, rather feebly called Pure (no match for the
Wynn's Tryst) – to alert the poker community to the £10,000
WSOP event to be held in London in September. Hosted
by the commissioner of poker himself, Jeffrey Pollack, the hot-
ticket do painted Britain in the theme-park, proto-Disneyland
colours (or should I say colors) through which America understandably sees its transatlantic cousins.

Scantily clad maidens – of whom I've seen a lifetime's worth
in the last two weeks – strutted around the room distributing
Pimm's as an iconic emblem of the mother country. Or, to
be honest, a feeble imitation of Pimm's. Other maidens in
minimally tight tops (and indeed bottoms), with Germany
or France or Sweden emblazoned across their ample breasts,
distributed schnapps, or champagne, or some cough-medicine-
like digestif, respectively. Best of all, of which I confess I drank
quite a few before writing this was the punchy grappa representing Italy.

People milled about. No one made any speeches. There was
no press kit. So I had to go to the internet to establish the dates
of the first WSOP Europe. There will be three events, starting
with Omaha and H.O.R.S.E., scattered around three casinos
(the Empire, the Sportsman and Fifty), climaxing in the £10,000

buy-in no limit Hold'em – yes, a gold bracelet event, the first to be staged outside the United States.

So there you have it. Just as I thought I'd got the point, and was wondering whether to go home, or maybe play some $2–$5 NLHE in the adjacent Caesar's cardroom, the Beatles appeared onstage in full sixties reincarnation. Or, to be precise, the Fab Four – Beatles impersonators, flophead wigs and all, unique to Vegas.

They were good. Very good. People began to dance. So good were they that, within a number or three, I decided they were miming.

The voices of 'John' and 'Paul' were extraordinarily like those of John and Paul. But their Liverpudlian accents – and I know whereof I speak, as that's where I come from – were hopeless when they were talking rather than singing. 'Ringo' was certainly drumming, for real, but I was sure the others were miming to pre-recorded tracks. I wandered over to the edge of the stage to check for myself. I could hear nothing coming from their mouths as they yelled through the loudspeakers.

Then I spotted Dave 'Devilfish' Ulliott, himself no mean guitarist and singer, looking at the stage so lustfully I realised that he would not be entirely happy, not really himself, until he replaced them upon it. I whispered my theory to Dave, and asked for his own, more expert judgement. No, said Dave immediately, he'd heard them before. They were good. The real thing. They weren't miming.

So I went back to recheck, and invited Dave to join me. That's when even the Devilfish began to wobble. When I bumped into Andy Bloch, himself something of a guitarist, Dave disappeared. I asked Andy for a definitive verdict, and he wandered around the stage for a while before confirming my own diagnosis.

Whatever the truth, we all agreed, the Fab Four were good. So good that we all began to dance. No matter that the party was sparsely attended. No matter that it should have been held the night before the main event, when most players were actually here, rather than the night before the final table, when most have already headed home. Thanks to the Fab Four, scores of Americans will head to the London WSOP – which may even secure more than the 150 starters foreseen by most Brits, if not the 750 predicted by Harrah's. Around 350–400 is my prediction for the likely number of £10,000 (or $20,000) contestants. [The number of starters turned out to be 362.]

18 July: WSOP 07 – The endgame

So it's true. Psychological savvy helps. For the superstitious (like me), it was also his commitment to giving 10% of his winnings to charity that saw 40-year-old psychologist Jerry Yang from Laos, now resident in California, arrive at the final table with by far the punchiest karma.

When play began at noon yesterday, Yang held the second-smallest stack, in eighth place out of nine with just 8.45 million in chips out of the 130 million in play. Sixteen hours later, at 4 a.m. this morning, he was the new world champion of poker, winning $8.25 million and a secure future for his large extended family, including a wife and six children.

At the most international final table of all time – four Americans, three Europeans, one South African and one Canadian – the youngest 22, the oldest 63 – Yang dominated from the off.

Within the first two hours, he had busted out three players, including two of the most fancied, and leapt into a massive lead with 62 million, almost half the chips in play. Over the subsequent 14 hours he would slip down as low as 40 million, but never lose the lead. Yang played super-solid poker throughout; but there were times he was helped by his opponents' remarkable recklessness.

First to go, astonishingly, was the chip leader when play began –
Philip Hilm, the Dane of Polish descent living in Cambridge.
Hilm managed to lose $20m in two consecutive hands. After
barely an hour's play, in only the 14th hand of the day, he
took his first dive after calling two bets totalling $5.5m from Yang
before and after a flop of Ah-Td-8s, then folding when Yang went
all-in on the turn, 3d. In the very next hand, Hilm himself went all-
in when 5d-8d brought him bottom pair and a flush draw, only to
be called by Yang with a paired eight that stood up.

Barely ten minutes later it was Yang's A-9 versus the all-in
A-7 of Lee Watkinson, the experienced pro from Washington,
who might have been expected to think twice about so rash a
move at such a crucial stage of the proceedings. 'What the hell
was he thinking?' asked Michael Craig on his blog for FullTilt,
Watkinson's own sponsors. 'What's on his mind? That he's got
a bracelet and a zillion big time final tables and 15 years of top
pro experience, so he better get all his chips in at once so the
amateur doesn't outplay *him* after the flop?' Again, Yang's hand
survived, and Watkinson was a goner. Few had expected action
of this scale so soon. But it was not over yet.

Next to go, after another half-hour, on Hand 28, was Lee
Childs, the wrestler from Virginia – and again Yang was the
executioner. When Childs raised 720k from the small blind,
Yang went all-in from the big. After a long think, with 5 million
left, Childs called, showing Kh-Jc to Yang's Js-8s. After the flop
of 6c-4c-4d, Childs had Yang dominated. But the turn brought
the 8c, giving Yang top pair and Childs a long-shot flush draw
on top of his possible boss pair. The river was the 9d. For the
third time in an hour or so, Yang ran to his jubilant Laotian
relatives for a mass hug on the rails.

At the first break, Yang has won 12 of the first 28 hands. His
62.3 million gives him a lead of 42 million over Canada's Tuan
Lam in second place. As play resumes, and the blinds rise to

150,000 and 300,000 with 40,000 antes, the pace slows for an hour and more before Yang dispatches his next victim. When he puts in one of his routine chip-leader raises to 1.5 million, this time from middle position, he gets his first action in a while from short-stack Hevad 'Rain' Khan, who raises from the small blind to 6 million. With Khan left holding just 3.5 million, Yang calls – and Khan sets himself in blind, before the flop. It comes Kc-4c-2d. Yang calls, and shows Jh-Js to Khan's As-Qs. The turn brings the 3c, giving Khan a straight draw to go with his chance of a Q. But the river is the 3s, sending an exuberant Yang back to the rail for more celebrations – and Poughkeepsie's all-singing, all-dancing Khan to the rail for good, out in sixth place, winning $956,243. All five survivors will now become dollar-millionaires.

As play resumes, Yang has 74 million, or 57% of the chips in play. Just four hands later, the 60th of the day, Britain's John Kalmar decides it is time to make his first big move. With Yang on the button, South African sexagenarian Raymond Rahme raises to 2.7 million and Kalmar goes all-in on the big blind – another 13.25m. Rahme calls, showing Jd-Js to Skalie's As-Kh. The board comes Tc-9h-6h, 3c, 3h, and Skalie is poker history, eliminated in fifth place, with a prize purse of $1,255,069 to take back to Chorley, Lancashire.

Not bad for a man who had been running so badly this WSOP that he wasn't going to play in the main event. When he learnt that changing his airfare home would cost $600, Skalie decided that the very last satellite might just be a better investment. He was right.

So it took just six hours and 60 hands to get rid of five players. But it would be another seven hours and 107 hands before the next one fell.

By 1 a.m., and the 100th hand of four-handed play, Jerry Yang was bleeding chips. At one point, he had held 60% of the chips in play; now he had slipped to 33%. He had won 63 of the 166 pots – but small ones compared to the few biggies he had lost. He was still the chip leader, but sexagenarian Raymond Rahme of South Africa was only 11 million behind him. After a rare burst of momentum the Russian, Alex Kravchenko, had again fallen silent. Then, on Hand 167, came Kravchenko's moment of truth.

With Rahme on the button, Kravchenko raises from the small blind to 2.1 million, Yang pushes from the big blind, and Kravchenko quickly calls all-in for almost 20 million. Yang shows 8c-8h, and Kravchenko As-Kd. It's a coinflip, which Kravchenko must win to stay alive. The flop comes Qd-9h-8s, sending Yang's fans crazy as he flops a set of eights. Kravchenko needs runner-runner – but the turn brings the 4c, leaving him drawing dead. The river is a meaningless 3s. Kravchenko is eliminated in fourth place, Yang's fifth victim of the day, earning $1,852,721. There is a jump of $1.2m between Kravchenko's fourth place and third.

Now Yang is back to holding more than half the chips in play. Two hands later, at 1.45 a.m., he raises from the button to 2.6 million. Raymond Rahme, the 62-year-old who is showing understandable signs of weariness, reraises from the big blind to 8.6 million. Yang calls, bringing the pot to 17.25m. After a flop of Ad-Jh-8h, Rahme checks, Yang bets 10 million, and Rahme moves all-in for 27.35m. Yang goes into the tank for several minutes, and the crowd falls silent, before he quietly says, 'All right, I call.' When Rahme shows Kh-Ks, an ecstatic Yang rolls over Ac-5s for top pair. The turn brings the 3s, the river the 2d. Yang jumps for joy and runs off the stage for yet more hugs with his family and friends. Tuan Lam walks over to Rahme to offer his congratulations, then Yang returns to give the old-timer a hug. On Nelson Mandela's 89th birthday, third-placed Raymond Rahme is going home to South Africa with $3,048,025.

As the heads-up begins, Jerry Yang has 104.5 million and

Tuan Lam just over 23 million. After seven hours of four-handed play, Yang has busted out two more players in just three hands. He has won 67 of the day's 169 hands, and holds 81% of the chips.

The 2004 WSOP head-to-head between Greg Raymer and David Williams lasted three hands. The 2005 heads-up between Joe Hachem and Steve Dannenmann took six. The 2006 endgame between Jamie Gold and Paul Wasicka was all over in seven.

This one would take 36, over three hours. Just before 4 a.m., on Hand 205 of the day, Yang raises to 2.3 million from the button, and Tuan Lam moves all-in for 22.2 million. Yang doesn't think long before calling. He shows 8c-8d to Lam's Ad-Qd. It's a race, which Yang is winning. Two-thirds of the crowd chants 'USA! USA!', the rest 'Canada! Canada!' The flop comes Qc-9c-5s, bringing bedlam as Tuan Lam takes the lead with top pair. He's a big favorite to double-up, and get himself right back in there. Yang needs an eight or runner-runner for victory. The turn is the 7d, giving Yang a gutshot straight draw. And the river comes . . . the 6h, giving Yang an unlikely straight and the 2007 world crown.

Chaos ensues, from which Yang eventually emerges to make a gracious speech thanking all concerned. Canada's Tuan Lam takes home $4,840,981 for second place, and Jerry Yang $8.25 million for first, minus 10% to the Make a Wish Foundation, Feed the Children, and the Ronald McDonald House.

Having earned his $10,000 entry via a $225 satellite, I doubt Yang will be parting with his unique WSOP gold bracelet. He has earned himself – and Laos – a lasting place in poker history.

POSTSCRIPT – JULY 2008

The 2008 world title was won by . . . well, for once, I can't tell you, because the organisers introduced a new twist this year, by freezing the final table on 14 July, when the tournament got down to the final nine, and postponing play – for TV's sake – until mid-November. That way ESPN could build up a back-story, i.e. suspense, and the finalists seek endorsements, advice, lessons, maybe even (said some doubters) cook up covert deals, before returning to play it out for the 2008 world title on almost-live TV.

On 14 July 2008, the dollar millionaires with four months to dream of poker glory were nine names we had never previously heard of: one Dane, one Russian, two Canadians and five Americans – all male, as usual (though one woman, Tiffany 'Hot Chips' Michelle, had come close, reaching the penultimate table but exiting in seventeenth place). As this book is published one of them will be carrying off a prize of $9 million for coming first out of 6844 starters.

I'm no longer there, alas; I was in July, again making it to the evening of the second day (and so the top third of the field), but not as far as the money – and I've since been too busy finishing this book. Next year, I'll be back in Vegas again for my umpteenth assault on the world crown – and I'll be hoping to see you at the final table.

In the meantime, may the flops be with you.

Appendices

Appendix A

Select (& Critical) Bibliography

(a) Manuals

BRUNSON, Doyle (ed.): *SuperSystem 2: A Course in Power Poker* (New York: Cardoza, 2005)
The pantheon of great poker names who contributed to this, the true Bible of Poker, reads like a list of first-ballot Hall of Famers. Its ambitious intent is to pass on the winning secrets of the world's best players in six poker disciplines popular at the time of publication: draw (Mike Caro), seven-card stud (Chip Reese), various forms of lowball (Joey Hawthorne), seven-card stud high-low split (David Sklansky), limit Hold'em (Bobby Baldwin) and no limit Hold'em (ed. Doyle Brunson). The book concludes with a glossary and tables of statistics decades ahead of their time.

Brunson's initial regret over its publication – too many secrets had been given away, too many poker players around the world were playing a better and more sophisticated game – is eloquent testimony to *SuperSystem*'s success. Almost thirty years after its publication, the book is finally showing its age. Many of the variants are no longer spread in cardrooms, and the advice is more intuitive than rigorous or academic. For 20 years after its initial publication, none the less, this was unquestionably the most advanced, comprehensive and instructional poker book.

CARO, Mike: *Caro's Book of Poker Tells* (New York: Cardoza, 2001)
The first and still the pre-eminent book on reading physical tells at the poker table. It contains hundreds of photos, each of which shows a different demeanour at the table that can be interpreted to your advantage. Caro explains what you are looking at, why your opponent is behaving that way (even if he or she is unaware), states how reliable the tell is and how it will impact on your long-term results. The book's strength lies in the simplicity of its principles, and the huge savings that can be made by their correct implementation.

This book will boost your live poker income more immediately than any other book on this list. An understanding of its lessons allows you to make consistently better reads and more accurate decisions. The first time you pick up a reliable tell and snap off a big bluff, or make a great laydown (and it will be in your first session after finishing the book), *Caro's Book of Poker Tells* will have paid for itself.

HARRINGTON, Dan: *Harrington on Hold'em vol. 1 Strategic Play, vol. 2 The Endgame, vol. 3 The Workbook* (Las Vegas: Two Plus Two, 2004/05/06)
With the number of Texas Hold'em tournament guides on the market when Harrington's first volume emerged, it had to be either innovative or superior to stand out. It was both. Although he acknowledges that he did not invent the concept of M and Q values, Harrington brought them to the attention of the masses. M and Q were immediately adopted by the tournament community as the universal method to talk about your status in a tournament.

As well as popularising M and Q values, Harrington's volume 1 set a new standard in the level of rigour and detail in discussing Texas Hold'em situations. Before giving the correct action, Harrington will tell you your chip stack, the status of the tournament, the stacks of your opponents, their playing styles and the dynamic of the previous few hours' play. Books that omit these details seem incomplete if not misleading by comparison.

SCHOONMAKER, David: *The Psychology of Poker* (Las Vegas: Two Plus Two, 2000)
Before this book's publication in 2000, it was no secret that every poker player had his or her own unique playing style. By introducing the loose/passive and tight/aggressive axes, it gave us the four quadrants by which all players are now categorised. It also gave us a guide

to adjusting to these specific styles at the table. Unique at the time, this classification system is now ubiquitous. Mention the difficulty in adjusting to a loose-aggressive player, and the chances are that every other player around the table will nod in agreement.

Schoonmaker also addresses for the first time the psychological pitfalls awaiting any aspiring poker pro. Knowing how to play correct poker is not enough to ensure a long and prosperous poker career. You must also be psychologically robust enough to deal with the frustrations and pressures attending even a top-class player's working life.

SKLANSKY, David: *Hold'em Poker* (Las Vegas: Two Plus Two, 1997, orig. pub. 1976)
Notable for its originality rather than its complexity or scope, Sklansky's 113-page manual introduced the Hold'em community to his pre-flop hand grouping system. For the first time, a Hold'em strategist could be entirely prescriptive about pre-flop actions in all situations. Recreational limit Hold'em players were stunned by how few hands a player like Sklansky played. Patience was crowned the principal virtue of low limit Hold'em for the next decade.

SKLANSKY, David: *The Theory of Poker* (Las Vegas: Two Plus Two, 1987, revised 1999)
Instrumental in poker's metamorphosis from hobby to intellectual pursuit and graduate career choice, this book's legacy is the fundamental theorem of poker.

Every time you play a hand differently from the way you would have played it if you could see all your opponents' cards, they gain; and every time you play your hand the same way you would have played it if you could see all their cards, they lose. Conversely, every time opponents play their hands differently from the way they would have if they could see all your cards, you gain; and every time they play their hands the same way they would have played if they could see all your cards, you lose.

To help a reader find the way we ought to play if we know our opponent's cards, the remainder of the book uses the theory of expected value. Now the dominant subject in poker conversation and analysis the world over, EV was then the domain of mathematicians and poker geeks. Finally, poker enthusiasts had a principle to play by in any situation in any variant of poker.

SKLANSKY, David: *Tournament Poker for Advanced Players* (Las Vegas: Two Plus Two, 2002)
Published in 2002 in response to the surging popularity of major tournaments, this book brought Sklansky's faultless poker logic to bear on the subtleties of winning tournament strategy. It was the first to look in detail at the adjustments a winning cash player must make when entering a tournament. Starting from the premise that a reader is already an accomplished cash-game player, this book articulates concepts that now underpin the basic strategy of most serious tournament players.

Also recommended:
CLOUTIER, T. J.: *How to Win the Championship: Hold'em Strategies for the Final Table* (New York: Cardoza, 2006)

GORDON, Phil: *Phil Gordon's Little Green Book* (New York: Simon & Schuster, 2005)

JONES, Lee H.: *Winning Low Limit Hold'em* (Pittsburgh: Conjelco, 2005)

McEVOY, Tom, and **CLOUTIER**, T. J.: *Championship Pot Limit and No Limit Hold'em* (New York: Cardoza, 2004)

——*Championship Hold'em*: *Tournament Hands* (New York: Cardoza, 2005)

RODMAN, Blair, and **NELSON**, Lee: *Kill Phil* (Las Vegas: Huntington Press, 2006)

SKLANSKY, David, and **MALMUTH**, Mason: *Hold'em for Advanced Players* (Las Vegas: Two Plus Two, 1999)

(b) Narratives, anthologies, fiction

ALSON, Peter: *Take Me to the River* (New York: Atria, 2006)
A self-styled 'over-educated under-achiever', rambling-gambling bachelor hits midlife crisis as he turns 50, finally pops the question to

his girlfriend and sets off to the 2005 WSOP to, er, win the money for the wedding. A witty, painful, beautifully written classic of the poker narrative genre.

ALVAREZ, Al: *The Biggest Game in Town* (Boston: Houghton Mifflin, 1983); *Poker: Bets, Bluffs and Bad Beats* (San Francisco: Chronicle, 2001) Alvarez wrote the first modern poker classic with his account of the 1981 World Series, which first introduced us to such legendary characters as Doyle 'Texas Dolly' Brunson and Jack 'Treetops' Straus. He also muses entertainingly upon the game in his lavishly illustrated 2001 book, and expertly in his 2007 anthology, *Risky Business*.

BRADSHAW, Jon: *Fast Company* (London: High Stakes, 2003) Three legendary poker players – Johnny Moss, Puggy Pearson and Titanic Thompson – join tennis player Bobby Riggs, pool player Minnesota Fats and backgammon player Tim Holland in this classic, first-hand, face-to-face account of what makes some men winners and some men losers.

CRAIG, Michael: *The Professor, the Banker and the Suicide King* (New York: Warner, 2005) Absurdly unpublished in the UK, this page-turner by a lawyer-turned-poker nut chronicles the biggest game ever played, when billionaire Texas banker Andy Beal took on a team of pros for tens of millions of dollars.

DALLA, Nolan, and **ALSON**, Peter: *The Man behind the Shades: The Rise and Fall of Stuey 'The Kid' Ungar* (London: Weidenfeld & Nicolson, 2005) The definitive biography of the definitive poker player – apart from his eventually fatal drug habit – this is the riveting life story, from New York rags to Vegas riches, of a poker genius but deeply flawed human being.

HOLDEN, Anthony: *Big Deal: A Year as a Professional Poker Player* (London: Bantam, 1990, Abacus, 2002–5; New York: Viking, 1990, Penguin, 1991, Simon & Schuster, 2007) Author tries and fails to win 1988 and 1989 world titles, but in the process describes what is now known as the 'old' world of poker.

HOLDEN, Anthony: *Bigger Deal* (London: Little, Brown, 2007, Abacus, 2008; New York: Simon & Schuster, 2007, 2008)
Author tries and fails to win 2006 and 2007 world titles, but in the process describes the genesis of the 'new' world of poker.

HUGHES, Johnny: *Texas Poker Wisdom* (Lincoln, NV: iUniverse Inc., 2007)
A racy, compelling Texas–Vegas poker novel, as full of good table tips as vivid descriptions of life on the road, with a denouement that proves how poker expertise can come in handy when life presents major problems.

KAPLAN, Michael, and **REAGAN**, Brad: *Aces and Kings* (New York: Wenner, 2005)
Chronicles the lives of poker's greatest characters, from old-time greats Pearson and Brunson to modern whizz-kids Negreanu, Lindgren and Ivey. Getting to 'know' poker's biggest stars – and learning as much from their mistakes as their triumphs – should be high on any serious player's list of priorities.

KONIK, Michael: *Telling Lies and Getting Paid* (Guilford, CT: Lyons Press, 2002)
As much about gambling as poker, this is another lively collection of articles and stories from the author of *The Man with the $100,000 Breasts and Other Gambling Stories*, also a TV poker commentator.

McMANUS, James: *Positively Fifth Street* (New York: Picador, 2003)
Chicago journalist is sent to Las Vegas to cover a murder trial, parlays his expenses into a $10,000 entry to the main event of the World Series – and gets all the way to the final table, winning $250,000 for fifth place. The poker equivalent of NASA finally sending a poet to the moon.

MAY, Jesse: *Shut up and Deal* (Harpenden: No Exit Press, 1999)
Before giving up the game to turn TV commentator, Jesse May wrote the finest poker novel since Richard Jessup's *The Cincinnati Kid*. As manic Mickey navigates his way through the shark-infested waters of 1990s, pre-internet cardrooms, you learn as much about luck as about life.

STRAVINSKY, John (ed.): *Read 'Em and Weep* (New York: HarperCollins, 2004)
The best poker writing ever – from Mark Twain and James Thurber to John Updike and Martin Amis, not to mention Al Alvarez and Anthony Holden, is collected in this indispensable anthology by New York writer and poker nut.

WILSON, Des: *Swimming with the Devilfish* (London: Macmillan, 2006)
Founder-director of Shelter, and former Lib Dem president, veteran enthusiast Wilson finally found his true vocation as a poker writer, with this compelling study of Dave 'Devilfish' Ulliott and other top UK players.

WILSON, Des: *Ghosts at the Table* (Edinburgh: Mainstream, 2007)
Sherlock Wilson turns detective to sleuth the true history of poker, visiting all points from Deadwood, Dakota, via the Mississippi to Texas and Vegas to tell it (very entertainingly) like it really was – and still is.

YARDLEY, Herbert O.: *The Education of a Poker Player* (London: Jonathan Cape, 1979, introduced by Al Avarez)
In the daddy of all poker books, first published in 1957, a cryptographer-turned-cardsharp teaches you to play while telling tall tales of wizened winners and losers around the smoke-filled rooms of the American West.

Appendix B

Glossary of Poker Terms

ACE-HIGH: a five-card hand containing an ace but no pair; beats a king-high, but loses to any pair or above

ACES UP: two pairs, one of which is aces

ACTION: the betting, as in 'The action's on you'

ADVERTISE: to show your cards after making a bluff, with the deliberate intention of being exposed as an apparently 'loose' player

ALL-IN: to bet all the chips you have left

ANTE: compulsory stake, for all players, before the deal

ANTE UP: dealer's request for antes to be paid

AVATAR: online poker term for a player's computer-generated image

B&M: online term for a real cardroom, short for 'bricks and mortar'

BACK DOOR: when a straight or flush is filled on the turn and river cards

BACK TO BACK: two paired hole cards, as in 'aces back to back' or 'aces wired' (also 'pocket rockets')

BAD BEAT: to lose a pot against the odds, the stronger hand being beaten by a lucky one

BELLY HIT: to fill an inside straight

BET INTO: to bet before an apparently stronger hand, or a player who bet strongly on a previous round

BET THE POT: to bet the total value of the pot (including the call)

BETTING INTERVAL: period during which each active player has the right to check, bet or raise; ends when the last bet or raise has been called by all players still in the hand

BICYCLE: the lowest possible straight, A-2-3-4-5

BIG BLIND: the bigger of the two compulsory bets before the deal – usually, in Hold'em, two seats to the dealer's left

BIG SLICK: A-K (also known these days as 'Anna Kournikova')

BLIND (1): the compulsory pre-deal bet(s) to the dealer's left

BLIND (2): to check or bet before receiving, or without looking at hole cards

BLOW BACK: to lose back most or all of one's profits

BLUFF: 'representing', with a bet, better cards than you actually hold

BOARD: the five communal cards revealed in the centre of a Hold'em table

BOAT: full house

BOBTAIL: see 'open-ended straight'

BOSS: the strongest hand at that stage, as in 'boss trips'

BRING IT IN: to make the first bet

BUBBLE: in a tournament, the last place before the money

BUCK: the rotating button used by a professional dealer to indicate which player is notionally dealing the hand, and so should receive the last card

BULLET: an ace

BUMP: to raise (as in 'bump it up')

BURN: to deal off the top card, face down, before dealing out the cards (to prevent cheating); or to set aside a card which has been inadvertently revealed

BUST: a worthless hand, which has failed to improve as the player hoped

BUST A PLAYER: to deprive a player of all his chips; in tournament play, to eliminate a player

BUST OUT, BE BUSTED OUT: to be eliminated from a tournament by losing all your chips

BUSTED: broke, or tapped

BUSTED FLUSH: four-to-a-flush, which failed to fill up

BUTTON: see 'buck'; also the seat before the blinds, i.e. prime position

BUY-IN: the amount of money required to sit down in a particular game or tournament

BY ME: a (dated) alternative to 'check' or 'fold'

CAGE: the casino's or cardroom's 'bank' where you exchange chips for cash or vice-versa

CALL: to match, rather than raise, the previous bet

CALLING STATION: a player who invariably calls, and is therefore hard to bluff out

CARDS SPEAK: refers to a face-up declaration at the end of a hand, by which, even if a player has not realised he holds the winning hand, the dealer or other players can point this out on his behalf

CASE CARD: the last remaining card of a denomination or suit, when the rest have been seen, as in 'the case ace'

CASH IN: to leave a game and convert one's chips to cash, either with the dealer or at the cage

CATCH: to 'pull' the card or hand you want

CHASE: to stay in against an apparently stronger hand, usually in the hope of filling a straight or flush

CHECK: to offer no bet, reserving the right to call or raise if another player bets

CHECK-RAISE: to check a strong hand with the intention of raising or reraising any bet

CHIPS: plastic discs of different colours representing different amounts of cash

CINCH HAND: a hand that cannot be beaten; see also 'nuts'

COFFEE-HOUSING: to attempt to mislead opponents about your hand by means of devious speech or behaviour

COLD: a bad streak, as in 'My cards have gone cold'

COLD DECK: a deck of cards 'fixed' in advance by a cheat; or a regular deck running cruelly against one player

COME: to play an as yet worthless hand in the hope of improving it, as in playing 'on the come'

COME OVER THE TOP: to reraise after the pot has been raised

CONNECTORS: consecutive cards, such as 9-10 or J-Q which might make a straight

COWBOY: a king

CUT IT UP: to divide, or split, the pot after a tie

CUT-OFF: the seat before the button

DEAD CARD: a card no longer legally playable

DEAD HAND: a hand no longer legally playable, due to an irregularity

DEAD MONEY: see 'fish', 'patsy', 'pigeon', etc.

DEALER'S CHOICE: a game in which each dealer, in turn, chooses the type of poker to be played for a round

DECLARATION: declaring by the use of coins or chips, in high-low poker, whether one is aiming to win the high or the low end of the pot, or both

DEUCE: a two, the lowest-ranking card in high poker

DOG: poker shorthand for 'underdog'

DONKEY: a weak or bad player, see also 'fish', 'patsy', 'pigeon', etc.

DOWN CARDS: hole (or pocket) cards

DRAWING DEAD: calling a bet, or drawing a card, on a hand that cannot win, whatever the 'turn', usually the 'river', may bring

DRAWING OUT: to win a hand on the last card or cards, after staying with an inferior hand, 'on the come' – in Hold'em, to 'river' or 'suck out on' your opponent

DRIVER'S SEAT (in the): said of a player who is making all the betting and thus appears to hold the strongest hand

DROP: to fold

ELGAR: twenty-pound (sterling) note

EPT: the European Poker Tour, a series of televised tournaments

FAMILY POT: a pot in which all the players are still 'in' before the flop

FIFTH STREET: the fifth and last communal card to be exposed in Hold'em, also known as the 'river'

FILL, FILL UP: to pull the card you are seeking for a straight or above; you fill up a boat

FISH: an inferior, losing player

FLAT-CALL: to call when a raise might have been expected

FLOOR-MAN: the cardroom employee supervising a group of tables, who is the ultimate arbiter of disputes

FLOP: the first three communal cards to be exposed in Hold'em

FLUSH: five cards of the same suit; ranks above a straight and below a full house

FOLD: to withdraw from, or give up, the hand

FOUR-FLUSH: four cards of the same suit, requiring a fifth to become a flush

FOUR OF A KIND: four cards of the same denomination; ranks above a full house and below a straight flush

FOURTH STREET: the fourth communal card to be exposed in Hold'em, also known as the 'turn'

FREE RIDE: to stay in a hand without being obliged to bet

FREEROLL: online tournament with no entry fee but cash prizes

FREEZE-OUT: a knockout game, usually a tournament, in which all players start with the same amount, and play until one has won the lot

FULL HOUSE: a hand containing trips and a pair. Between two full houses, the higher trips win. Beats straights and flushes, loses to four of a kind

G-NOTE: a thousand-dollar bill

GRAVEYARD: the pre-dawn shift in a Las Vegas casino

GUTSHOT: the card needed to fill an inside straight

HEAD TO HEAD: see 'heads-up'

HEADS-UP: a game between just two players, often the climax of a tournament

HIGH ROLLER: one who gambles for large amounts of money

HIGH-LOW: a species of poker in which the highest and the lowest hands share the pot

HIT: to fill, or obtain the card you are seeking

HOLE CARDS: in Hold'em, the two concealed cards dealt to each player at the start of a hand; see also 'pocket'

HOT: said of a player on a winning streak

HOUSE: full house, or 'boat'

IGNORANT END: the low end of a straight

IMPROVE: to pull a card or cards that better one's hand

IN: a player is 'in' (the hand) if he has called all bets

IN THE DARK: to check or bet blind, without looking at your cards

INSIDE STRAIGHT: four cards requiring (an unlikely) one in the middle to fill a straight, viz. 5-6-7-9; see also 'open-ended straight'

INTERVAL: the length of time before the blinds go up in tournament play

JUICE: see 'rake'

KIBITZER: a non-playing spectator, or railbird

KICK IT: to raise

KICKER: the subsidiary or 'side' card to a more powerful card or cards

KNAVE: a jack

KNOCK: to check; see 'rap'

LAY DOWN: to reveal one's hand in a showdown

LEAK: a tendency to lose poker winnings at other forms of gambling, such as dice or sports betting

LEVEL: the level of each (escalating) set of blinds in tournament play, or the time allowed for it (see 'interval'); or the stakes in a cash game

LIMIT POKER: a game with fixed betting intervals, viz. £10–£20, £20–£40

LIMP (IN): to call, rather than raise, a bet

LITTLE BLIND: see 'small blind'

LIVE ONE: an inexperienced, bad or loose player; a sucker who apparently has money to lose

LOCK: a hand that cannot lose; see also 'cinch' and 'nuts'

LOOK: to call the final bet (before the showdown)

LOOSE: liberal play, usually in defiance of the odds

LOWBALL: a form of poker in which the lowest (or worst) hand wins

MAKE (the deck): to shuffle

MARK: a sucker

MARKER: an IOU

MECHANIC: a cheat who manipulates the deck

MEET: to call

MONSTER: a powerful hand, especially used of starting hands

MOVE IN: to go all-in

MUCK: the discard pile, in which all cards are dead. Also used as a verb

NLHE: no limit Hold'em

NUT FLUSH: the best available flush, i.e. an ace-high flush

NUTS: the best, unbeatable hand at any stage of a game

OFF-SUIT: hole cards of different suits

ON THE COME: to bet with four cards to a straight or a flush, in the hope that it will 'come' on the turn or river; also called a semi-bluff

ON TILT: playing badly, often because of a bad beat, or being 'stuck'

ON YOUR BACKS: to turn your hole cards face up in a hand where there can be no more betting, i.e. after one or more players are all-in

OPEN: to make the first bet

OPEN-ENDED STRAIGHT: four consecutive cards requiring one at either end to make a straight, viz. 5-6-7-8; also known as a two-way straight or a 'bobtail'

OUTS: the cards still available that could, in theory, improve your hand

OVERBET: in no limit, a bet bigger than the pot

OVERCARDS: in Hold'em, cards higher than the flop cards, or those in your opponent's hand, played in hope of catching a higher pair

OVER THE TOP: to reraise

PAINT: any picture or court card

PAIR: two cards of the same denomination

PASS: to fold; occasionally (wrongly) used for 'check'

PATSY: an inferior, losing player

PICTURE CARD: king, queen or jack, also known as court or face cards

PIGEON: an inferior, losing player

PIP: the suit symbols on a non-court card, indicating its rank

PLAY BACK (at): to reraise

POCKET (in the): synonym for 'hole', as in 'pocket nines'

POCKET ROCKETS: a pair of aces in the hole

POSITION: your seat in relation to the dealer, and thus your place in the betting order, an important tactical consideration

POT: the total of the chips at stake in the centre of the table

POT LIMIT: a game in which the maximum bet is the total of the pot after a player has called

POT ODDS: the ratio of the total size of the pot to the bet you are required to call

PUT DOWN: to fold

QUADS: four of a kind

RABBIT-HUNT: looking (when permitted) to see what the turn and/or river would have brought when a hand ends after the flop

RAGS: low, bad, unplayable or irrelevant cards

RAILBIRD: a non-playing spectator or kibitzer, often used of a busted player

RAINBOW: a flop of three different suits

RAISE: increase the previous bet by at least as much

RAKE: chips taken from the pot by the dealer on behalf of the house, or from tournament entries by the organisers

RAP: to knock the table, to indicate a check

READ: to try to figure out the cards your opponent is holding

RE-BUY: to start again, for an additional entry fee, in tournament play (where permitted)

REPRESENT: to bet in a way that suggests you are holding a particular (usually strong) hand

RERAISE: to raise a raise

RIFFLE: to shuffle chips

RING GAME: American term for cash games (as opposed to tournaments)

RIVER: in Hold 'em, the fifth and final communal card to be exposed, also known as fifth street

RIVERED: beaten on river (fifth) card, usually a bad beat

ROCK: an ultra-tight, conservative player

ROLL (a card): to turn a card face up

ROUNDER: a poker-player who makes his or her living at the game

ROYAL FLUSH: A-K-Q-J-10 of the same suit. The best possible poker hand in all but wild card games

RUN (1): synonym for a straight

RUN (2): a run of good cards, see also 'rush' and 'streak'

RUNNER-RUNNER: improving your hand on both the 'turn' and the 'river'

RUNNING BAD: on a losing streak

RUNNING GOOD: on a winning streak

RUSH: a run of good cards see also 'run' and 'streak'. A player 'on a rush' may well 'play his rush', i.e. play an indifferent hand because he's feeling lucky and might win against the odds

SANDBAG: (a) to check-raise; (b) to get caught between two players who are raising each other

SATELLITE: a small-stakes tournament whose winner obtains cheap entry into a bigger tournament

SCHOOL: collective noun for the players in a regular game

SEE: to call

SEMI-BLUFF: see 'on the come'

SET: three of a kind or 'trips' (in Hold'em, normally used of a pair in the hand and one on the board)

SET YOU IN: to bet as much as your opponent has left in chips

SEVEN-CARD STUD: a poker game in which players make their best five-card hand out of seven they are dealt, four showing and three hidden

SHILL: a cardroom employee, often an off-duty dealer, who plays with house money to start or fill up a game

SHOWDOWN: showing hole cards, after betting has ceased, to see which of the remaining players has won the pot

SIDE CARD: an unmatched card which may decide a pot between two hands otherwise of the same strength; see 'kicker'

SIDE POT: a separate pot contested by other players when one or more players are all-in

SIT-AND-GO: a tournament that begins as soon as all seats are filled

SLOWPLAY: to disguise the real value of a high hand by underbetting it, to tempt players with worse hands into the pot

SMALL BLIND: the smaller of the two compulsory bets; in Hold'em, the player on the dealer's left

SOFTPLAY: to play gently against a friend

SPLIT (POT): a tie, or stand-off. Occasionally this can be agreed between two players before the hand is ended

SQUEEZE (CARDS): to look slowly at the extremities of your hole cards, without removing them from the table

STACK: the pile of chips in front of a player, as in 'short stack'

STAND-OFF: a tie, in which the players divide the pot equally

STARTING HAND: the two hole cards in Hold'em

STAY: to remain in a hand with a call rather than a raise

STEAL: a bluff in late position, attempting to 'steal' the pot from a table of apparently weak hands

STEAMING: playing badly or wildly, to go on tilt

STRADDLE: to make a voluntary blind raise (if allowed) before the deal

STRAIGHT: five consecutive cards, not of the same suit; beats trips, but loses to a flush and above

STRAIGHT FLUSH: five consecutive cards of the same suit. Beats everything but a higher straight flush, viz. a royal flush

STREAK: a run of good (or bad) cards, see also 'run' and 'rush'

STRING BET: an illegal bet in which a player put some chips in the pot, then reaches back to his stack for more. He should declare a raise verbally before calling

STUCK: losing

SUCK OUT: to 'river' a player, or beat him against the odds on the last card to be dealt

SUIT: one of the four suits: hearts, diamonds, clubs or spades

SUITED: cards of the same suit, as in 'A-Q suited'

SWEETEN (the pot): to raise

TABLE: can be used as a collective noun for all the players in a game, as well as for the green baize itself

TABLE STAKES: a poker game in which a player cannot bet more than the money he has on the table

TAP CITY: to go broke

TAP OUT: to bet all one's chips

TAPPED OUT: broke, busted

TELL: a giveaway mannerism or nervous habit which reveals the strength or otherwise of an opponent's hand

THREE-FLUSH: three cards of the same suit

THREE OF A KIND: three cards of the same denomination with two 'side' cards; beats two pairs, but loses to a straight or above. See also 'set' or 'trips'

TIGHT: a conservative player who tends to play only strong hands

TILT: see 'on tilt'

TOKE: a tip to the dealer (illegal in Britain)

TRAP: to check, or make merely a token bet, when holding a strong hand (with the aim of suckering another player into betting, then raising)

TREY: a three

TRIPS: three of a kind or a set. Beats two pairs but loses to a straight or above

TURN: the fourth communal card to be revealed at Hold 'em, also known as fourth street

TWO PAIRS: a hand containing two pairs plus a kicker; beats a pair but loses to trips or above

UNDER THE GUN: the player who is first to bet, after the two blinds

UNDER-RAISE: to raise less than the previous bet, allowed only if a player is going all-in

UP CARD: an 'open' or exposed card

UTG: under the gun

WHALE: a fish of giant proportion, i.e. a major casino punter, or high roller, who is usually a loser (used less about poker players than other gamblers)

WHEEL: the lowest straight possible, A-2-3-4-5, also known as a bicycle

WHIPSAW: to raise before, and after, a caller who gets caught in the middle

WILD CARD: a card designated as a joker, of any value

WIRED: said of two paired hole cards, as in 'aces wired' or 'aces back to back'

WPT: the World Poker Tour, a series of televised tournaments

WSOP: the World Series of Poker, held in Las Vegas each summer

Appendix C

Probability and Guide Tables

Probability tables

Total possible hole-card combinations: 1,326

Odds of getting ANY specific pocket pair: 220-1

Hand	Combinations of this (or higher) pair	Probability	Odds (1 in X)	Odds (X to 1)
AA	6	0.004524887	221.0	220.0
KK	12	0.009049774	110.5	109.5
QQ	18	0.013574661	73.7	72.7
JJ	24	0.018099548	55.3	54.3
TT	30	0.022624434	44.2	43.2
99	36	0.027149321	36.8	35.8
88	42	0.031674208	31.6	30.6
77	48	0.036199095	27.6	26.6
66	54	0.040723982	24.6	23.6
55	60	0.045248869	22.1	21.1
44	66	0.049773756	20.1	19.1
33	72	0.054298643	18.4	17.4
22	78	0.058823529	17.0	16.0

Odds of getting ANY specific suited connector: 330-1

Hand	Combinations of this (or higher) suited connector	Probability	Odds (1 in X)	Odds (X to 1)
AK	4	0.003016591	331.5	330.5
KQ	8	0.006033183	165.8	164.8
QJ	12	0.009049774	110.5	109.5
JT	16	0.012066365	82.9	81.9
T9	20	0.015082956	66.3	65.3
98	24	0.018099548	55.3	54.3
87	28	0.021116139	47.4	46.4
76	32	0.02413273	41.4	40.4
65	36	0.027149321	36.8	35.8
54	40	0.030165913	33.2	32.2
43	44	0.033182504	30.1	29.1
32	48	0.036199095	27.6	26.6

Odds of getting ANY specific off-suit hand: 110-1

Hand	Combinations of this (or higher) off-suit ace	Probability	Odds (1 in X)	Odds (X to 1)
AK	12	0.009049774	110.5	109.5
AQ	24	0.018099548	55.3	54.3
AJ	36	0.027149321	36.8	35.8
AT	48	0.036199095	27.6	26.6
A9	60	0.045248869	22.1	21.1
A8	72	0.054298643	18.4	17.4
A7	84	0.063348416	15.8	14.8
A6	96	0.07239819	13.8	12.8
A5	108	0.081447964	12.3	11.3
A4	120	0.090497738	11.1	10.1
A3	132	0.099547511	10.0	9.0
A2	144	0.108597285	9.2	8.2

Total possible flop combinations: 19,600

Chance of flopping . . .	Probability	Odds (1 in X)	Odds (X to 1)
Quads with a pocket pair	0.00245	408.3	407.3
Flush with suited cards	0.00842	118.8	117.8
Straight with 95o	0.00327	306.3	305.3
Straight with 85o	0.00653	153.1	152.1
Straight with 75o	0.00980	102.1	101.1
Straight with 56o	0.0131	76.6	75.6
Three of a kind or better with a pocket pair	0.118	8.5	7.5
One pair with AK/AQ/AJ or AT	0.290	3.5	2.5
Flush draw with suited ace	0.109	9.14	8.1
2 card open-ender with off-suit connectors	0.0980	10.2	9.2
2 card open-ender or flush draw with suited connectors	0.203	4.9	3.9

Miscellaneous	Probability	Odds (1 in X)	Odds (X to 1)
Any suited hand	0.235294118	4.3	3.3
Any ace (including AA)	0.149321267	6.7	5.7
Any suited connector	0.036199095	27.6	26.6
Any off-suit connector	0.108597285	9.2	8.2
Any connector	0.14479638	6.9	5.9
Any pair or ace	0.20361991	4.9	3.9

Frequent Hold'em match-ups

	Two big missed cards	TPTK	OP	Top two	Top set
FD	X	37.1 – 62.9	36.7 – 63.3	33.1 – 66.9	24.6 – 75.4
FD + 1 LC	48.4 – 51.6	44.9 – 55.1	45.3 – 54.7	X	X
FD + 2 LC	54.0 – 46.0	52.9 – 47.1	54.1 – 45.9	X	X
FD + GS	X	47.3 – 52.7	46.9 – 53.1	39.9 – 60.1	33.8 – 66.2
FD + GS + 1LC	56.3 – 43.7	55.2 – 44.8	47.0 – 53.0	X	X
FD + GS + 2LC	62.5 – 37.5	62.2 – 37.8	56.1 – 43.9	X	X
FD + OE	X	56.8 – 43.2	56.3 – 43.7	52.7 – 47.3	42.4 – 57.6
FD + OE + 1LC	61.1 – 38.9	62.9 – 37.1	63.0 – 37.0	X	X
FD + OE + 2LC	70.0 – 30.0	68.9 – 31.1	X	X	X
OE	X	34.3 – 65.7	34.3 – 65.7	30.0 – 70.0	25.8 – 74.2
OE + 1LC	41.6 – 58.4	41.5 – 58.5	41.8 – 58.2	X	X
OE + 2LC	49.9 – 50.1	50.0 – 50.0	X	X	X
Pair + 1OC	77.9 – 22.1	22.6 – 77.4	20.2 – 79.8	19.1 – 80.9	4.0 – 96.0
Bottom 2 pair	95.1 – 4.9	74.6 – 25.4	74.5 – 25.5	8.2 – 91.8	0.2 – 99.8
Top 2 pair	95.1 – 4.9	84.3 – 15.7	74.5 – 25.5	X	0.1 – 99.9
Bottom set	100 – 0	89.1 – 1.9	90.8 – 9.2	82.2 – 16.8	4.4 – 95.6

TPTK = Top pair
top kicker
OP = Overpair
FD = Flush draw
GS = Gutshot
OE = Open-ender
LC = Live card
OC = Over card

Your own hand is listed down the left-hand side. Your opponent's hand is listed along the top. The figures given are your percentage chance of winning the pot to your opponent's chance of winning the pot. X indicates that it is impossible for those two hands to be matched up. For example, you cannot hold a flush draw against two missed big cards without yourself having at least one live card. Hence the top-left box contains an X.

Guide tables

Hands in the north-east section of the table are suited; hands in the south-west section are off-suit. The pocket pairs are within the bordered diagonal. Each hand has three cells within its box. The top cell represents the action you should take if you are the first to enter the pot. The middle cell represents the action you should take if there is one or more caller before you. The bottom cell represents the action you should take if there is one or more raiser before you.

Key to actions:
F = Fold
C = Call
R = Raise
RR = Reraise

Of course, your action will depend on what position the caller(s)/raiser is in, and how many callers or raisers there have been, so this is just a guide for average situations. Also, as already mentioned, it is a personal idiosyncrasy of mine to rate pocket pairs much more highly than most strategists, so calling from early position with 2-2, etc. will probably contradict a lot of other manuals.

Early	A	K	Q	J	T	9	8	7	6	5	4	3	2
A	R R RR	R R C	R R F	C C F	C C F	F F F	F F F	F F F	F F F	F F F	F F F	F F F	F F F
K	R R C	R R RR	C F F	F F F	F F F	F F F	F F F	F F F	F F F	F F F	F F F	F F F	F F F
Q	C C C	F F F	R R C	F F F	F F F	F F F	F F F	F F F	F F F	F F F	F F F	F F F	F F F
J	F F F	F F F	F F F	R R C	F F F	F F F	F F F	F F F	F F F	F F F	F F F	F F F	F F F
T	F F F	F F F	F F F	F F F	R R C	F F F	F F F	F F F	F F F	F F F	F F F	F F F	F F F
9	F F F	F F F	F F F	F F F	F F F	C C C	F F F	F F F	F F F	F F F	F F F	F F F	F F F
8	F F F	F F F	F F F	F F F	F F F	F F F	C C F	F F F	F F F	F F F	F F F	F F F	F F F
7	F F F	F F F	F F F	F F F	F F F	F F F	F F F	C C F	F F F	F F F	F F F	F F F	F F F
6	F F F	F F F	F F F	F F F	F F F	F F F	F F F	F F F	C C F	F F F	F F F	F F F	F F F
5	F F F	F F F	F F F	F F F	F F F	F F F	F F F	F F F	F F F	C C F	F F F	F F F	F F F
4	F F F	F F F	F F F	F F F	F F F	F F F	F F F	F F F	F F F	F F F	C C F	F F F	F F F
3	F F F	F F F	F F F	F F F	F F F	F F F	F F F	F F F	F F F	F F F	F F F	C C F	F F F
2	F F F	F F F	F F F	F F F	F F F	F F F	F F F	F F F	F F F	F F F	F F F	F F F	C C F

Middle	A	K	Q	J	T	9	8	7	6	5	4	3	2
A	R R RR	R R C	R R F	R C F	R C F	F F F	F F F	F F F	F F F	F F F	F F F	F F F	F F F
K	R R C	R R RR	R C F	F F F	F F F	F F F	F F F	F F F	F F F	F F F	F F F	F F F	F F F
Q	R C F	F F F	R R C	C C F	F F F	F F F	F F F	F F F	F F F	F F F	F F F	F F F	F F F
J	C F F	F F F	F F F	R R C	F F F	F F F	F F F	F F F	F F F	F F F	F F F	F F F	F F F
T	F F F	F F F	F F F	F F F	R C C	F F F	F F F	F F F	F F F	F F F	F F F	F F F	F F F
9	F F F	F F F	F F F	F F F	F F F	R C C	F F F	F F F	F F F	F F F	F F F	F F F	F F F
8	F F F	F F F	F F F	F F F	F F F	F F F	R C C	F F F	F F F	F F F	F F F	F F F	F F F
7	F F F	F F F	F F F	F F F	F F F	F F F	F F F	C C C	F F F	F F F	F F F	F F F	F F F
6	F F F	F F F	F F F	F F F	F F F	F F F	F F F	F F F	C C C	F F F	F F F	F F F	F F F
5	F F F	F F F	F F F	F F F	F F F	F F F	F F F	F F F	F F F	C C C	F F F	F F F	F F F
4	F F F	F F F	F F F	F F F	F F F	F F F	F F F	F F F	F F F	F F F	C C C	F F F	F F F
3	F F F	F F F	F F F	F F F	F F F	F F F	F F F	F F F	F F F	F F F	F F F	C C C	F F F
2	F F F	F F F	F F F	F F F	F F F	F F F	F F F	F F F	F F F	F F F	F F F	F F F	C C C

Late	A	K	Q	J	T	9	8	7	6	5	4	3	2
A	R R RR	R R RR	R R RR	R R F	R R F	R C F	R C F	R C F	R C F	R C F	R C F	R C F	R C F
K	R R RR	R R RR	R C C	R C F	R F F	R F F	F F F	F F F	F F F	F F F	F F F	F F F	F F F
Q	R C C	R F F	R R RR	R C F	R F F	F F F	F F F	F F F	F F F	F F F	F F F	F F F	F F F
J	R F F	R F F	F F F	R R RR	R C F	F F F	F F F	F F F	F F F	F F F	F F F	F F F	F F F
T	R F F	R F F	F F F	F F F	R R C	R C F	F F F	F F F	F F F	F F F	F F F	F F F	F F F
9	R F F	F F F	F F F	F F F	F F F	R R C	R C F	F F F	F F F	F F F	F F F	F F F	F F F
8	R F F	F F F	F F F	F F F	F F F	F F F	R R C	R C F	F F F	F F F	F F F	F F F	F F F
7	R F F	F F F	F F F	F F F	F F F	F F F	F F F	R C C	R C F	F F F	F F F	F F F	F F F
6	R F F	F F F	F F F	F F F	F F F	F F F	F F F	F F F	R C C	R C F	F F F	F F F	F F F
5	R F F	F F F	F F F	F F F	F F F	F F F	F F F	F F F	F F F	R C C	R C F	F F F	F F F
4	R F F	F F F	F F F	F F F	F F F	F F F	F F F	F F F	F F F	F F F	R C C	F F F	F F F
3	R F F	F F F	F F F	F F F	F F F	F F F	F F F	F F F	F F F	F F F	F F F	R C C	F F F
2	R F F	F F F	F F F	F F F	F F F	F F F	F F F	F F F	F F F	F F F	F F F	F F F	R C C

Blinds	A	K	Q	J	T	9	8	7	6	5	4	3	2
A	R R RR	R R C	R R C	R C F	R C F	R C F	R C F	R C F	R C F	R C F	R C F	R C F	R C F
K	R R C	R R RR	R C C	R C F	R C F	R C F	R F F	F F F	F F F	F F F	F F F	F F F	F F F
Q	R C C	R C F	R R RR	R C F	R C F	R C F	F F F	F F F	F F F	F F F	F F F	F F F	F F F
J	R F F	R C F	R C F	R R C	R C F	R C F	F F F	F F F	F F F	F F F	F F F	F F F	F F F
T	R C F	R C F	R C F	R C F	R C C	R C F	F F F	F F F	F F F	F F F	F F F	F F F	F F F
9	R C F	R C F	R C F	R C F	R C F	R C C	R C F	F F F	F F F	F F F	F F F	F F F	F F F
8	R C F	F F F	F F F	F F F	F F F	R C F	R C C	R C F	F F F	F F F	F F F	F F F	F F F
7	R C F	F F F	F F F	F F F	F F F	F F F	R C F	R C C	R C F	F F F	F F F	F F F	F F F
6	R C F	F F F	F F F	F F F	F F F	F F F	F F F	R C F	R C C	R C F	F F F	F F F	F F F
5	R C F	F F F	F F F	F F F	F F F	F F F	F F F	F F F	R C F	R C C	R C F	F F F	F F F
4	R C F	F F F	F F F	F F F	F F F	F F F	F F F	F F F	F F F	R C F	R C C	R C F	F F F
3	R C F	F F F	F F F	F F F	F F F	F F F	F F F	F F F	F F F	F F F	F F F	R C C	F F F
2	R C F	F F F	F F F	F F F	F F F	F F F	F F F	F F F	F F F	F F F	F F F	F F F	R C C

Acknowledgements

In the spring of 2006, while I was living and writing *Bigger Deal* for Time Warner UK (now Little, Brown), another publisher asked me to write a beginner's guide to poker for people who had seen it on TV but might feel nervous about taking the plunge. I felt honour-bound to seek the permission of Ursula Mackenzie, publisher and CEO of Time Warner Books UK, and the fairy godmother of *Big Deal* who had also commissioned *Bigger*, to interrupt my work on a poker book for her to write another for a rival publisher. Charm personified, as always, Ursula said she herself had no problem, but she had better check with her (then) immediate superior in New York, our mutual friend David Young.

Back came an email from David, saying: 'Damn. A rival publisher has had a good idea. Tell Tony it's fine for him to do it – but get him to do a bigger and better version for us further down the line.' This book is the result of that email.

I am therefore pleased to express my public gratitude to David Young and Ursula Mackenzie for having this idea in the first place. At Little, Brown UK I am also grateful to Stephen Guise for supervising the project until his recent departure, handing over to Tim Whiting and Iain Hunt, whose editorial support and interventions have been invaluable. I am also grateful, as ever, to LB's design department for the style with which the book has been produced, especially its terrific jacket (is it master-caricaturist Phil Disley's fault or mine that my face is so chubby?); and the publicity department led by Rosalie Macfarlane, who again entrusted me to the safe hands of Jenny Fry.

The commission had just come in when I played for England in the 2006 World Cup of Poker in Barcelona (as immortalised in Chapter 10 of *Bigger Deal*). Over a delightful alfresco dinner in the harbour beside Barcelona's Gran Casino, I talked it over with Tamar Yaniv, then marketing director of PokerStars.com, and her colleague Conrad Brunner, communications director. I was looking for some way to breathe life into a project that might otherwise dwindle into just another unreadable manual. We agreed that one way of gathering good material would be for me to play on the European Poker Tour, which is sponsored by PokerStars.com. So Tamar offered me sponsorship to play in half a dozen EPT tournaments, as described in Chapters 10–14, and the 2007 World Series of Poker (diary, Chapter 15). I am especially grateful to her (who has since moved on to another, more spiritual life), to Conrad and to all their colleagues in the London office of PokerStars.com, who were also generous enough to sponsor the first year of life of the website that spawned *Bigger Deal*, www.BiggerDeal.com. The EPT's founder-director, John Duthie, was always great company on my travels, as was PokerStars' former cardroom manager, then EPT honcho Lee Jones, now returned to his natural habitat in the United States. I am also pleased to thank Courtney Yamron, head of PokerStars' celebrity player management, and her colleagues for since continuing my sponsorship as a 'Friend of PokerStars' and the exclusive partnership with my website – where you can take on me and my fellow bloggers in monthly online tournaments.

I have received invaluable help in the compilation of this book from two young players with highly distinctive skills: my son Ben Holden, director of development at Hammer Films, who has (with a little help from his stellar wife, Salome) made me a proud grandfather while assisting in the chronicling of the EPT tournaments, Chapters 10–14; and his friend (and now mine) Oliver Chubb, whose poker brilliance was first quoted in *Bigger Deal*, and who has now made a huge contribution to the instructional red meat of this book, Chapters 3–9. I am hugely grateful to them both for working closely with me on both the content and structure of the finished product, which has been vastly improved by their contributions. We had a few good meals together, too.

I thank poker writer Johnny Hughes for permission to quote in Chapter 3 from his entertaining 2007 novel *Texas Poker Wisdom*; and my friend Michael Craig for permission to quote his Full Tilt blog on Lee Watkinson's 2007 WSOP final table exit in Chapter 15. My buddy James McManus was kind enough to interrupt work on his forthcoming *The Story of Poker* to review an early version of Chapter 1, and offer helpful suggestions. Victoria Coren was also kind enough to lend a hand with Chapter 10, immortalising her victory at the London EPT event, and to give me permission to quote from her own writings on it, while understandably keeping her powder dry for her own forthcoming poker book. After the publication of *Bigger Deal*, Roland De Wolfe approached me during a break in a tournament at London's Loose Cannon club, with a polite if firm enquiry as to why he wasn't in it; I promised him his very own chapter in my next book, and am delighted to honour that promise in Chapter 13.

Some material in Chapter 2 has been adapted from my 2006 book *All In*; and much of the material in Chapter 15 first appeared in a series of blogs I wrote from Las Vegas, during the 2007 World Series of Poker, for www.BiggerDeal.com.

Anyone who has ever played poker with me will know how absurd it is for me to be offering anyone strategic advice. Mustering the presumption to do so, however, also enables me to thank the people whose books taught me everything I'm supposed to know – Doyle Brunson, Mike Caro, David Sklansky, Mason Malmuth, Tom McEvoy, T. J. Cloutier, Dan Harrington; to thank my friends and fellow poker-writers Peter Alson, Mike Craig, Jim McManus, Jesse May, Nolan Dalla and Des Wilson for their ace-high company on the road; the original 'Moll', Cindy Blake, for her continuing presence in my life; and, last but never least, my pal of forty years, Al ('The Crony') Alvarez, for introducing me to poker in the first place. Fans of the Tuesday Night Game will be pleased to know that Al and I still play in a London home game together, if now (alas) on Fridays.

Finally, it seems appropriate to thank all the people who have knocked me out of all those tournaments over all these years, especially the main event of the World Series of Poker – for giving me such good copy as well as hard-earned lessons in the University of Life, where I am still hoping one day to be appointed Dean of Poker Studies.